KERRY BROWN is the Director of the China Studies Centre at the University of Sydney and Associate Fellow of Chatham House, London. With 20 years' experience of life in China, he has worked in education, business and government, including a term as First Secretary at the British Embassy in Beijing. He is the author of *Contemporary China* (2013), *Friends and Enemies: The Past, Present and Future of the Communist Party of China* (with Will Hutton, 2009) and *Struggling Giant: China in the 21st Century* (with Jonathan Fenby, 2007).

'So many people I meet often discuss China in their own Western context, and few say that the Chinese Communist Party is essentially the biggest business organisation in the world. Kerry Brown's book is a must read for anyone who needs to understand China's complexities, which given how important the country is becoming to the world, means the other 5 billion plus of us that don't live there.'

– Jim O'Neill, former chairman of Goldman Sachs

'Kerry Brown plumbs the murky depths of power, networks, and influence of the newly installed Chinese leadership under Xi Jinping. The result is an insightful framework for understanding how they got there and – importantly – how they intend to stay there.'

– Bates Gill, University of Sydney

'Kerry Brown's account of China's power elite is sweeping, topical and accessible, and a most valuable addition to our knowledge of the rising superpower.'

– Jonathan Fenby, author of *The Penguin History of Modern China* and *Tiger Head, Snake Tails*

THE NEW EMPERORS

EMPERORS

POWER AND THE PRINCELINGS IN CHINA

KERRY BROWN

I.B. TAURIS

LONDON · NEW YORK

Published and reprinted in 2014 by I.B.Tauris & Co. Ltd
6 Salem Road, London W2 4BU
175 Fifth Avenue, New York NY 10010
www.ibtauris.com

Distributed in the United States and Canada
Exclusively by Palgrave Macmillan
175 Fifth Avenue, New York NY 10010

ISBN: 978 1 78076 910 3
eISBN: 978 0 85773 383 2

A full CIP record for this book is available from the British Library

A full CIP record is available from the Library of Congress
Library of Congress Catalog Card Number: available

Typeset by Out of House Publishing

Printed and bound by CPI Group (UK) Ltd, Croydon, CR0 4YY

Dedicated to my colleagues at the China Studies Centre at Sydney University, and to the Vice Chancellor, Dr Michael Spence

CONTENTS

ACKNOWLEDGEMENTS

I am grateful for the assistance of Xin Zhao (Caroline Xin) for selection of Chinese language material and for research assistance for this book, to Tzu-hui Wu for work on the bibliography, and to Dr Shi Li for comments on the first chapter. My thanks also go to Tomasz Hoskins at I.B.Tauris for commissioning and giving support and feedback with his team, and to Robert Whitelock for copy-editing the manuscript.

ABBREVIATIONS

CCDI   Central Commission for Discipline Inspection
CCTV   China Central Television
CIC   China Investment Corporation
CPC   Communist Party of China
CPPCC   Chinese People's Political Consultative Conference
CR   Cultural Revolution
CYL   China Youth League
DPRK   Democratic People's Republic of Korea
DRC   Development and Reform Commission
GDP   gross domestic product
PLA   People's Liberation Army
PRC   People's Republic of China
RMB   Renminbi
SARS   Severe Acute Respiratory Syndrome
SEZ   Special Economic Zone
SOE   State-owned enterprise
TVE   Town and Village Enterprise
WTO   World Trade Organization

INTRODUCTION: THE NETWORKED LEADERSHIP

On the night of 14 November 2011, Neil Heywood – a British businessman and consultant, resident in China for over a decade – was staying in the Lucky Holiday Hotel, a fading three-star residence in the suburbs of Chongqing, a province-ranked city in south-western China. He was there, according to documents issued by Chinese authorities later in 2012, at the behest of Gu Kailai (sometimes called Bogu Kailai), wife of the most powerful man in the city, Communist Party Secretary Bo Xilai. Heywood reportedly had an association with the Bo family going back to his time when he was resident in Dalian in the north-east of China earlier in the decade.

According to the official Chinese news agency, Xinhua, which reported at the trial of Gu Kailai nine months later in Hefei, Anhui province, some time on the evening of 14 November Gu poisoned Heywood. During the trial, Gu testified that 'Heywood had threatened the personal safety of her son and decided to kill [him]. "To me", she was reported as saying, "that was more than a threat. It was real action that was taking place. I must fight with my death to stop the craziness of Neil Heywood." '[1]

The report continued with the direct testimony of the man who it was claimed had been her accomplice, Zhang Xiaojun, a member of her security detail:

On Nov. 12, 2012, Bogu Kailai asked me to contact Neil Heywood, saying that she wants to meet him and I shall pick him up and bring him to Chongqing. She instructed me repeatedly that I should accompany Heywood to Chongqing. I called Heywood and he [...] replied that he also wished to see her, but had to check his schedule. Within half an hour, Heywood called me back, telling me he would be available the next day and asking me to book a flight for him.[2]

Zhang stated that at 9 p.m. in the evening of the next day, after Heywood had taken the two-hour flight from Beijing to Chongqing, Bogu Kailai went to the Lucky Holiday Hotel with drinks. She took these to Heywood's room, Zhang waiting outside until Kailai summoned him a little later that evening, commanding him to bring prepared cyanide in a glass container. This she personally administered to the British man, who was by that time so drunk he was vomiting copiously. She then 'told hotel waiters to leave the guest alone in Room No 1605, after hanging the "Do Not Disturb" sign on the door when she left, according to testimony of a hotel waiter'. There Heywood's body lay until hotel personnel finally forced the door down and found him, spread on the bed, two days later.

The August trial of Gu resulted in her admission of full guilt, along with her claimed accomplice, and a suspended death sentence. But the trial also raised a whole series of questions, some of them relating to the murder, and others relating to the very function and exercise of power in contemporary China. The reason that Heywood's tragic fate, and the whole set of circumstances around Gu's involvement and the final trial, mattered was their link to the political ambitions of one of the most ambitious and talented politicians of his generation in modern China, Bo Xilai. The simple fact was that the trial occurred at a moment in Bo's life when he had the chance to reach the summit of power – the Standing Committee of the Politburo of the Communist Party of China (CPC). His wife's activities were the first in a series of events that were to cause this to unravel, and for him to end up felled and disgraced, facing charges of corruption, his Party membership revoked, and his political hopes eradicated.[3]

The Heywood case aroused most interest after Bo Xilai's chief security assistant, and one of his faithful allies, Wang Lijun, fled to the US Consulate in Chendu on the night of 6 February 2012. He stayed there for only 24 hours, before personnel from the central Ministry of State Security in Beijing came to pick him up. While details of what Wang told his American interlocutors have never been issued, a clear link with the Heywood case and the involvement of Gu Kailai and Bo was made, with some accounts saying that at the time that Wang had been in charge of public security as one of Bo's deputy mayors in late 2011 he had been entrusted with the post-mortem of Heywood and establishing the reason for his death. It soon became clear that Bo Xilai's wife was involved in this. The final encounter between the two ended in Bo slapping the face of Wang and banishing him from his sight.[4]

Heywood's demise was a personal tragedy. At the age of 42, he had left a widow and young children in Beijing, and a family grieving in Britain. Questions swirled around the real reasons for his death, and the links he and others had had with the Bo family. Conspiracy theories proliferated, ranging from the bizarre claim that – on the back of the fleeing of the blind rights activist Chen Guangcheng to the US embassy in April 2012 – there was an American directed covert campaign to destabilise China at a moment of vulnerability while it was undergoing a leadership change, to more grounded speculation that Gu's misdemeanour, whatever its real motives, had been exploited to the full by Bo's many enemies.

That Bo had accrued enemies during his political career was clear. His sterling family background, with his father Bo Yibo one of the so called 'Eight Immortals' who had been active politically from the earliest era of the Communist Party before it even came to power in the 1920s to the first few years of the twenty-first century, meant that he belonged to the elite of the elites. Chosen over his brother in the 1980s at a time when Party elders were made to retire and were only allowed to nominate one of their offspring to carry on their interests by having positions of influence and power in the Party, Bo had risen through provincial and national positions to be on the full Politburo, and to be one of the most talked about figures for promotion in 2012 at the Party Congress then due.

Bo had promoted eye-catching campaigns in Chongqing, the city he had been made Party head of in 2007, in a move that surprised many. The debate about the 'Chongqing model' will be covered later. But Bo's drive to strike down on the mafia, his resurrecting the atmosphere and some of the style of revolutionary campaigns from the late Maoist period, and his pro-poor housing and social welfare programmes had captured the imagination and attention of commentators within and outside China. Most members of the Politburo, with the noticeable exceptions of Hu Jintao and Wen Jiabao, had visited Chongqing during his period there, with figures like the then head of the powerful Organisation Department, Li Yuanchao, lauding the reforms being implemented with warmth. According to one senior politician I spoke to in Europe in late 2011, 'Bo Xilai is the only politician in China now who we can say really tries to reach out to capture the emotions of the people in ways that Western politicians aspire to. He is the one we feel as European leaders we can relate to.'[5]

The Bo case revealed a great deal about elite Chinese politics and indeed about the distribution of power generally in contemporary China. It was perhaps the most significant in a series of events over the period of leadership transition through 2011 and into 2013. This transition was eagerly awaited, and was the first that would be undertaken without the influence of a central strong man like former paramount leader Deng Xiaoping, whose choice of Hu Jintao, a young official in the early 1990s, was taken as giving Hu a crucial piece of support in becoming leader first of the Party and then of the government and the military a decade later in the early 2000s. One of the most striking aspects of the Bo case, however, was the way it showed how we, observers, analysts, and those generally interested in politics in the world's second largest economy and most populous nation, really don't know or understand power in China now.

This book will focus on the new leadership elite of contemporary China – those who finally emerged at about noon on 15 November 2012 in Beijing, in the Great Hall of the People, as the 'winners' in the process to enthrone a new Standing Committee. In this book, as I will argue in Chapter 1, I will treat these leaders as the first building blocks in a system of interlinked patronage, tribal, factional and institutional links, which reaches out from Beijing into the five-level-strong governmental structure of China, into the 84-million-strong membership of the CPC itself, and through the whole of society. The ancient Greek philosopher Archimedes asked to be given one place to stand to be able to create the world. In this book, the still point I will move from is the seven members of the new Politburo Standing Committee of 2012. They are the final clue to how power is evolving, developing, renegotiating its parameters and evolving in modern China. I will progress from models of how power is distributed and structured in this system into the lives, the networks and the biographies of these and other key figures, looking in particular at the paths they have taken to get where they are, the things they have had to say, the debts they have accrued, and the things they are owed. In many ways, the CPC now operates like a ruthlessly successful multi-national corporation, its output gross domestic product (GDP) figuring like profit for the bottom line of a company, but its values and future profitability under threat from new challenges. I will therefore also try to make sense of the future political programme these leaders will need to adopt, and the ways they will need to change the Party in order to preserve this profit.

One thing is for sure. While this leadership transition was finally successful inasmuch as it produced a new line-up of leaders nationally, and then down to the provinces, its legitimacy in the long term is an open question. 'Sealing the deal' with a broad constituency of people is easy enough in democracies, where election outcomes tend to decide this (even though these have become increasingly contentious in recent years, producing coalitions and split administrations that have highly qualified mandates). In the recent leadership transition, precisely who decided, for what reasons, and the defensibility of those reasons, is a highly contested question.

At the heart of this is the nature of the CPC itself. This is a question that will be returned to throughout the book. The Party, which came to power as a revolutionary force, lives uncomfortably with its violent past.[6] In the last decade, excellent historians in China like Yang Jisheng have been asking tough questions of the ways in which the Party exercised power in the six decades since its victory in 1949. Yang's monumental *Tombstone* calculates deaths from the great famines in the early 1960s, and imputes blame to the officials who blindly implemented destructive policies and were wilfully dismissive of the human costs they finally brought about.[7] Work on the Cultural Revolution (CR) from 1966, at least within the People's Republic, has almost become taboo in the last two decades, as figures who cut their first political teeth during this period, amongst them Bo Xilai, have occupied positions of increasing power. One of the intriguing aspects of the new generation of leaders in China is their links to this period of zealous and divisive activism and the intense politicisation. Those who were adolescents at this time were excluded from education from 1966 and involved in deeply unsettling mass campaigns. For them, the traces of the CR period have not been erased.

The man who would end up as the Party and country leader after 2012, and who is central to the book's subject, is Xi Jinping. His narrative over this period is interesting – a sort of case of 'opting out' because of the marginalisation of his father from 1964 during an earlier, less dramatic political campaign targeting enemies by Mao Zedong. But as the profile of Xi will show when it is given later, the CR has had a more complex impact on his life.

For while Xi may well belong to Party royalty because of his father, he was also a man of the people, working in humble positions as a teenager, with a tale of hardship much less contentious than Bo Xilai's (around whom there were uncomfortable rumours of violent zealousness and excess, dating from his association with the radical student activist movement in the late 1960s).[8]

The Party's complex internal arguments in the early twenty-first century about how it should now articulate its history and identity prior to the onset of the reform and the opening-up of the economy that started in 1978 offered one set of difficult questions. But everything that has happened post 1978 has only made this issue of the Party's already complex self image and its political narrative even more conflicted. In the Party's own internal assessment of President Hu Jintao and Premier Wen Jiabao's period in power from 2002 to 2012, these elemental battles over what the real values of the Party actually are are never far way. Is the CPC guided by a utopian vision borrowed from regime founder Mao Zedong, striving to push society towards becoming a perfect Socialist heaven on earth? Or are its values pragmatic, national ones – simply aiming for the delivery of certain key outcomes and leaving the grand ideas to a future that will never come? Is the Party simply – as a prominent intellectual from Beijing University, Wang Hui, argued – a sort of evaluative, structural entity that needs no real ideology but just allows space for people to thrive and prosper, or is it something more – embodying a coherent belief system that has real traction emotionally and intellectually over the enormously complex society of modern China?[9] The Party looks in terms of its structure and institutional cohesiveness and organisation like something very focused and tangible. But closer analysis of what this leadership transition has exposed shows something less solid – an entity that is surprisingly brittle and fragile, and that evidently, going on some of the events from 2011 to 2013, came close to imploding, acting at many times like an entity under threat.

Throughout this book, I will argue that the only way to get to grips with the ambitions and aims of the Party is to look at the people within it, and at their objectives and values. That leads once more back to the elite in Beijing, and the seven men (no women have ever served on the Standing Committee since the first Congress in 1921) who now count themselves its members. Open talk of the leadership and their inner lives is one of the most sensitive issues in modern China. Like the cardinals of the Catholic Church, the members of the Central Committee seek to present themselves as embodying the values and aspirations of the Party as a whole. This reaches its culmination in the Standing Committee of the Politburo. Membership of these bodies has immense spiritual as well as political meaning. They not only seek to lead China, but to represent its values and its identity. And yet, for all the grand ambition behind this, backed up by the abstract talk so popular during the Hu and Wen period of scientific principles being the guiding lights of political life in China, this is a system run at its centre by the personalities and ambitions of a small group of people and the networks around them, a group I will quantify and define precisely later. Behind the stiff and unyieldingly impersonal language that they use in the twenty-first century, we have to try to discern these personal stories and the very real tensions and clashes that exist between elite figures, looking beyond the symbolic sheen around them.

The structure of this book is deliberately simple, despite the fact that it seeks to understand a complex organisation during a bewildering time in its development. In the first chapter, I look at the issue of power and networks within the new leadership, and at the very concept of what a network in modern China actually is. I take inspiration in this chapter from the great work of Fei Xiaotong, the father of modern Chinese sociology whose wonderfully provocative works remain as fresh and stimulating now as when most of them were written from the 1940s onwards. In particular I look at the concept of liquidity in Chinese social relations, seeing how this relates to the surprisingly small elite that live at the very top of this system, and I discuss models of how to understand power in contemporary China. I will argue against the somewhat ossified and static notion of faction-loyalty, and will instead try to create a framework that is more fit for purpose in capturing the fluidity and energy of relationships and how they are associated with different types of power in a China undergoing rapid and sometimes bewildering social and economic change.

In the second chapter, I get down to details, by looking at the processes by which the leadership transition over the period from 2011 to 2013 actually worked. This entails looking at the mechanics of this change, the impact of the Bo case and other extraneous and unexpected events, and the forms of negotiation over the period. The figure of the former President of China, Jiang Zemin, and what has sarcastically been called in the Hong Kong press his 'resurrection' after reports of his death in 2011, and the meeting at the seaside town of Beidaihe in late August 2012 will figure large in this chapter, as will an assessment of the Hu and Wen legacy. I will argue that the final result of the leadership transition within the Party can be seen as a highly negative criticism of Hu and Wen's 'Do Nothing' era in politics, but that it also contains the seeds of reform – if the conditions are right. The influence of Hu and Wen, therefore, as I will show here, cannot be said to have ended.

In the third and fourth chapters, I will come to the people – the life stories and political trajectories of the 'winners' of this process, of their provincial and personal careers, and of the networks around them. I will look at the key events and people they have been associated with, their family and educational backgrounds, and particular campaigns they have been a part of. Building out from detailed analysis of the careers of Xi Jinping and Premier Li Keqiang, I will then construct a narrative around networks of the other five members of the Standing Committee. Amongst these superficially very similar looking ethnically Han Chinese men I will show a surprising level of diversity in the ways in which they have acquired power and the routes they have taken to get here.

My fifth chapter will move from the personal to the ideological and political. From 2002 to 2013 leaders in the new line-up have made pronouncements about their political ideas and the key elements in their world views. These give some clue to possible programmes of action they may take now they are in power. I will in particular assess the work of the most active writers and speech makers in this new leadership – Xi Jinping, Li Keqiang, and their chief ideologue, Liu Yunshan. I will give an assessment of their public statements and utterances over the last decade, and then look at some of the challenges that they have articulated, and what they have started to say about how they will approach these. I will then attempt to draw some conclusions about what the elite networks show us about where China as a polity and a society might be heading, and how this will impact on the world beyond the country's borders.

China in the twenty-first century more and more resembles something akin to what the great Russian philosopher Mikhail Bakhtin called a 'carnival' society – a place of rich paradoxes and immense energy, full of potential and struggle, as much with itself as with the outside world. Elites, of course, are not the only story. There are divisions and layers and interlinks through Chinese society that spread in every conceivable direction. But this elite, sitting like a small island in the vastness of what China is, and is aspiring to become, allow insights into at least how some of the machinery of the country work. Their life paths, networks and the ways they have risen to the top tell us some helpful things. This is an attempt to understand them and the amazingly dynamic society within which they operate.

A NOTE ON SOURCES

In this work, I have heavily used two sorts of sources. Wherever possible, I have tried to rely only on Chinese-language sources for information about the leaders, what they have said and their careers. Some of this material has been produced in Hong Kong and Taiwan, or outside China. Writing on leadership issues in China, while no longer the huge taboo it once was, is still a hazardous game. Lives of key figures are often swathed in mystery. I am aware of the issues of reliability with some Chinese-language material published outside China on leadership issues. I have tried to ensure, therefore, that for factual claims made in this book I have been able to find two different sources. Beyond this, I have taken the narrative and analysis provided by Chinese-language material on its own merits. Some is highly partisan, but some is no more nor less speculative than commentary produced in the English-language press. The huge advantage of this material is that it allows for a more linguistically intimate insight into the ways in which Chinese politics might work, and how relationships are evaluated, written about and understood within this linguistic environment.

For the thinking of the leaders, I have used an archive of their essays and speeches published over the last decade from the official Communist Party ideological magazine, *Qiushi* (*Seeking Truth*). Some of this may be edited, and there are inevitable questions of its original authorship. Because there are differences in the ways leaders write in this material, however, I am inclined to detect in it some explicit and engaged authorial direction. All translations from Chinese to English given in this book are by me, unless otherwise stated.

1

POWER AND THE POLITBURO

The world of the super elite in modern China is a strange one. It has a specific geography and ritual, and even its own kind of language. The rhythm of daily life is set out according to meetings of the Politburo, audiences with foreign dignitaries, and liaison with and speeches made to local leaders, along with carefully planned domestic and international visits.

Sometimes the members of this world try to come down to a more demotic one. The tale of a taxi driver issued through the Hong Kong newspaper *Ta Kung Pao* in April 2013 illustrated this. Late one evening by the Drum Tower in Beijing a driver named Guo picked up two men, one who sat in the front of the cab, one in the back. Not taking much notice of them at first, he started off some chit-chat about the recent very severe pollution in the city. 'I said,' Guo was reported by the paper as saying,

> that there had been so much smog in Beijing this year, and that now the air pollution was really serious, and that was causing a lot of anger in society, and making common people get a poor idea of the government. The guy beside me said 'It's an easy thing to make pollution, but hard to manage it. You can make pollution in a minute, but it takes ten minutes to clear it up. People's lives now are prosperous. You had to take care to look after society's progress, and it was tough to

balance on the one hand the management of pollution and
on the other the production of pollution.'

Betraying immense powers of understatement and light irony,
the driver was reported as having responded to this homily by
observing to himself that 'the way this guy talked was different
to someone off the street'. It was only a few minutes later that he
observed the man behind him, who he could see in the mirror
looked very much like the newly appointed president, Xi Jinping.
The paper went on to report that only when he dropped the customer off at the gates of the State Guest House did he realise that
it was the one and only Xi Jinping – president of the People's
Republic of China (PRC).[1]

Tai Kung Pao is regarded as a paper close to the Chinese government. This, along with the fact that the official State news
agency, Xinhua, had initially seemed to confirm the story, created
fevered excitement. Surely this encounter had been for real? And
yet the idea of the most powerful man in China simply travel-
ling incognito on the streets of Beijing ran against everything that
had been assumed about the ways leaders at this level operated in
the country. Even the most insignificant of the 200-strong Central
Committee permanent members tended to travel in ways that
closed down large parts of the air and land transport system when
they descended on a place. The length and breadth of the land
had privileged areas reserved for the accommodation of these god-
like figures. For a Politburo member, let alone the highest ranking
ones, to be apart from a squadron of security officers and protection police was revolutionary news. That Mr Guo had only a scrib-
bled note on which the customer had written 'Serve the people'
without even signing it, and a couple of anonymous cab tickets as
evidence of his claimed encounter, gave some pause for thought.
But the odd way in which the story was first confirmed and then
denied by people who should have known what was happening
complicated things. Maybe the denial meant the opposite – that

in fact the Party secretary had broken free of his usual minders, and in the fashion of a modern-day Peter the Great of Russia from three centuries before, had gone anonymously amongst the people to find out what they were really thinking.

'Once elevated to join the twenty five members of the Politburo,' Australian journalist Rowan Callick, who was based in Beijing for a number of years, wrote in a book on the modern CPC, 'a Chinese leader and his – it is almost invariably his – spouse will probably never again eat in a restaurant, stay in a hotel, fly in a plane or even drive on a road at the same time as any member of the public'.[2] The oddly isolated world of these figures is only testified to by a senior journalist based in China who said that one of the few ways the members of this elite club were able to try to peer back into the world they had just left was to have an hour a day during which, on open-access computers able to operate outside the parameters of the great firewall of China, they could surf the internet, checking the public pulse on issues, trying to work out what the country they led actually thought. In the 2000s, in the era of Hu and Wen, there had been information that in a single county in Inner Mongolia, out of a population of 400,000, 12,000 supplied information to various government agents. Hu Jintao, in his work report at the Seventeenth Party Congress in October 2007, had stressed the need for getting good-quality public feedback on government and Party services, and allowing people to participate more in decision making. But it was clear that in the new networked China, while information flowed through the air, what could be trusted, and how it would be interpreted usefully and reliably, were matters of deep contention.

SMASHING FACTIONS

Most accept that China's political system is a hierarchical one topped by a small and very powerful super elite. But defining the unifying characteristics of these elite political groups in modern China is an issue dominated by lively argument. Right from the

1970s, scholars in the West have come up with various models to try to make sense of how elite politics works and what holds groups together. Factional models have been very popular. Experts have articulated models that show the links between political careers in the elite and important entities like the Party Youth League or the military or powerful ministries.[3] Assumptions about the importance of factions in explaining elite careers are part of the landscape of trying to understand contemporary Chinese politics. But getting clarity on how factions work proves more elusive.

It is clear that Chinese politics is a world dominated by figures and groups who have shared cohesive and interlinking bonds. After the era of strong-man politics, which reached its acme under Mao Zedong, but still lingered up to a point in paramount leader Deng Xiaoping's period of domination from the end of the 1970s into the 1990s, elite leaders have had diminishing political capital. Individuals needed to form into groups promoting common interests rather then aiming to control everything themselves. The main configuration of factions, it is argued, occurred during the Jiang Zemin period from 1989 to 2002.

One of the most easily identifiable is the Shanghai faction. When Jiang Zemin was unexpectedly elevated to Party secretary after the demise of his predecessor as national CPC secretary, Zhao Ziyang, during the Tiananmen Square uprising in 1989, he came to Beijing after a long career mostly spent in the great coastal city of Shanghai. It was here that he had been mayor and then Party secretary. He was surrounded by important figures there, like Zhu Rongji, who was to serve as his premier later in the 1990s, but also fellow national leaders after 1997, Wu Bangguo and Huang Ju. All of these were to come to Beijing from Shanghai to work alongside him. He also raised Wang Huning, originally at Shanghai's Fudan University but then lifted to direct the Central Research Office and become, in many ways, the Party's chief strategic thinker from the late 1990s onwards. The other key member of the Shanghai group was Zeng Qinghong, Jiang's chief lieutenant and right-hand man, who reached the level of vice president from 2002 to 2007, and whose influence on elite politics and policy throughout the Jiang and early Hu period was immense. Such a cluster of people who had worked so much in Shanghai naturally created talk of a 'Shanghai gang'.

Then there are those associated with the China Youth League (CYL) faction, the branch of the CPC for people under 26, which had, as of 2010, over 90 million members. The importance of the League became clear in the Deng period in the 1980s, because it was seen as the training ground for future leaders. The former leader of the League, Hu Yaobang, had himself ended up as Party secretary from 1980. His successors – particularly Hu Jintao, who had been brought from one of the more remote western provinces, Gansu, to Beijing – were able to use their leadership of the League to capture the attention of the elder leaders, who at that time had mostly retired from politics but still exercised immense influence. The Youth League faction of the current generation of leaders is claimed to include figures like Premier Li Keqiang, who was active in the League at the same time as Hu Jintao. With its national networks, its immense importance in inculcating Socialist values in young cadres, and its ability to figure as a training ground for future elite leaders, the CYL became viewed as one of the chief power fiefdoms of modern Chinese politics.

We can add to this the princeling faction. Arguments about the definition of princelings continue to this day. The principal idea here is to track a cohesive group of current leaders who have family links going back to early generations of elite figures in the PRC. The idea of 'a bloodline inheritance' for Party membership reared its head at the very beginning of the CR – the long decade from 1966 – with class membership being viewed as a critical constituent of one's Party fidelity and fitness to be called a Communist.[4] Links to elite officials at this time were a double-edged sword. Originally, they were seen as potential sources of protection as the mass-mobilisation characteristic of that time got under way. This quickly became more complicated once the initial guise of the CR as a cultural campaign gave way to what turned out to be its real objective – at least in Mao Zedong's mind.[5] This was to attack the vested interest of the Party itself, and especially the bureaucracy that had built up around specific ministries and power centres. Figures at the very head of the Party like country president Liu Shaoqi and general secretary Deng Xiaoping were felled, and their families subjected to humiliation and sometimes physical violence. The impact of the CR on the Chinese elite was very deep and traumatising, and will be looked at in more detail later. But through their shared experience of suffering, it created a cohesive group of people. In the late 1970s and early 1980s, after the great rectification campaign largely spearheaded by Hu Yaobang with Deng Xiaoping's support, elder leaders returned, but at a time in their lives when some of them were deep into their 70s and 80s. There was a decision in 1982 to ask leaders to retire from executive positions at the age of 70, but to allow each family to choose one younger member to carry on their interests. Bo Xilai was one of the beneficiaries of this. By the late 1980s, therefore, there were a select group of new leaders who were the children of former senior leaders, and the concept of a Party family aristocracy took root. Princelings became defined as those with blood links to people who had served at vice-ministerial level or above in previous administrations. Of the seven-strong Politburo Standing Committee from 2012 it could be argued that four, either directly or through marriage, are princelings. But as I will argue later, the term princeling raises more issues than it settles.

A more business-orientated group is the oil faction. As the Party defined its role more precisely in society from 1978, it became clear that there needed to be more clarity about the division between State-owned enterprises (SOEs) within the centrally planned economy, and political or administrative entities. Despite this commercialisation and reform, SOEs continue to have immense political importance, and their most senior management are still appointments made directly by the Party from officials within its ranks. The huge oil industry in particular, with what ended up as three key large State companies, has become important as a foundation for political power and careers. The most representative figure from this faction is Zhou Yongkang, Politburo member from 2007 to 2012, whose career in the oil industry lasted several decades before he became China's security czar in the Seventeenth Congress. Another example is Zhang Gaoli, a member of the Politburo from 2012, and someone with 17 years in the petrochemical industry leadership, who was elevated onto the Eighteenth Party Congress.

Finally, there is the Qinghua University faction. Qinghua, Beijing is one of modern China's top universities. At least under the Hu Jintao leadership, those who had been educated there became significant. Hu Jintao and his premier, Wen Jiabao, were both graduates in the 1960s. Xi Jinping was also a graduate. The rise of the Qinghua group represented for some analysts the appearance of a better-educated, technocratic generation of leadership, many of whom were graduates in the hard sciences. Qinghua figured as a training ground for the new elite in the same way as Oxford University in the UK (responsible for all but three post-war British prime ministers) and the *grandes écoles* in France.

Looking at the leaders in this way at least allows us to get some purchase on their careers and the rationale behind them getting into the final elite in contemporary Chinese politics, and provides some initial organising principles. But it clearly also has limitations. Many elite figures transcend boundaries between factions easily. Liu Yandong, a Politburo member from 2007, is perhaps the most representative. Liu is a princeling (or at least the female equivalent) through her father, Liu Ruilong, a former vice minister of agriculture, who had been instrumental in introducing Jiang Zemin into the CPC[6] (thereby giving her a link to the Shanghai faction; her father had also worked there in the early 1950s and spent five years in jail there during the CR from 1967[7]). Liu was at Qinghua University from 1964 to 1970, overlapping with Hu Jintao, and took a series of positions in the Youth League from 1982 to 1991 in Beijing. The only faction that Liu does not seem to belong to is the oil one. Looking at other key figures, one sees similar interlinking networks. Xi Jinping is a princeling par excellence, a Qinghua graduate and, through his brief period in 2007 as the Party secretary there, arguably a member of the Shanghai gang. Making sense of leaders by using factionalism in China is therefore a hard business.[8] Not many figures easily belong to one particular group. And some belong to almost all of them.

Factionalism as a means to understand elite politics in China probably reached its zenith in the build-up to the 2007 Party Congress that year. Throughout 2006 and into 2007 there was talk of a grassroots faction versus an elitist one. President and Party secretary Hu Jintao was seen as exemplifying the first. He was portrayed as coming from a modest background politically, with his father noted simply as a tea merchant, and his mother dying when he was not yet ten years old.[9] He stood in stark contrast to someone like Jiang Zemin, his predecessor, who was portrayed as the son of a Party revolutionary martyr, and therefore a member of the elite. At this time, the elitist-versus-grassroots model worked nicely enough, and everyone could be shuffled into one or the other. But a few years later there were figures like Li Keqiang, who seemed not quite to fit in either. His background was modest enough, from a small town in Anhui. According to some reports he had relied on only his own abilities to get into the national elite Beijing University.[10] But his father in law, Cheng Jinrui, had been a leading member of the very earliest Youth League established after 1949, working from 1952 as a representative on the second Zhengzhou City Youth League delegation, staying in the League locally into the CR until he worked in a national agricultural organisation in the 1980s. While he was not at vice-ministerial level, it is clear that Li was also linked to someone with a significant career in the Party bureaucracy.[11] Did that mean he was an elitist grassroots faction member? The only conclusion one can draw from all of this is that we need much more sophisticated categories to try to capture the links between leading political figures in China.

SO NO FACTIONS, BUT DEFINITELY ELITES

Factionalism might not help much, but we still have a definite elite
to try to make sense of. China remains a highly hierarchical political system. To try to get to grips with understanding this elite we
need to work out whom we are dealing with. One of the first questions is how big this group is, and how it is constituted. Research
by Kjeld Eric Brødsgaard on the CPC organisation history showed
that in 1998 there were 40.5 million cadres in China running the
country. 'Leading cadres' constituted a little over 1 per cent of these,
92 per cent of whom were working at provincial level and below.
That meant 0.1 per cent were in the centre in Beijing. And in this
group, those working at ministerial level and above constituting the
'high-level cadres' (*gaoji ganbu*) came to a national total of 2,562,
of whom a third were in Beijing.[12] There is a clear conclusion to be
drawn from these statistics: China is a vast country, run by a small
group of people.

The genealogy of this elite can be tracked back to the 11 Chinese
members of the First Congress in 1921: a sort of gene pool of Party
aristocracy, many of whom were felled in purges or destroyed in
war before a second wave of elites appeared through the 1930s.
Most of the new elite were linked to patronage networks around
Mao Zedong as he rose to Party leadership dominance. These second generation elites turned on themselves in purges of various
completeness and depth in the Maoist period from 1949 to 1976,
the most serious and extensive being the CR. Those that finally
emerged from this back into positions of power after 1978 became
the basis for a new wave of elites, more often than not with links
to the old. Deng Xiaoping's attempts to introduce fresh blood into
the Party simply created a new elite sitting alongside the old.

There is nothing as solid and well defined in modern China as
a standard group of people operating like an aristocracy as part of a
highly unified elite with a set identity and firm rules of how power
can be passed from one to the other. There is, rather, a much more

dynamic and changing network of different elites with porous boundaries that, with political skill and the cultivation of the right patronage networks, people from diverse backgrounds can enter. The one feature that holds this diverse clustering of elite groupings together is fidelity to the Party and defence of its monopoly on power. Even about the best means of attaining this fundamental end, there are, within these different elites, splits, fractures and frequent clashes. We have to know better what holds these groups together, and, when things get tough, what splits them apart. They are the masters of the country we call China – a country run by a group of people that is smaller than most villages in Europe. They deserve closer attention and more sophisticated understanding than the oversimplified language of factionalism can supply.

GETTING PERSONAL: JIANG AND HU

The era of power based purely on the networks around one man, as Mao had brought into existence, is long past. There is more competition in the power market in China now that Maoist centralisation is gone. Sources of power are no longer in one place but dispersed through different institutions and bodies, locally and nationally. Aspiring politicians have to 'canvas' amongst these different sources, recruiting support in order to have a chance to join the 'club of 3,000' high-level cadres outlined above. Zhao Ziyang's brief tenure as Party secretary from 1987 to 1989 proves that, without the time and the opportunity to build up a network in the ministries, provinces and the other key organisations around you, your core support at the centre when a major challenge comes can be very shallow. Perhaps Bo Xilai also proves this. His fall was remarkable for the lack of meaningful opposition to his removal amongst his peers. The most enduring figures in modern Chinese politics from 1978 therefore have been people who have managed to create this wide, supportive, enabling network. This 'political feudalism' of power lords and serfs is something that will be looked at in depth below.[13]

When one looks at analysis of the leadership elites since 1990 as they have appeared in the various Central Committees of up to 350 alternate and full members of the CPC, and of the Politburos that have come from these, one sees increasing talk of 'Jiang's men' and 'Hu's men'.[14] The standard explanation for Jiang Zemin's ceding the key Party leadership position to Hu Jintao in 2002 is that the former generation of Party elders around Deng Xiaoping had ordered this, and it was therefore something Jiang did not have the political capital to overrule. The elders had aimed in this way to support the institutionalisation of leadership succession so that never again would the Party be hijacked by the influence of a single man as it had been under Mao. One means to achieve this was stipulating a fixed retirement age for Party leaders. Jiang was therefore required to retire after two terms as Party secretary even though this was not written down anywhere (the Party Constitution, unlike the State Constitution, sets down no term limits on Party secretary occupancy). A process of succession started from the Fifteenth Party Congress in 1997, the first step of which was the elevation of Hu Jintao to vice president, then to vice chairman of the Central Military Commission, and finally to Party secretaryship itself in 2002. That this was a process where the rules were being made up as things went along was clear at the time, with heavy speculation before and after 2002 about just how much Jiang was really able to withdraw from political influence. In the ensuing decade, Jiang continued to occupy an ambiguous place, out of office but often imputed with influence. This, as will be shown later, became most visible at the very end of the transition between Hu's leadership and Xi Jinping's, where Jiang played a critical brokering role. Jiang's role post 2002 proves that political capital is a substance that, once created in Chinese politics, is hard to destroy.[15]

Jiang Zemin had been an unexpected leader. Being regarded as something of a buffoon and a political lightweight as mayor, and then Party secretary of Shanghai from 1985, his elevation to Beijing in 1989 very soon after Tiananmen Square erupted in protests in June that year was regarded with widespread surprise. The sole credible explanation for this sudden elevation offered by commentators at the time was that he was the least objectionable candidate in a highly unappealing field. While the leadership in Beijing, divided at the time because of the student rebellion crisis, did not strongly support him, they also certainly disliked any other possible contenders more.[16] Jiang's early period in power was unsurprisingly lacklustre, and he was to tell a future interviewer that when the call came for him to come to Beijing to national leadership, he was as astonished as anyone else.

Jiang had luck, but he was at least able to seize this and show remarkable adeptness over the coming decade. In that sense, as those who tried to face Jiang off even in his retirement found out, his achievements while he was in charge of the Party over 13 years, and the wide networks of people who owed him because of their promotion and elevation during this time, were immense and continuing sources of influence. He carried these with him even after stepping down from formal positions of power. Jiang could invoke as achievements during his period in power the strong growth of the Chinese economy from 1989 to 2002 while he was in charge, despite the threat posed by the Asian financial crisis over 1998. He had also seen through the final period of negotiations successfully for the World Trade Organization (WTO) in 2001, and managed to secure the Beijing Olympics the same year. But there were deeper achievements. He had managed to push the military out of commercial activities in 1998–9, reining them in after a particularly bellicose period over Taiwan in 1995, introducing principles issued by the government in 1998 whereby the People's Liberation Army (PLA) had to desist from low-level money-spinning activities. He had also completed the successful 'rehabilitation' of non-State-sector business people, devising the 'three representatives' theory, which had allowed some of them to join the Party in 2002 after years of disenfranchisement, acknowledging their role in producing GDP growth and productivity. He had brought down the corrupt

Party secretary of Beijing, Chen Xitong, in 1996, without great danger. He had managed to see off the danger when the US-led NATO forces had accidentally bombed the Chinese embassy in Belgrade, Serbia in 1999, a time when Chinese public anger and nationalism could have caused huge problems for relations with the US. Finally, Jiang had been instrumental during the risky and delicate transition of power to Hu Jintao, a period fraught with issues because of the very poor record of the Party before in trying to choose a successor. Jiang's achievements while in power were impressive, and things that gave him continuing credibility and clout even after his ostensible retirement.[17]

Hu had never been Jiang's man despite working with him from the Fourteenth Party Congress in 1992 after returning from Party leadership of Tibet. His own greatest power base was in the CYL, which he had headed from 1982 to 1985, during which time he had attracted the admiration of Deng Xiaoping and other senior Party leaders, but also managed to start building his own patronage network amongst younger officials. His great asset when he came back to national leadership in 1992 was a long and diverse provincial career in which he had proved that he fitted the new leadership template of being someone who was able to deal with a range of challenging administrative tasks in charge of difficult provinces. Even so, his first period as Party secretary from 2002 was beset with feelings that he was surrounded by those who owed their real allegiance to his predecessor rather than him. Zeng Qinghong, who served as his vice president, was the most controversial: a man who was seen as belonging to the princeling faction through his father but who was also inextricably linked to Jiang Zemin from their time together in Shanghai, and who was regarded in many ways as Jiang's most loyal advisor. Of Hu Jintao's first Politburo Standing Committee from 2002, seven of the nine members could be clearly linked to Jiang Zemin by patronage and promotion lines. In 2007, Hu was accorded a victory in the fact that finally Zeng Qinghong retired from the new Standing Committee, and at least four of the nine new members were not clearly linked to Jiang. From this period, too, there was a stronger sense that figures like future premier Le Keqiang were at least 'Hu's men'.

This idea of 'belonging' to someone in this way is, at least on the surface, a strange one. The means by which figures are appointed in the Party and government in China is highly opaque. The actual ways in which officials are finally elevated above their peers to win key positions remains largely a mystery. Even so, the transition from the fourth to fifth generation, with the high-level meeting held at the seaside resort of Beidahe in the autumn of 2012 (see later) offers a little insight into the ways in which consultation with former leaders and taking into account their opinions are strong factors in favour of someone's promotion. What we are less clear about in this system is the criterion by which people are given a clear advantage over others, and the ways in which elite conflict and disagreement are brokered. Certainly, a sense from former senior leaders that candidate X is 'a good guy' and up to the job is a major step towards success. For that reason, Jiang and Hu, simply from the positions they occupied at the summit of the Party, have the most clout. Jiang in particular had decades to build a strong network, stretching back to the 1950s – something that will be illustrated later. But he also seemed to share, with US president Ronald Reagan, a disarming disconnect between his somewhat comical outer image, and evidence that he was a far shrewder judge of people and their abilities than he was ever given credit for. While it might not therefore be written on the job description of Party leaders in China (if there is even such a thing), one of their key tasks, and one Jiang performed well at, is talent spotting.

It is inevitable in view of the age bands by which leaders on the whole rise up the Party and government system in China that a former leader's networks bear fruit before those of current leaders. Hu's men, therefore – those presented in the Chinese and international press as people with strong links to him – are ones that might have strong careers in the future (with the exception of Li Keqiang,

who is now premier). The most favoured of these have been Hu
Chunhua and Ling Jihua, both full Politburo members after 2012
(although, as will be explained later, the death in uncertain circumstances of Ling's son in a car accident in Beijing in early 2012
may have blighted his future). Their political personalities perhaps
reflect the influence of their ostensible patron – quiet, administratively gifted, seemingly able to deal with crises. But they remain, at
least for today, tomorrow's men, their potential not yet realised.

Does relating people's careers to evidence of patronage by significant serving or retired Party leaders help us much in understanding
the dynamics of the leadership elites in modern China? The Jiang-
versus-Hu competition was interesting to watch over the decade
from 2002 and there are parts of it that help explain, up to a point,
why certain things happened when they did. Even so, just like factional analysis, this still seems a simplification. What precisely was
the political standpoint of the Jiang period, the ideological or policy
content, as it were, that would divide a Jiangist from from a Huist?
Where did they differ on policy issues so that you might actually
be able to tell them apart, in the ways that you could a Democrat
from a Republican in the US? Beyond owing their promotion and
appointments to the involvement of particular people, how can they
be said to 'belong to the same camp' as them? This also overshad-
ows the idea of a Shanghai, Qinghua, or oil faction set out above.
Is there any way we can group these figures in such a way that they
are linked not just by institutional or tribal features of their careers,
but by a meeting of the minds, a common political approach, something approaching political orientation in multi-party democratic
systems where you can try to split the right from the left, and then
find segments and shades of opinion in each of these based on a
combination of ideas as well as personal links?

Trying to identify a specific 'Jiang' vision of the world that differs
from a 'Hu' one and therefore gives not just institutional but ideological content to belonging to the one rather than the other faction
is not so easy. The greatest concern over the 2002 political transition

was to avoid Party fracturing. The likeliest way to cause this to happen would have been to resurrect some of the key ideological battles
of the past that had split the Party so severely during its history.
Finding consensus and means to deliver that consensus therefore
was a big challenge, and ability to deliver this made up a major part
of the CPC leadership skills. Jiang's battle to allow entrepreneurs
into the CPC was greeted with dismay by leftists around influential
Party ideologue Deng Liqun, who attacked it as conceding the heart
and soul of the whole Socialist experiment in the late 1990s. Beijing
University professor Wang Hui stated elegantly that all conflicts in
recent Chinese history have had, at their heart, a major ideological
component.[18] The most elemental of these have been between those
who stood by the conviction that the State was best placed to plan
and direct the economy, and those who embraced deeper marketisation.[19] Ultra-leftism remained a dog that still had teeth to bite even
after 2002.[20] Bo Xilai was accused of using Maoist messaging to
promote a more equal, equitable society based on communal values. Fundamentally, the political argument in contemporary China
boils down to the same debates between left and right over the final
role of the State versus the market that occur across the world –
with the major difference in China of this all occurring within one
political party. Factionalist allegiance underestimates this ideological dynamic, emphasising the ways in which people act from tribal
and personal-interest-driven links rather than ideational ones.

Leadership in the period of Jiang and Hu, and in Xi's so far,
has been based on the belief that there is a central political ground.
Finding consensus about where this ground is has become akin to an
elite counterpart of the 'pro-stability' policy increasingly promoted
by Hu in the later part of his period in office. Policy evolution
and growth, rather than sudden innovation and change, have been
the name of the game. The 'Three Represents' ideology supporting non-State entrepreneurs becoming members of the Party grew
over the late 1990s, till it was finally put in the Party Constitution
in 2002. The 'Scientific Development Theory' and 'harmonious

society', which were Hu Jintao's signature ideas, were announced in 2003 and 2004, and finally given formal constitutional status from 2007. Slow announcement of policies in order not to disrupt or upset has been a common feature from the early 1990s. One of the illuminating issues about Bo Xilai's case is how it showed that policy innovation and then promotion, when done too overtly and quickly, were read as both threatening and disruptive. This was not the way to do things in modern Chinese politics.

IDEOLOGY MATTERS: THE CASE OF PREMIER WEN JIABAO

Despite this, there has been fierce debate about ideology or at least political positioning in China, but at a much more granular level than simply saying that Jiang and Hu represent two easily identifiable approaches to policy and policy development. In 2012, the National Development and Reform Commission (DRC) and the World Bank produced a report on the challenges facing the country in the coming two decades up to 2030. The conclusions of the report will be discussed in Chapter 5. It was a broadly reformist document, which in its executive summary proposed six major areas for future reform, running from deeper marketisation of the economy and the factors of production, to a larger role for the non-State sector, and a wider reform of government and administrative functions.

The issuance of the report offered an opportunity for 1,644 prominent economists within China to produce their own open letter on 15 July 2012, directed particularly at Premier Wen Jiabao, who was viewed as the primary political patron of the report, despite its falling more under the immediate jurisdiction of the vice premier in charge of macro-economic affairs at the time, Li Keqiang. The letter interpreted the report as a direct challenge to the Chinese Socialist system. It was, the letter said, 'an attempt by Wen Jiabao to introduce multi-party capitalist politics' into China, and to attack public and State-owned enterprises. The authors of the report found that this had been a consistent trend of Wen throughout his period as premier, with only 27 per cent of the economy in 2010 in the hands of the State sector, and 73 per cent in the non-State. The State enterprises, in the energy, chemicals, materials, telecoms and construction sectors were, however, 'critical to preserving the independence of our economy'. State enterprises were presented as the most competitive in taking on enterprises outside China, and the major source of profits for the country. The most powerful attack in the document, however, was a statement that the DRC and the World Bank were nothing more than the front for American-led capitalist infiltration into China, and into the Chinese economy, which they were covertly seeking to weaken and destabilise in the same disastrous way that had happened after the fall of the Soviet Union and the central planning system in 1991. Continuous analysis and focus on this event in China from the early 1990s had concluded that the involvement of foreign, and mostly US, economists had visited on Russia almost complete disaster.[21] 'As a member of the Standing Committee of the Politburo, and for a decade Premier of the State Council, Wen Jiabao in his time in power has pushed forward revisionism, and surrendered national interest to foreigner colonialists', the letter declared. He had 'promoted privatisation, turned over Socialism and committed a series of massive mistakes'. As evidence for this the letter claimed that in his decade as a leader in the Centre Wen had never once, in a speech, report or interview, mentioned the name of Mao Zedong. 'In his time as leader, management problems in our society have increased, and criminal acts risen to a level never seen since the period of liberation [in 1949].' Quoting figures from the *Chinese Annual Legal Yearbook* (*Zhongguo Falu Nianjian*) from 2003 to 2010, the critics of Wen stated that in 2003 there were 4.8 million 'social management' issues, but this had increased over 2.5 times to 12 million by 2010. In 2003 there had been 730,000 crimes prosecuted in China, but by 2010 this had risen to 1.05 million, up 1.4 times. One of the signatories of this report, Ma Bing, was nearly

100 years old. The whole letter was a forceful reminder that supporting state enterprises and holding foreign cooperation in deep
suspicion still had traction within some intellectual communities
in the country.[22]

That Wen had tried to articulate more broadly 'reformist' language towards the end of his time as premier is true. But there were
also a swath of issues about both his own political networks and
his family influences that come into this, which will be looked at
later. The key point here is that ideological positioning, while not
blatant, is important amongst elite politicians.[23] Factional analysis
fails to reach this, with no real idea of what precisely the policy
unity might be between Qinghua-group people, princelings and
youth leaguers, nor for that matter between those who are seen as
owing most to Jiang's patronage, and those who owe more to Hu.

DYNAMIC NETWORKS: POWER AND PROFIT

How do we make some sense of why certain people get in and why
others remain outside the political leadership elites in contemporary
China? I want to propose three key ideas to help here. Each one
tries to capture one of the unique features of this elite firmament in
slightly different ways – and that is its extreme dynamism. One of
the criticisms I will make of factional analysis is that is comes across
as too static. Are leaders really coopted into these groups and then
settled in them for good, like life membership of organisations or
clubs? Is there really that strong a sense of membership, that once
one joins a group in this way one somehow never really leaves it?
And does factionalism adequately capture how, even in a way very
diluted from the period of Mao and Deng, individuals can really take
and shape particular power bases, and profoundly change and adapt
them? Factionalism fails to capture the very personal nature of power
in modern China, and goes too far towards stressing the strength
of politically ill-defined blocs. For an easier life, we might want to
see Chinese politics evolving in this way. But to underestimate the

power of personal impacts and directions within this system would be a big mistake. The challenge is to find a model that somehow captures the personal, the ideological and the institutional, and captures something of the dynamism within this system. In the era of almost ubiquitous social media in China, we might at least have a good model to start out with in the notion of networks, and use this as an explanatory tool to understand better the dynamic, person-centred nature of Chinese elite political allegiances.

First of all, however, we have to start off by looking at power itself. The political elite in China are mainly in the business of negotiating, trading, sometimes accruing and sometimes losing power. That much seems clear. We can track this through money, legal impact, through their ability to support particular political programmes, and other tangible manifestations. As I will argue later, the remarkable thing about the Socialist system that has developed in the PRC in the last decades after Mao has been the ways in which, for all the sophistication and complexity of marking out policies, patronage networks, vested interest and political priorities, profit, and in particular money profit, has become the great leveller. It may be concealed and hard to dig out, but money and profit have become overwhelming features in this system. One of the great political skills found in figures like Xi Jinping is their ability to navigate between the rhetorical positions of the Party in articulating public disdain for this outcome, even at the same time as there is almost universal indulgence in its promotion.

One way to understand the dynamic property of power in China can be found in French philosopher Michel Foucault, who argued that power operated more like a kind of energy, or a field of forces.[24] Foucault's descriptions of power captured its dynamism and steered away from the notion that power was something fixed and ossified. On one level, the modes of how power operates in contemporary China can be mapped through its material institutional 'delivery' mechanisms. The relationship between the Party as a source of power, and the government as an entity on which this power operates, is the prime example. Through looking at this we get some insights into how the Party is able to maintain its distinctive position in society through its pre-eminence as a means of brokering consensus and compromise amongst key political elites and then mandating governmental implementation. Power can be mapped through the occupation of specific positions and territories within the Party's national and provincial apparatus, and through understanding their discrete enabling networks. But power also lies outside designated Party or government positions, and sometimes remains in the gift of people who have influence but do not occupy an easily defined space within the formal structures of administrative and political power. Retired senior leaders are trickiest to catch when trying to map configurations of power. Figures like Deng Xiaoping in the 1980s and 1990s, then Jiang Zemin in the 1990s and 2000s, and after 2013 Hu Jintao, had power through influence, though this is something very hard to tabulate and give evidence for. The CPC's opacity is in some ways one of its key strategic assets. External observers therefore often either underestimate or overestimate the intent behind particular actions and how best to interpret them, whom to impute them to and how to understand either the calculus of winners or losers, or the guiding intention behind them.

Foucault's almost poetic description of power as a kind of energy source captures the dynamism and amorphousness of power in modern China well. Far from flowing from a single legitimated source, power in China comes from various origins, flowing out through various tributaries. Some of these are linked to control over narratives of the past and the rise to power of the CPC promoted through propaganda and information networks, some of them to domination over the actual apparatus of information control such as the internet, some of them to control over resources like rights to land and its use, and some of them to leadership of institutions used for the coercion or attack of subversive elements like the Ministry of State Security or the Public Security Bureau. A major source of power simply flows from the ways in which the unified operations of the central and provincial Party propaganda machinery have been able to promote the idea of its delivering since 1978 a better life for people, and its strenuous efforts to have consistent narratives of the aim towards a better life and an almost utopian Socialist outcome for everyone. An elite figure in this system can in some senses be seen as trying to capture as many of these sources of power as possible, moving across different areas, using different institutions, slipping into different narratives, and acquiring the right to use different contested but highly privileged vocabularies and modes of expression in ways that promote their personal interests and that of their associated networks.

ECONOMIC CHANGE: THE BIRD IN THE CAGE

The political and linguistic environment in modern China is profoundly penetrated by the notion of a market, and of fulfilling financial and economic objectives. The elites, politically and administratively, have embraced hard-nosed capitalism to such an extent that even the most zealous supporters of the dream of world Socialism's final victory have huge problems aligning the reality they meet in contemporary China with the CPC's remnant of outward commitments to Marxism-Leninism in the speeches of its leaders and the constituent elite guidance documents issued by the State Council and other government and Party organs. In this context it is perhaps appropriate to look at the concept of liquidity of relations in modern China, just as one can talk of liquidity of capital in a market. This is especially so because the Party's dominant discourse, at least as it appears in many of the speeches by figures like Hu Jintao in the last decade, presents itself as at the vanguard of modernity.[25] The liquid nature of modernity has been well described by sociologist Zygmunt Bauman, who in his classic work on this talks of the way that fluidity is a quality of liquids and gases, and how this distinguishes them from solids because 'they "cannot sustain a tangential, or shearing, force when at rest" and so undergo "a continuous change in shape when subjected to such a stress" '.[26] Bauman talks in his book of 'the melting of bonds' and 'releasing the breaks' between people and institutions in post-modern societies in the developed world: of processes of 'deregulation, liberalization, "flexiblization"', which increase fluidity, and are manifested through, amongst other things, the unbridling of the financial, real estate and labour markets. In this society, power and authority are marketised, and people are located in highly flexible and self-creating networks, where they are able to negotiate identities, statuses and personal narratives as never before.[27]

Arguably no society has undergone such large-scale and rapid change as that of modern China. Since 1949, in two very different phases of modernisation, it has seen revolutionary social and economic transformations. These have had a profound effect. Prior to 1976, one could argue that the dominant polity was to accept mass social mobilisation (there were 16 mass campaigns from 1951 onwards to bring about change, the largest of them the CR), to sanction the resolution of contradictions in society through violent struggle, and to subscribe to a Sinified version of Marxism located in Mao Zedong's canonical works. Over the final years of the 1970s, this was replaced by a new consensus in which economic development of the country as a means of restoring it to national greatness was viewed as the more effective strategy. That involved the embrace of foreign capital, marketisation, and a loosening and redefinition of the State's boundaries and the Party's function. This process is still ongoing. At the heart of the changes since then is the framework put most famously and crisply by Chen Yun, a Politburo member in the 1980s, of the 'bird in the cage' vision of economic development – controlled, strategic industrial and market models that allowed State ordering and direction but also made space for entrepreneurialism, the private sector, and some limited and non-threatening social liberalism. The battleground has strayed back and forth across this turf, with liberals sometimes in the ascendant (as they were over the entry into the WTO up to 2001) and then more conservative groups gaining the upper hand (as during handling of the student unrest in 1989 and its final outcomes).

The leadership elite, particularly in the Politburos or in the Central Committees, appear like a still centre in this vortex of activity, the real emperors of control, whose language, customs and habits are reassuringly static despite the almost constant change around them. In 2011, a Politburo member told a delegation of which I was part that, since 1978, there had been change every day in China, physically transforming the environment and the world, and that this change had operated on the visible, but also 'on those places we cannot see – people's hearts'. These two zones of profound change, the physical world and the inner world of Chinese people, have been the sites of renegotiations, contestation and transformation. The elite have sometimes acted as though they were above and somehow outside all of this, imperiously directing and commanding, from another world. This is most visible in the ways in which they speak, with their highly controlled and somewhat unnatural love of a bureaucrat 'socio-dialect' that is far away from the street language of the rest of society – a sort of professional 'language of power'.

Despite this, the leadership transitions of 2012–13 and the ways in which elite figures related to each other during this process, as this book will aim to show, have in fact changed along with society. How could they not? Elites might be different from others, but they are part of a greater society despite occupying a specific space in it. The neat way in which Bauman captures the dynamism of modernity and its impact on the social and intellectual as well as the material sphere helps when we look at the ways in which leaders are appointed, legitimised, and how they need to operate in a system in which many of the former 'solid' structures of authority have been eroded. Just as the economy of the PRC over the last three decades has been marketised, so have the power structures. There is now a power market, along with money and goods ones. Within the elite, people's stock rises and falls, the capital of their power and influence increases and then declines. In this system, there are investors, stakeholders, those who put some kind of influence and 'capital' into it and therefore wish to see a return. Like any market in any context, this one is dynamic and ever changing. Not the least of the paradoxes of modern China is that the State Socialist system, with its Party enjoying a monopoly on power, is in fact profoundly marketised. What is difficult is to stand outside this system and work out the modes of investment, the ways in which political capital is acquired and lost, and the means by which particular key careers are conducted. If we had a way of calculating this then we would be well placed to try to understand the advancement of certain figures, and the falling behind of others. We would also see how their bonds into certain loose networks that we have called factions up till now sometimes assist them, sometimes are of no use, and sometimes are an impediment. What we see in this system is an attempt to be collectivist and joined up from outside, but a system that is strongly driven by individual actors and their capacities, personal networks and strategies. Why we cannot map out more clearly the likely winners and losers in this game is because the number of variables is almost infinite. The best we can do is to use this model of liquidity and of a 'market of power' as a useful descriptive framework.

FEI XIAOTONG: NETWORKS FROM THE SOIL

As one comes closer to looking at networks built around particular people, one also comes perilously close to the exhausted notion of *guanxi*. Endlessly discussed and analysed, and a concept fondly embraced by business people and consultants, *guanxi* has become so broad in its usage now as to verge on the meaningless. As one commentator caustically remarked after a presentation on the importance of connections in China during a seminar I attended held in Vancouver late in 2012, 'What society doesn't put a premium on connections? In fact, what human behavior in the end does not involve notions of socialisation and building interpersonal links?' In that sense, *guanxi* belongs to a fading menu of orientalist vocabulary, now slowly sinking into self-caricature.

A richer sense of the networks that might operate in Chinese society comes from the immensely important work of the great sociologist Fei Xiaotong. Fei is regarded as the father of Chinese sociology, and enjoyed an academic career that spanned London in the 1930s to China in the first decade of the twenty-first century. Fei's work allows precision to be put on the notion of what a Chinese social network might be. And despite the fact that his work was done mostly before the rapid changes from 1978, it still gives rich insights into the way in which networks operate in modern China, and how individuals are able to move and navigate between these.

From the Soil is one of his most celebrated works, written in fact in 1947, and therefore predating the foundation of the PRC by two years. The first sentence of this wonderfully lucid book sets out the critical contention: 'Chinese society is fundamentally rural.'[28] Perhaps at best in 2013 we can update this to say that the roots of contemporary Chinese society are still fundamentally rural, despite the processes of urbanisation and industrialisation that have occurred in the last six decades. Fei continues:

> Life in rural society is very parochial. Villagers restrict the scope of their daily activities; they do not travel far; they seldom make contact with the outside world; they live solitary lives; they maintain their own isolated social circle. All of these characteristics contribute to the parochialism of rural China.

This is, Fei concludes, 'a society without strangers, a society based totally on the familiar'.[29] Trust in rural societies like these is 'based not on the importance of contracts but rather, on the dependability of people, people who are so enmeshed in customary norms that they cannot behave in any other way'.[30]

In this society without strangers, with profound familiarity, 'everyone stands at the centre of the circles produced by his or her own social influence. Everyone's circles are interrelated. One touches different circles at different times and places.'[31] In Chinese society:

> the most important relationship – kinship – is similar to the concentric circles formed when a stone is thrown into a lake [...] Each network is like a spider's web in the sense that it centres on oneself. Everyone has this kind of kinship network, but the people covered by one network are not the same as those covered by another.

In such a society, 'Each web has a self as its centre, and every web has a different centre.'

Unlike Bauman's liquidity, Fei uses the term 'elasticity'. This captures the dynamism within this system:

> [The] pattern of organization in Chinese traditional society has the special quality of elasticity. In the country, families can be very small, but in the wealthy landlord and bureaucratic classes, families can be as big as small kingdoms. These highly elastic social circles [...] cause the Chinese to be particularly sensitive to changes in human relationships.[32]

Social relationships in China, Fei concludes, 'possess a self centred quality'.[33]

The metaphor of a series of circles on water emanating from a centre is a powerful one. And looking at a group like the political super elite within contemporary China, the people who occupy the Central Committee of the CPC, one at least has some chance to plot these links between different groups and networks, while never losing sight of the fact that each one is based on the centrality of an *individual*. If we look closely at the individual, we can work out some of the personal links and terrain around them, capture the dynamism of this system, and free ourselves from restrictive and static frameworks implied in using concepts like factions.

A FAMILY BUSINESS

One of the most natural networks to look at is that of the 'imperial families' of the Party – the descendants of the 'Eight Immortals' as they were informally called – Deng Xiaoping, Chen Yun, Yang Shangkun, Wang Zhen, Bo Yibo, Li Xiannian, Peng Zheng, and Song Renqiong. The 'Eight Immortals' is a term referring to figures in Taoism, but it has been appropriated here to speak of elite figures from the earliest period of the CPC's rise to power who were able to maintain influence deep into the final decade of the twentieth century. Their longevity and the fact that they survived purges, dangers and challenges gifted them with immense political capital. According to some reports, their direct descendants have sought to translate that into material gain and financial wealth. The claimed behaviour of the families of the Immortals as a controlled group gives some flavour to how networks are inherited, built, mobilised and, increasingly, monetarised in contemporary PRC.

Bloomberg's celebrated analysis of the wealth of the 'Immortal' network in 2012 showed that of the 103 descendants they looked at, 23 had been educated in the US, 18 worked in American companies, and 12 had property there. Out of the 103, 43 had their own companies, or significant stakes in others, and 26 had a role in a major Chinese State-owned enterprises. A report by the Hong Kong-based newspaper *Mingbao* in January 2010 described the ways in which the Immortal descendants had managed to stake out powerful interests in specific industrial and financial sectors. More recent political families had leveraged the influence of (usually) their patriarchs in order to create new forms of economic control and vested interest. Jiang Zemin's son Jiang Mianheng had become a major player in telecoms, Li Peng's family have

significant interest in the energy sector (with his son Li Xiaopeng
appointed in 2012 as acting governor of Shanxi province after a
career in the Shenhua energy company), and Zhu Rongji's family are highly active in the finance sector, along with relatives of
Zeng Qinghong.[34] Of the 2,900 sons and daughters of high-level
officials, according to a report issued by the Chinese Academy
of Social Sciences in 2008, their collective wealth was RMB
2 trillion. In Guangdong, of the 12 major property companies,
all were employed or had links with the children of high-level
officials – usually officials who were members of the local political
Standing Committees, or deputies of the national or local people's
congresses, or the local Chinese People's Political Consultative
Conference (CPPCC). This close link between property companies and the relations of elite members of local Party committees,
congresses or consultative congresses ran across the country, from
Shanghai to Gansu.[35]

In this context, the families of the Eight Immortals occupy the
most prime territory. Looking at the case of Deng Xiaoping – 'chief
architect of reform and opening up', as one of the official phrases
describes his immense achievements – one Chinese commentator
caustically remarked that 'his catchphrase of letting a few get rich
first' might better be translated as 'but first of all, let the family of
Deng get rich', then everyone else can try to follow.[36] Bloomberg
reported that Deng Rong, Deng's daughter, and his son Deng
Zhifang, 'were among the first to enter real estate, even before new
rules in 1998 commercialised the mainland's mass housing market'.
In 1994, Deng Rong became head of a development in Shenzhen,
with apartments at that time valued at up to USD 240,000 each.
Deng's son-in-law Wu Jianchang, an executive in a State-owned
metals company, went on to become vice minister of metallurgy
and head of the Chinese Iron and Steel Company. According to
Bloomberg, he and another of Deng's sons-in-law, Zhang Hong,
ran companies that 'teamed up to buy up one of the key produc-
ers of material for rare-earth magnets from General Motors Co.'.

This 'helped China fulfill Deng's aim of dominating the market for the minerals, now used in US smart bombs, wind turbines and hybrid cars'.[37]

The family of the former great military leader Wang Zhen has been particularly successful in business. According to Bloomberg, two of the sons have interests in a valley in north-west China that, it is planned, will be turned into a USD 1.6 billion tourist attraction. Wang Jun, one of the sons, was a senior leader of the Citic Group Corporation, a major State-owned enterprise, and China Poly Group, a commercial entity linked to the military. Wang is now active as a golf course developer in China, and his daughter Jingjing owner of a USD 7 million house in Hong Kong.

As the Bloomberg report makes clear, the wealth of the Immortal families was prompted by the key role that they took in the first wave of commercialisation and marketisation of SOEs in the 1980s. Someone was likely to get rich from this period of liberalisation, and it might just as well have been the families of leaders who were in charge of the Party then, who were, after all, most trusted, and the ones who had sacrificed the most to get where they were.

The cohesive yet flexible dynamism of this network is the main takeaway point here, coming back to Fei Xiaotong's notion of a society of elasticity where the individual sits at the centre of a shifting focus of energies, all rippling out from where they are, and all in flux. Not all descendants of the Immortals decided to act commercially, showing that there are no hard and fast rules in this networked elite, despite the fact that it is one of the most tightly defined central elite bands. Song Kehuang, son of Song Renqiong, was quoted by Bloomberg expressing profound distaste for how most of the others had behaved: 'My generation and the next generation made no contribution to China's revolution, independence and liberation. Now, some people use their parents' positions to scoop up hundreds of millions of yuan. Of course, the public is angry. Their anger is justified.'[38]

MISTRESSES AND CONCUBINES:
THE NETWORK CORRUPTING

A network is a network. It has no intrinsic moral value. It is a field of energies, where forces can be felt, or withdrawn, formations made, and then unmade, and constellations established. It is a functional system with no moral viability or worth in and of itself. There are good, effective networks, and there are bad, ineffective networks. But there are also immensely powerful networks where at the heart are programmes or objectives that have highly destructive social outcomes.

The modern elites in China and the networks that surround them, with all their elasticity and flexibility, have a specific geography, and this helps us initially to address the issue of what moral worth networks might have. Once more we have to take inspiration from descriptions of more remote periods in strands of Chinese history in order better to understand today. In his study of the early Qin and Han dynasties (897 BCE–220 CE), historian Mark Edward Lewis discussed the issue of gender and spatial structuring of power. 'From earliest times,' he writes,

> Chinese political power was articulated in terms of the authority of the inner over the outer. Temples, palaces, and houses in early China and throughout its history were walled on the outside, and the first buildings encountered after entering the gate were the more public ones.

During the Warring States period, he continues:

> political power was walled off and rendered invisible, or visible only in the walls and towers that were its outer manifestations. This was true particularly of rulers, who for security and cultivation of an aura of spiritual power were hidden from the outside world [...] Power was hidden behind not

one wall but a whole series; those of the city, the palace district, the palace itself, the court, and finally the inner chamber. Passage through each was controlled, and each movement closer to the centre was reserved for a smaller number of people. Power and prestige were marked by an ability to move ever inward into the holy of holies that was the imperial presence.[39]

This relates to the highly ambiguous role of women within this male-run political culture and geography:

It was theoretically powerless women who occupied inner spaces, while men were assigned to the outer public realm. Thus, the Chinese world was marked by a contradictory set of equations in which power was located in the hidden depths of the interior, women were also located in the interior, but women were to be excluded from power. The institutional expression of this contradiction was that as power flowed inward toward the hidden emperor, it flowed away from male officials in the outer public realm and into the hands of women, their kin, and the eunuchs, who shared their physical space [...] This spatial ordering of political authority linked power with interiority, secrecy and origins. Since women occupied the deepest interior and the place of greatest secrecy, and since they were the physical origins of male heirs, their place within the structure of the Chinese household represented both a restriction and a source of power. It was a hidden power, however, kept secret rather than acknowledged. Whenever knowledge of this hidden power seeped into the public realm, it was greeted with outrage.[40]

Two millennia divide the world described in this passage from the China of today. And yet, there are haunting parallels. The geography of power in China in the twenty-first century is still clear, with designated private spaces and privileged zones for Party leaders, and even the most humble country or prefecture Party boss having a small world to move in, largely policed by security agents and servants, some bureaucratic, some personal. This world was alluded to in the passage used earlier from journalist Rowan Callick, who talks of the very particular, and somewhat isolated, world that members of the Politburo join when they cross the line from being mid to senior members of the super elite. They move about society in a sort of well-guarded corridor, their visits to inspect places minutely choreographed, and the notion of thir somehow breaking away from this world, as the Xi Jinping taxi-ride story showed, both unthinkable and unbelievable.

This geography is not easily mapped out. Richard McGregor, in his book on the Communist Party, talks of how the key buildings for Party power in Beijing or elsewhere in the country bear no outward sign of what they are.[41] The mighty Organisation Department headquarters in Beijing, for instance, has no signs on it, and other security and strategic departments, for the Party and even sometimes for government, enjoy anonymity. Breaking through the constraints and barriers in this system to get to the truly powerful who sit at its centre is an immense challenge, and one that has led Beijing to be called 'the lobbying capital' of the world, because of the industry of consultants, fixers and key holders who promise some kind of route into the people whom one needs to talk to. It was to this legion of actors that the tragic Neil Heywood belonged.

And it is in this world, but in a highly ambivalent space, where the wives, lovers and modern concubines of the Chinese super elite operate. The Standing Committee of the Politburo has never, in its history, had a female member. Even the wife of Mao Zedong, the formidable Jiang Qing, stayed on the outer perimeter of super-elite formal power. Rumours in 2012 that finally Liu Yandong, the one woman on the full Politburo from 2007, would be taken into the innermost seat of power in the Standing Committee were finally scotched. Of the 84 million members of the CPC, only one-fifth are women. In the Central Committee, it is approximately the same proportion. Of the 31 provinces, autonomous regions and cities directly under the central government, only one has a female Party secretary as of 2013, and of all of these, only twice since 1949 have there been female governors. The upper echelons of Chinese power in the Party and government are overwhelmingly dominated by men. This is a gender-skewed world. Only in business have women been better represented, despite the efforts put into addressing this inequality by the CPC when they came to power with their celebrated slogan that 'women hold up half the sky'.

In the modern context, access to the inner sanctum of power with its restricted geography and its very small number of people can sometimes be delivered along unorthodox routes. In the mid 2000s, a journalist who had been resident in Beijing for many years told me that they were working on a study of two 'modern concubines' – women who were able to build up an access and consultancy business on the back of their intimate relations with powerful men. For both, Western and local business people were willing to pay as much as USD 50,000 in order to get access to members of the highest reaches of the government or Party.

In 2011, the campaigning magazine *Caijing* (meaning 'wealth' in Chinese) was able to produce a groundbreaking study of the modern 'queen of the lovers', Li Wei. Journalists Luo Changping and Rao Zhi, in an article simply entitled 'The public mistress' described the story of the Vietnamese-born migrant who came to China to live in the south-western province of Yunnan in 1970.[42] If any figure symbolises the ups and downs of a fluid lifestyle in modern China, then the tale of Li Wei does. Going under one name and one set of identity documents in her early life, over the course of the next three decades she assembled a series of passports and identities, from Shenzhen, or Guangdong, or Hong Kong, as she grew closer to a number of powerful officials, and 'assisted' them in their work. Involved in this were her sister and her initial patron, who also happened to be her husband – an official from the Yunnan province local tobacco bureau.

According to *Caijing*'s report, after an initial start in trading in tobacco, Li Wei moved to creating links with Li Jiating, a man who ended up as governor of Yunnan, helping him with a small investment in 1995 in property. Her activities soon expanded to getting false Hong Kong identity documents, and dealing with smuggled oil. Li Jiating was caught and put on trial in 2001, during which he was given a suspended death sentence. Li Wei's conclusion, as the *Caijing* report acidly states, was that after his fall 'she could not put all her eggs in one basket'. There followed a decade of building up an extraordinarily diverse patronage network that may well have reached deep into the innermost recesses of the Party.

Li's real ability was to use her sexual appeal to get senior leaders to leverage business deals. She was also able to gain their trust. *Caijing* states how 'she wore clothes like they were weapons'. Her involvement soon extended into the areas of water treatment plants – which became big business for local government as the 2000s went on – and property. For all of this, she was either given introduction fees or consultation fees. The figures reached into the millions, with one deal in 2002 alone securing her RMB 1 million. The best business, though, was in establishing a network of petrol stations that started to secure multi-million-dollar returns.

Li Wei's network was exposed in 2010, after which she went to Hong Kong, becoming in the course of this something of a folk hero in China. But her name was linked to figures like Wang Qishan and Yu Zhengsheng, both of whom were claimed, in some speculative reports issued outside China, and by covert voices within, to be people who had 'political marriages' that had largely ceased to mean anything, and who were therefore obvious patrons for trustworthy figures who were able to supply them with feminine emotional and material comfort.[43] Whether credible or not, as we look at the specific stories of the super elite later, it is important that we bear in mind the ways in which the network can easily be corrupted and has no intrinsic moral qualities of its own. This is especially important to remember when we try to unpick the moral language that elite figures in China use, and the ways in which this stands in stark contrast to their own behaviour. In this power culture, there is surprisingly high tolerance of people doing one thing and saying another. In fact, in many ways this has become almost an expectation.

Li Wei is a highly symbolic figure in another way. Her identity, her mode of operating, her ability to shift between different networks around her, from officials, to national and local provincial leaders, business leaders, and the families and tribal loyalties they inspired, were liquidity personified. She had changed her name, acquired different identities and picked up multiple links in diverse fields as she progressed towards her final business destination, Qingdao. Were the political figures she grew close to and worked with in a sense buying into her elusiveness, and her ability to move more freely than they in the various zones around them? Was she some kind of relationship entrepreneur, an emissary from one kind of relationship type to another, allowed to work in this way because of her evident talents in concealment? In some ways, Li Wei, in her multiple identities and names, carries shades of a previous generation, of leaders from the revolutionary period before 1949, when to have a settled identity was in fact to be vulnerable, identifiable and unsafe. Jiang Qing, Mao Zedong's wife, is an appropriate figure to mention here: someone who had been linked to the father of Yu Zhengsheng, a figure himself linked to Li Wei. Jiang had also lived a highly liquid and mobile life, born as Li Shumeng, then changing her name at elementary school to Li Yunhe, and adopting the stage name Lan Ping before adopting her final name, Jiang Qing. Figures from her generation commonly accumulated a range of acquired names. Her great mentor, Kang Sheng, the godfather of China's intelligence services, was also known as Zhang Zongke, Zhao Rong, and Li Jushi.

The crises and dangers of revolution forced these changes of name and identity, place and allegiance on this generation. Over eight decades later, the world of fifth-generation leadership in the China they founded was engaged in a different revolution – but some of their tactics of concealment and their habits of quick removal and obfuscation were eerily similar.

TIES THAT BIND

Taking the seven members of the Eighteenth Party Congress Standing Committee of the Politburo as the key figures to analyse, with their personal world of networks and links around them, we have to pay particular attention to the differing levels of relationships and the intensity that these bring – along with their relative visibility.

The first of these is blood ties, the links that elite leaders have with their immediate families and family networks. This might be through being sons, daughters, cousins or other kinds of direct relations with former elite leaders, and is connected to the concept of princeling. Here, however, it has a broader meaning, and embraces the links that leaders have through their spouses or children. Spouses in particular will be the focus of attention in some of the analysis below, with the wives of Xi Jinping and Li Keqiang offering different kinds of spouse career, and different dynamics from that of their husbands. Blood links can also be inherited through marriage, as Wang Qishan shows – someone who is widely regarded as having 'married' into the Party elite rather than being born into it. Looking at just what sorts of support this might give an elite career, and in what ways the political capital of a former elite leader can somehow be 'transferred' via marriage or other relations to a younger generation will be an important dynamic to capture. The relationship of parents to their children is also important, with the strength of this bond lying in a system in which trust comes from family closeness more easily than via any other route.

There are also political links. These relate to the ways in which elite figures have been able to pick up capital and influence while working in specific government or Party entities. Some elite leaders, such as Zhang Gaoli, having enjoyed business careers (in his case after a career in the State-owned oil industry), have also been associated with long service in particular central ministries. For Zhang this was the State Planning and Development Commission of the 1990s, which became the National DRC in 2002. These links have allowed them to build up good enabling networks for their future careers. Party networks through organisations like the CYL, the Party Organisation Department or the State Security Apparatus have also been a good source of influence and networking opportunities. Finally there are provincial-based networks that help careers. Leaders who are in charge of provinces still make up the biggest constituency in the Central Committee.[44] Some provinces, like Shandong and Jiangsu (both Jiang Zemin and Hu Jintao were actually born in the latter) have particularly high success rates at getting leaders who have spent significant periods of time there into the national upper levels of the Party. It has become a feature of promotion of fourth- and fifth-generation leaders over the last two decades that experience as Party leaders of provinces is considered critical to their final elevation – though there are, as will be explained later, exceptions.

There are also friendship and non-blood kinship ties. Through their experiences as youths, at university, and in other social areas outside the purely political, these figures have a less easily traceable world around them. They acquired links and affective bonds in the time before they went into politics, and some of these still operate despite the highly regulated and politicised world they have now moved into. Some gained experience as journalists, or as youth leaders, or as academics, and in that life made connections. We have an image of Politburo leaders being friendless, and somehow isolated. But they would be located within a universe in which some early links are still important to them, and in which the sense of obligation and connectivity to these is still alive.

Then there are business links. These overlap with provincial
links. Generically, however, they cover two areas. One is in the
SOEs. Networks acquired here support links derived from careers
that in the modern Party career system can elide between Party and
SOE work. The most well known of these are Zhou Yongkang from
the Seventeenth Party Congress Politburo, who had enjoyed a long
career in the State oil sector, and Zhang Gaoli of the Eighteenth
Party Congress Politburo, who had also come to Party positions
after 17 years in the same industry. There are also non-State activities. These are less analysed and include links into new areas of business activity that leaders might have treated favourably and built
links with during their provincial and then national careers. The
power of the non-State sector is little understood. Political prejudice against non-State companies is still powerful. Even so, these
private companies are important employers, sources of growth and
of profit, and the cultivation of links with them would be a natural
development for ambitious politicians in China.[45]

Intellectual and academic links are also important. These would
be intellectual influences on leaders, and people to whom they have
turned for advice or ideas. In particular, Wang Huning, with his
connection to Jiang Zemin and then Hu Jintao, is the classic modern case of a political career that grew from what was originally
intellectual and academic influence. Around leaders are formal and
informal networks of advisors, from economists to social scientists,
some located in the traditional advice-giving insitutions such as
the Chinese Academy of Social Sciences, or the universities like
Qinghua and Beida, and others in more esoteric areas – some of
them even abroad. There are differences in the ways in which elite
leaders have come to view the world, and the articulation of these
in the written work will be important. Some, like Zhang Dejiang
and Wang Qishan, even worked as specialists in universities or
think tanks before starting their official careers. In that sense, to a
lesser or greater degree, leaders do have intellectual influences, and
tracking these is important in trying to understand them.

Another group are army links. The current so-called fifth-generation leadership is wholly civilian, and maintains the tradition of the Party 'controlling the gun', as the Maoist phrase from the 1930s put it. However, some in the current leadership are linked to the army apparatus, and the army still maintains a formidable lobbying or influence power. The clearest such link is through Xi Jinping, who alone of the Politburo Standing Committee worked directly in a military entity in the early 1980s before going into civilian leadership. It was also clear during the period of Bo Xilai's demise in early 2012 that he too enjoyed, through his father's immense historic influence, appeal to sectors of the military. He went, after all, to address an army garrison in Sichuan in February 2012, even as the turmoil mounted up over his wife's involvement in murder and Wang Lijun's fleeing to the American Consulate in Chengdu.

The hardest of these fields to write and gather much evidence about is that of intimate links. However, as the Li Wei case described above helps to show, in this largely male-dominated polity the intimate lives of this group of people, who live in such a controlled and particular way, merit investigation. As one anthropologist noted at a meeting I attended in London in 2009, these are people who on the whole live together in the highly secure compounds in Beijing, work together, are meeting each other all the time, engage with each other very deeply, do whatever socialising they can together and also tend to have sex together. Their 'physical needs' are either satisfied within their marriages or, as mostly circumstantial evidence suggests, through networks of lovers and intimate physical friendships, some of which are translated into political and business activity along lines similar to Li Wei. Speculations about the intimate lives of modern Chinese leaders are legion. In his time in office, Jiang Zemin was persistently linked with the famous singer Song Zuying, despite there being not a shred of evidence that this was ever the case. Very briefly, even the famously straitlaced Hu Jintao was linked to a China Central

Television (CCTV) newsreader, though what weak legs this tale ever had soon exhausted themselves on the shoals of improbability. A prurient and slightly titillating atmosphere bubbles around discussion of senior leaders' private lives, probably inflamed by the fact that they remain such a taboo subject. And yet the very pragmatic arrangements that it seems some of the elite political leaders have made over their marriages, the evidence of long absence from each other and the occasional signs of indiscretion all show that while these intimate networks are a hugely challenging area to write about, they cannot be ignored.

In the detailed analysis of each of the figures looked at in this book from the fifth-generation top leadership, I will draw lines of relationships falling into the spheres above. The kinds of kinship and relation types mapped out above often fall into each other, invade each other's boundaries and do not respectfully observe neat divisions. Provincial business links sometimes morph into ministerial or Party links later on; family links can also become business ones; and intellectual links, as Wang Huning showed when he joined the official hierarchy, can become political ones. There are strategies of cooption, or outright annexation, by members of some networks to those of others. This is a system without open competitive elections and easily described processes of gaining influence and power. In each of the spheres listed above there are hierarchies, different shades of intensity and different levels of reliability.

One key group that doesn't figure above but which almost certainly does preoccupy the thinking and strategy of all elite leaders in China is that of enemies – groups of people who have been alienated, offended or damaged by the rise of leaders, and who are seeking ways of redressing their grievances or seeking revenge. Once more Bo Xilai's case is illustrative. The spite and opposition of enemies might be manageable when the going is good, but once trouble appears then they can be the source of alliances that can topple and end promising careers. Bo's famously bad relations with Premier Wen Jiabao had been known for a number of years (Wen famously never visited Chongqing when Bo was Party boss there). But it was only when Bo had been compromised and wounded by the activities of Gu Kailai and Wang Lijun that Wen was able to deliver the final ringing *coup de grâce*, during his press conference at the National People's Congress of 2012 when he indirectly denounced Bo. After that, Bo's fate was sealed.

THE NETWORKS SOCIETY MADE FLESH

We are helped in this task by something that, more than anything else, assists us in visualising and understanding the networked nature of modern Chinese society – the arrival of the World Wide Web. Long gone are the fond liberal dreams nurtured by some in the West that the internet would open China up and lead to the triumph of democracy along American or European lines (a view expressed with particular conviction by media mogul Rupert Murdoch in the 1990s).[46] In China, the internet has certainly had a wide and profound impact, but this has not been straightforward to quantify or describe. In the space of a little over a decade from 2000, China's internet has become a place that is at the same time highly policed, contested and contentious, a bewildering mixture of freedom and coercion, liberation and surveillance. In this sense, it maps out virtually some of the paradoxes of the society that it belongs to, reflecting that society's contradictions and complexity.

The Caustic comment from author Yu Hua that elite political leadership was the final great taboo in a society now riddled with 'flesh searches' (a popular term for the exposure of officials and figures in authority online), internet lynchings and a wholly libellous atmosphere was partly challenged, partly supported by the case of actress Zhang Ziyi. When connected by websites in China to Bo Xilai after his downfall in 2012, she threatened to prosecute. While speculation about an elite figure was now permissible because he had been felled, the bedlam of libel-producing internet users in China meant her attempt to prosecute anyone or hold them to account was regarded as hopeless. China has moved from a society where almost total control of news management was possible over three decades before to one now where information circulates within the hundreds-of-millions-strong community of those linked to the internet and active online, in ways that mean some ideas go viral in seconds, and where the relationship of these to standards of evaluation or fact are dizzyingly variable. In such an environment, the truth is almost always remote. Even the outcome of the trial of Bo Xilai's wife, Gu Kailai, was infected by the conviction of large numbers of net users that it was not her but a body double who had appeared in the court room in Hefei.

In this sort of environment, leadership rumours occur either in deeply encoded language, or briefly before being taken down. Media like the Chinese version of Twitter, Weibo, or Weixin, are subject to powerful, State-run search engines that constantly hunt out materials about elite leaders, along with clever ways of disguising this.[47] In a society that US academic Yang Guobin described as going through a period of deepening contentiousness, the internet has, by the very diversity of its contents and the ways in which it can illustrate the battles over specific knowledge and values terrains, become a massive, virtual monument to this.[48]

What looks like information on the internet may be profuse, but relying on it alone is treacherous. In a society where nothing is certain, everything gains some kind of credence. Levels of trust in what the government or officials state is the case have plummeted. In this book, the internet can only sensibly be posited as evidence for the extraordinary complexity and diversity of ideas in China from varying communities, groups, subgroups, interest factions and other actors. In that sense, as Liu Xiaobo, the Nobel Prize for Peace winner, eloquently stated, it is almost as though the internet had been created for China: a virtual network for a networked society, one that is able to map out the links and interlinks of this dynamic, changing, evolving world.

IT'S THE PEOPLE, STUPID

One of the biggest impressions made on me when I started to work for the British Foreign Office in the late 1990s was by a course on working for ministers. The teachers put up a diagram on the board, the centre of which was occupied by a box representing the minister. Around this they then placed different figures who were important in their world. There were their fellow ministers, and members of the government they served in. There were their political advisors, their Party officials, the officials of the ministries, and then the voting constituents whom they represented. And out on a separate limb on this diagram were the members of their families, their friends from their past, their relatives. The trainers allowed us to absorb how busy and interlinked this diagram was, and then pointed out that as people working as civil servants and officials with these individuals, we were only one of a number of contesting groups who were trying to get access to their time and attention.

Ministers in the British government system have power, but it is minuscule compared to that of a Politburo member in contemporary China. In China, the legal, institutional and social constraints on what they do are much weaker. While unable to work with complete abandon as Mao Zedong had been able to, Chinese elite politicians still have immense clout when they choose to use it. And the networks within which they operate are far denser and more interlinked than those of a politician in a Western liberal democracy.

One of the key messages of that training course taken in the late 1990s as a new government official was to reflect on how, at least till then, I had largely thought of politicians in the UK system as wholly public figures, people who operated in a public realm in which their private lives and their more intimate relations were not important. That one was always, even in the most structured system, dealing in the end with fallible, often emotional, sometimes not particularly rational, and vulnerable human beings, despite the immense façade put up between them and the outside world, was a revelation. Within the carapace of the formal trappings of power – the buildings in which these people worked, the assistants around them, the institutions in which they operated, and the language they had to use – there was still a human. In the current Chinese system, the humanity of leaders is even more remote. They speak, talk and act in ways that are far removed from others even in their own society. A business man from China tapped into this when he chided me, after I had given a talk to a group of which he was a member in London in 2012, that I 'needed to hang out more with normal people and stop being too involved with those people a million miles away from us who run our country. They are not real people.'

But getting to grips with these people who seem so remote and act in a world in which there are many layers of ritual and formality is important. It is clear, as some of the analysis in this study will show, that their privileged space in society, and that of the Party they seek to represent, is under threat as never before, and not from some powerful political opponent out in the open, but from the extraordinary forces of social transformation that their own economic policies have unleashed. The exclusive zone of the Party and of elite leadership is being compromised, questioned and invaded bit by bit each day. Trying to work in this extraordinary dynamic situation must be hugely challenging. This book, therefore, is written in the conviction that despite all the trappings and structures around them, it is the individual humans, their experiences, challenges, aspirations and dreams, that constitute the heart of this, which we must not lose sight of.

2

THE LONG AND WINDING ROAD TO THE EIGHTEENTH PARTY CONGRESS

At around 11.00 a.m. on 15 November 2012, I was sitting in the lobby of a major five-star hotel in Beijing, waiting for a friend. Above me in the lobby area was an enormous TV screen hung on the wall for guests and visitors to look at as they came in and out, or milled around waiting. As I sat there I realised I was looking at a live broadcast of the final day of the Party Congress. The images showed a simple stage with a red carpet, filmed continuously despite the fact there was no one standing on the stage nor any sign that someone was about to come. On the Twitter feeds I could get on my mobile phone (Twitter is blocked in China, but foreign phones with internet capacity are still able to receive it) I saw comments posted about the events taking place in the Great Hall of the People (for that was, indeed, where the live coverage was coming from). They reported increased anxiety and concern as the appearance of China's new leaders grew more delayed. An event that had been expected at 11.00 was put off to 11.30. Finally, at around noon, seven figures appeared from the right side of the stage, the one leading them climbing up and placing himself in the centre while the other six formed in a row either side of him.

The world's second largest economy and its most populous nation had just come to the end of a transition in the top leadership of its sole governing political party. Many of the seasoned journalists in the hall, and many watching this moment across the world, had wondered whether it would ever happen. The final stretch, from February onwards in 2012, had been rocky, with murder, the felling of major political actors, intrigue and in-fighting reaching fever pitch. The original plan may well have been for China to have a transition so quiet and unspectacular that hardly anyone noticed. However, in reality the event had been more of a roller coaster. And during its course, one of the world's more opaque political systems had at least opened up to reveal a few of its secrets.

The thing that struck me most powerfully in the hotel lobby while this drama was reaching its denouement however was the attitude of the people around me. Most of them were Chinese, some working in the hotel, some waiting for people to come, some passing through. The images beamed on the TV screen watched so closely across the world merited barely a second's attention from almost all the people around me. While I absorbed the line-up, revealed finally after so much speculation and analysis, I was surrounded by people who evidently felt the whole process so unimportant and disengaging that they didn't even glance at the attention-hugging screen, even though it was likely to impact on them directly. From their outward behaviour, everyone around me regarded this as a major non-event.

Elections in liberal democracies, of course, are milked by the media when they reach their culmination for every ounce of drama and excitement. They become like a kind of grand public theatre. But the leadership change over 2012 in China was different. The process by which it was achieved, the ways by which figures were winners and losers in this process, and the communication of the final outcome to a broader domestic and international audience, were all highly particular. Leaders were appearing that day who were almost certain to be amongst the most powerful people in the world – participating in decisions that would impact on the global economy and geopolitics for the next five to ten years. And yet, even amongst the most eagle-eyed of specialist observers in

Chinese politics, there was widespread confusion over precisely how this whole process had been undertaken, and which rules were ostensibly being followed.

Perhaps it was this opacity that meant that when the fifth-generation leadership finally emerged, they had long exhausted the feeling of engagement by the vast majority of the Chinese people. On that historic day in mid November 2012, apart from increased security in the town centre and roads that seemed suspiciously free of cars because of the need to carry high-level figures in cavalcades of vehicles, Beijing looked eerily normal, its inhabitants going about their business with apparent nonchalance.

FOLLOW THE LEADER: A LAMENTABLE HISTORY

The leadership succession of 2012 leading into 2013 perhaps interested non-Chinese observers as much because of its novelty as because of the likely impact they thought it was going to have. The simple fact was that, for all the reassuring noises about this being a process built on precedent, in many ways this was the first rules-based, consensus-led transition of elite leaders the CPC had ever had in its nine-decade-long history. Transitions between generations of leaders in the past had all been highly specific and all too often involved real conflict and problems.

Mao Zedong's search for a successor had been the most prolonged, the most unsuccessful and the most draining. Choice number one, Liu Shaoqi, was Mao's almost exact contemporary, but was brutally felled in the CR and treated so badly after his removal from office he died within three years. Choice number two, the infamous Lin Biao, had been one of the greatest military leaders of the 1946–9 Civil War. But he enjoyed only a five-year period as successor-designate before dying in a plane crash in the Mongolian People's Republic while fleeing the country in 1971. The much younger Wang Hongwen appeared fleetingly in 1973 at the Tenth Party Congress as a possible successor – but the final decision was fixed on Hua Guofeng.

In what sense Mao even contemplated someone replacing him one day is a moot question. His megalomania had reached monstrous proportions by the mid 1960s, so there are valid questions to ask about whether the Party and its leaders then were even able to think about a leader after his death. Hua Guofeng himself lasted six years, and there is growing appreciation now for his role in supporting the reforms from 1978, and in stabilising China in a transition that could, at some points, have caused the fall of the Party from power, or the collapse of the State itself.[1] Hua's engagement in a process of transformation that culminated for him in the elimination of the very position he relied on for power – chairmanship of the Party – was perhaps more selfless than hapless. In the end, his decision to cede to the new Deng Xiaoping-centred leaders allowed China to rebuild its economic capacity and modernise. One further serious factional fight in the late 1970s would have seen China plunged into terminal turmoil, something to which there was profound opposition after the hard years of the CR.

For Deng Xiaoping himself at the end of the 1980s, finding a successor, despite all the effort his leadership had put into institutionalising structures in the Party – making congresses more regular and ensuring that things were run with more orderly rules – proved challenging. This was in different ways from Mao but just as frustrating. Leaders seemed incapable of handing on what political capital they had accrued to their chosen successors. Hu Yaobang, Deng's main choice up to 1987, had to resign ignominiously over mishandling of student unrest that year. Deng's second choice, Zhao Ziyang, lacked any meaningful patronage and support network in Beijing beyond Deng himself and was floored by the dramatic impact of the June uprising in 1989. Jiang Zemin, as described in the previous chapter, was a surprise choice, and finally a successful one. But few would claim that this was originally Deng's preferred option had there not been the immense shock of the events of 1989.

It might be that Chinese elite leaders of the first and second generations, as we now call them, were incapable of thinking in terms of a succession. The world ended with them, in their own minds. So thinking seriously about how the Party and country functioned once they were gone took up far less time in their minds than it ever should have. Successions in the Soviet Union had been messy, and in the Democratic People's Republic of Korea (DPRK) the whole problem was solved by simply making it an inherited leadership, passed from father to son. Deng's writ was able to extend to the choice of Hu Jintao, which was determined quite early in the 1990s. Once more this was a wholly new departure, with the idea that a former leader could choose not only a successor, but a leader after the retirement of that successor.

With only a handful of successions, it is very hard to extract easy rules. This is especially the case in view of how different each succession has been. The most one can say is that this has proved itself in the past to be a dynamic and evolving situation, and one where significant changes have happened each time. The question from the Hu and Wen leadership, therefore, to the new ones – the fifth generation – was in what ways precedents existed that could be used, and how these would be applied. The variable this time was that there was no easy way of factoring in, at least formally, the views of former leaders. Jiang Zemin, for all his great political talents, was not able unilaterally to exercise the same influence as Deng. Times had changed. There were more contending forces and voices to be listened to.

The Constitution of the Communist Party of China offered precious little help. The amended text of 2007 had, under Article 11, the stipulation that 'The election of delegates to Party congresses and of members of Party committees at all levels should reflect the will of the voters. Elections shall be held by secret ballot.' Article 18 lays down the regulation that national congresses of the Party, from which a new Central Committee are to be elected, need to be held every five years. Such congresses 'hear and examine the reports of the Central Committee and Central Discipline and Inspection Commission, discuss and decide on major questions concerning the Party, revise the Constitution of the Party, and elect the new Central Committee and elect the Central Commission and Discipline Inspection.' Article 22 states that the Political Bureau, Standing Committee and general secretary get elected by the Central Committee.[2] Nowhere in the Constitution, however, does it say precisely how members of congresses then elect members of the Politburo, how many should be on the Politburo, and then how the Standing Committee itself gets elected and how many can serve on this. The only widely accepted issue was that despite there being no constitutional limit to their five yearly terms as Party secretaries, precedent meant that after two of these there needed to be a changeover. The political logic looming behind this was the need to prevent the recontamination of Chinese politics by the dominance of one specific figure. Mao's shadow figured here. These 'checks and balances on power with Chinese characteristics' were unable, however, to militate against the informal and back-channel influence of figures who had accrued in their previous careers large amounts of political capital. The Constitution therefore describes a highly abstract process, a framework within which succession is meant to work, with no real detail. Consensus on this had yet to be reached. The Party leading up to the Eighteenth Congress had a clear end objective but no map by which to reach that.

Speculation about who the leaders after Hu and Wen might be started very early on in their period in power. In 2002, attention had focused quickly on Li Keqiang, then the Party Secretary of Henan province, as a very strong possible contender. Li had the support of Hu Jintao, and was one of the youngest ever local Party leaders.[3] Like Hu he was well linked into the CYL, and also like Hu he came from a relatively modest background. At this time, the main other contender was Li Yuanchao, also a reformist-minded leader linked to the CYL with extensive and deep Party links through his father, who had attained high position in the Party in Shanghai.

The leadership transition a decade on from 2002, however, was located deep within the unknown territory of the future. There was a sense early on, and with increasing intensity before the Seventeenth Congress in 2007, that this was a potentially treacherous process for the Party. There were many variables and a lack of consensus amongst the serving leadership over what sort of leader the Party, and therefore the country, needed. This lack of clarity meant that the CPC was looking at a potentially very risky moment, when there were choices to be made that ran the risk of splitting and dividing the whole organisation and destroying its hard-won unity. At this time, few would have suspected how large the role of retired elder leaders would be in this process, or the huge impact of wholly unexpected and dramatic events. But each of these things proved to be important.

THE RUN UP: THE SEVENTEENTH PARTY CONGRESS

The greatest clue to who might eventually prevail came in October 2007, when, a couple of days later than expected, the Seventeenth Party Congress ended, and finally a reconfigured leadership appeared. The members of the new Standing Committee were largely seen as closer to Hu Jintao than in the earlier leadership. From 2002 to 2007 Hu was seen as being surrounded by people who were more politically aligned to predecessors Jiang Zemin and Zhu Rongji: figures like Zeng Qinghong and Huang Ju, both with long careers in Shanghai, or the more mysterious Wu Bangguo, also a Shanghai man, though less committed to Jiang and far more conservative in his outlook. Of the Sixteenth Party Congress leadership of nine, there was a turnover of five in 2007. The greatest surprise was the retirement of Zeng Qinghong himself, despite being just under the age threshold of 68. An interpretation given at the time for leaving power like this was simply that he had made way for Xi Jinping.

Zeng Qinghong has become one of the legendary political operators of modern China, admired both within and outside the country for his silky political skills. His background was a rich one.

His father, Zeng Shan, was a minister of the interior in the early PRC period. His mother, Deng Liujin, established an orphanage in the 1940s and 1950s for children whose parents had been killed in the revolutionary struggle in the north-east, or who were off-spring of leaders of this area, looking after over 100 infants. It was here that the future Politburo leader Liu Yandong was cared for with her brother, establishing a relationship with Zeng from this early on.[4] Zeng became an official in the State DRC just after the reform era started in 1978, and worked in the State petrol industry before moving to Shanghai. In these positions he established his relationship with Jiang Zemin from 1984. Zeng was never a popular figure. Willy Lam, in an analysis in 2002, stated that 'one of the many ironies [of modern China] is that most of the prospects for political reform may hinge on one of the least popular cadres of the Communist Party', Zeng. He went on:

> The Jiangxi [province] native is such a controversial figure that while he was made an alternate (second tier) member of the Politburo at the 15th Party Congress in 1997, Jiang's [Standing Committee] colleagues have repeatedly prevented him from giving his faithful follower full Politburo status.

His main crime for other colleagues in the elite was his position at that time as someone who could play a role 'in ensuring that the retiring president can maintain his influence after the 16th Congress'.[5]

Zeng was to serve under Hu Jintao for one term, occupying the symbolically important position of vice president. But on 21 October 2007, despite wide predictions that he would continue in place, his name did not appear on a list of the 200-plus members of the new Centre Committee. That put him out of contention for the Standing Committee. 'No one knows better how to ride the political winds within China's Communist Party than Vice President Zeng

Qinghong,' Reuters reported on 21 October. 'But as the country's Communist Party Congress closes, the 68-year-old has bowed out.'[6] Perhaps this was just as well. A *Caijing* report issued in 2008 on the privatisation of a State enterprise in the power sector Luneng, in Shandong province, showed that enormous numbers of assets had been transferred at the time to private companies.[7] A further report in *Foreign Policy* found that the most sensitive individual linked to this was Zeng Wei, son of Zeng Qinghong. Zeng had already been linked to a USD 32 million house in Sydney. 'According to a family friend of Zeng Qinghong, the notoriety of his son's financial dealings [...] was one factor in his decision to retire after he handed the vice presidency to Xi in 2007.'[8]

The more political reason was that Zeng had always been a patron of Xi Jinping, and it was Zeng's hand that was seen most strongly in the machinations around who would win out between Li Keqiang and Xi in the build up to the Congress in 2007. As leader of the CPC Central Organisation Department from 1999 to 2000, Zeng had overseen the important transition by Xi from Fujian province, where he was governor to the Party secretaryship of the economic powerhouse of Zhejiang.[9] This proved the patronage link. The argument used for why he would support this line-up was a simple one: Zeng had selflessly felt it better for the Party that new leaders be settled in and that a succession process be well established before 2012, when the transition was due. For this to happen, there needed to be clearly marked successors for both Party and State Council leadership. Zeng's role as kingmaker at this stage was signified by his support for the removal of Party secretary of Shanghai and Politburo member, Chen Liangyu, in the social welfare and housing fund scandal in the city in 2007, and his replacement at short notice in March that year by Xi. With senior leadership experience in three major political centres – Fujian, Zhejiang and Shanghai – Xi had the suite of qualifications to justify his return to Beijing central politics after over two decades' absence.

Speculation in reports issued in Hong Kong in 2007 stated that as chair of the preparatory committee for the Seventeenth Party Congress, Zeng was in a major position of influence over the eventual outcomes. Speaking in a meeting before the Congress that year, Zeng referred to the duty to the Party in living up to certain standards and models of behaviour that had been established by Deng Xiaoping's leadership. These involved restraints on power and on terms of people in power. The need therefore to choose a clear successor was set out.[10] In *Asia Weekly* another report stated that during the preparatory meetings for the upcoming Congress, Zeng had simply given a letter in the spring of 2007 to Hu Jintao and other members of the Politburo Standing Committee stating the reasons for this retirement: he was 68, he had been working in the central government for 18 years, he had occupied all the major positions of responsibility he felt qualified in, and he wanted to consider the needs of the future and to see younger leaders promoted.[11] Zeng's political objective, however, was, through this 'sacrifice', to see Xi – a person who was tribally and politically far better able to look after his own interests and those of the family and network of his great patron Jiang Zemin – prevail over the main competitor, Li Keqiang. The end result in October 2007, therefore, was to see Xi emerge before Li in the final line-up of the new Standing Committee, despite the fact that in many ways Li was the better qualified, administratively and academically, and the one that seemed much closer to Hu Jintao.

THE 'UNHAPPY' HU ERA

This thwarting of Hu's succession intentions provides insight into one other framework by which to interpret the outcomes of the Eighteenth Party Congress in 2012. This is to look at it as a very early, initial assessment of the Hu Jintao era and of Hu's leadership. What analysis appeared in 2012, as will be shown later, largely judged the events of that year as showing Hu in a negative light, and as monuments to his failure to demonstrate leadership in the Party and to achieve hard political goals.[12] Hu had presided over a period in which China's economy had increased in size over four times, and in which the country had grown richer and stronger. And yet, there was a sense in which, as authors of a book in 2009 argued, China was not happy, and its leader even less so. 'Unhappy Hu' was a man who, in the words of one Hong Kong-published book, 'feared losing power, feared the military, feared the rights movement, feared the Charter 08 activists, feared Jiang Zemin, and feared the princelings'.[13] Yan Jiaqi, historian and author of one of the earliest accounts of the CR, banned in China over two decades earlier, wrote an article simply entitled: 'Why is old Hu so miserable?'[14] In this article, Yan acidly related four main reasons for Hu's unhappiness. Drawing a parallel between Hu's namesake (but not a relative) Hu Yaobang, a man who had been a patron of younger Hu before his felling in the 1987 student unrest, Yan pointed out that while Hu Yaobang had had the political courage to rectify the cases of those misjudged during the CR a decade before, to release those placed in jail in the anti-rightist campaign of 1957–8 (these included the pupil of the great writer Lu Xun, Hu Feng), and even initiated discussions again over the future of Tibet, Hu Jintao had done nothing over Tibet despite the uprising there in 2008, freezing the little dialogue both sides had from 2011, crushing any moves towards liberalisation, putting Liu Xiaobo in jail after Charter 08, and generally refusing even limited moves to reform the political system. The second reason Yan pointed to was Hu's stiff and uncomfortable public persona, meaning that at moments of national crisis and tragedy, like the Wenchuan earthquake of 2008, Hu's involvement in comforting people had been brief and peremptory, whereas his Premier Wen Jiabao had at least tried to show some human empathy and engagement. This connected with the third criticism: that Hu had no energy and gave no sense of a political personality or charisma. This had created a politics of 'empty gestures' and bureaucratic speech, which emanated from the still centre in which nothing seemed to be happening because of Hu's 'do nothing, stop everything' predispositions. The final criticism was that his evident lack of political charisma, and anything approaching a clear Huist message, meant that the only other thing he might hope to rely on to achieve anything was a network of powerful patrons and family links within the Party and society in general, but as someone who had come into central leadership as an outsider, whose career had been spent in Gansu during its most formative years from 1968 to 1982, Hu clearly lacked even these. His outsider credentials may have made him an attractive proposition at a time when alliances and elite formations were less secure than they became in the 2000s, but as these strengthened, his ability to create coalitions in order to achieve anything more than straightforward economic target goals was hopeless.[15]

Those that criticise Hu for his stiff public manner and his public demeanour are in many ways using a coded means of pointing to far deeper criticisms. According to one, in both the Jiang and the Hu era there were three hard issues that neither had been able to do much about. The first was that for all the 'intra-Party democracy reforms' that had been promoted at the expense of township elections from the early 2000s, accountability in the Party, and particularly in the governing elite, was highly rudimentary. In such a system, crises were dealt with as and when they occurred, with no pre-emptive constructive strategy to make sure they didn't happen in the first place. Worse still, nothing was done to ensure that they didn't reoccur. Crisis and its impact on the elevation of some of the leaders will be looked at later, as the role of these in shaping modern Chinese politics is still strong.[16] A second issue was that, in a territory as vast as China, the ways in which the central government was able to impose any form of control over localities was limited. Fiscal restraint was one way, but the means by which provinces and then sub-provincial entities were able to get their own way and run things as they wanted to were legion. The third was official corruption. With no accountability, with weak links in many key areas between central and local forms of government, and the rise of local strong men and 'barons', the natural outcome of all of this was a system where, to those who were unconstrained by any highly internalised codes of moral propriety and good behavior, modern China with its galloping economy offered a field day for venality and greed.[17] The Hu response to the inability to build consensus in the Party on these three tough issues listed was to use immense amounts of repression: through State agents; through blocking avenues to expressing opposition; and through creating an oddly contradictory atmosphere in which, on the one hand, society, social media and the economy were riddled by evidence of dynamic change, and yet on the other the 'fiefdom' of the political elite at the centre was increasingly isolated and reliant on a vast apparatus of control. The price tag for this was to exceed that for national defence. By 2012, as the National People's Congress publicly admitted that year, China was spending USD 5 billion more a year on protecting it from itself than on safeguarding itself against the aggressive intent of outsiders.

This era of new repression had intensified as a result of the impact of the Tibet, Xinjiang and Inner Mongolia unrests of 2008, 2009 and 2011 respectively. The failure both to see these coming, and then to deal with them effectively, were black marks against Hu's record. A critic in the magazine *Big Issues*, published in Hong Kong, listed the full 'shortcomings' of the Hu era – specific things that he had failed to achieve:

> The tainted milk scandal, tainted foodstuffs, the Tibet uprising of 2008, the Xinjiang uprising, Yang Jia's killing of a policeman, Deng Yujiao's killing of the official in a nightclub, the killing of an official by a construction worker, the murder of numerous school children by crazed knife attackers [...][18]

The explosive growth of China's economy had also brought with it extreme pollution, but the strategy of the elite leadership around Hu had been to 'do nothing' – and for this reason, Hu had never been accorded in official documents the honorary title 'core of the fourth-generation leadership' in the same way that Jiang had been called core of the third generation.[19] The ideological statements he was mostly closely associated with and that he sponsored – 'scientific development' and 'harmonious society' – figured outside the official reports and speeches in which they were solemnly declaimed as 'sarcastic phrases', used with deft irony by many Weibo and Weixin users.

Hu had all the main levers of power by 2012. He was head of the Party; head of the Central Military Commission, which commanded the army; and president of the country. But he was also someone who clearly believed that the processes of the Party were paramount and that they needed to be strengthened and deepened. He supported the campaign for 'intra-Party' democracy from 2004 as a way of strengthening this internal self-governance and institution building, weaning the Party from the drug of personal patronage. From this angle, a merit-based leadership succession free of the intervention of powerful figures and their patronage networks was the ideal outcome. But in this endeavour, Hu failed. The heavy involvement of his predecessor, Jiang Zemin, in the 2012 line-up showed that individual power still trumped process. The immensely capable Hu protégé, Li Keqiang, was beaten into second place finally by a man who was in many ways, at least on paper, far less able than he – Xi Jinping. The reason for this was simple – the support of Jiang Zemin.

Hu had to contend with three specific issues that set the odds against him in this aspiration to strengthen process and get away from power located in the hands of specific strong individuals. The first of these was the persistent meddling and involvement of Jiang Zemin even after his supposed full retirement from all positions in 2005. Hu was always in Jiang's shadow, even after having secured a more open space for his leadership after 2007. Part of the problem here was that Jiang had seniority, and was accorded second rank in official listings even after his ostensible retirement as Party secretary in 2002. The second issue was Hu's poor status with the military. Before becoming vice chair of the central military commission in 1997, Hu had no formal links with the PLA at all. He had never served as a soldier, nor worked as assistant to any major army figure, and had no family links into this network. And while the PLA were in no way the political power block they had once been in the Maoist period, they were still significant and needed someone who at least showed they were able to fight their corner and understand their needs. Hu's final great problem, alluded to above, was that he was the poorest communicator ever to have been leader of the PRC, and his evident reticence and dislike of any show of public emotion, excitement or engagement became a major political liability, particularly in moments of crisis when China needed a leader's voice to speak on its behalf. This mattered as much in how China came across to the rest of the world as it did in how leaders within bridged the vast and growing gap between themselves and the people around them.

The handling of dissident Liu Xiaobo was perhaps the worst example, exemplifying the problems caused by the extreme sensitivity and risk aversion of the Hu leadership. Liu's informal detention after issuing the Charter 08 document arguing for greater democratic freedoms in late 2008 had been clumsy, with no clear idea of what was happening to him nor any clarity about the legal basis under Chinese law for what was, in effect, his house arrest. When it happened, his trial oozed cynicism, with his sentence of 11 years announced on Christmas Day 2009 when it was likely that critical Western audiences would be distracted by their own festivities. Things only worsened when, despite a pre-emptive lobbying campaign by Chinese diplomats, the Nobel Prize for Peace was awarded to Liu in late 2010. The same Chinese diplomats then created even greater problems by strenuously leaning on foreign governments not to send representatives to the award ceremony in Oslo in November that year, placing most of them in an impossible position because, once this pressure was exposed, no one could accede to it without making themselves look weak. Billions of dollars spent on the splendour of the Beijing Olympics in 2008, with its images of harmonious Chinese culture that could inspire and reach out to everyone across the globe, were undone by the simple image at the Nobel Ceremony of an empty chair where Liu was unable to sit. The ensuing campaign of vilification of Liu only worsened this diplomatic own goal. Throughout this, Hu Jintao remained silent. He said nothing, did nothing, not once expressing any opinion. His silence became an enormous burden. Even putting forward strongly China's opinion on the issue and making it clear that they did not view the Nobel Prize Committee as legitimate would have served to help. But blanket silence was the worst of all options.

BLOOD ON THE TRACKS

Hu's final problem was simply to have bad luck. Early in the morning of 18 March 2012, while the turmoil around Bo Xilai was still swirling, a Ferrari car was found with a dead young man and two semi-naked, badly injured women who were reported to be of Tibetan ethnicity. Ferraris, with their astronomical prices, occupy a particular place in the symbolic firmament of corruption in contemporary China. This one was estimated to have a price tag of RMB 5.6 million (USD 600,000). That the post-mortem showed the dead driver was heavily inebriated only added to the sense of this being a tragic monument to the wholly out of control way in which the young wealthy in China were behaving. News of the crash was suppressed for some weeks. Speculation afterwards linked this to ferocious efforts by the leading security official Zhou Yongkang to protect the father of the dead driver, Ling Jihua.[20]

If there was one official linked most closely to Hu Jintao from the time he had become Party leader, then that was Ling. Always at

Hu's side wherever he went, Ling had shared his patron's humble beginnings. Born and brought up in Shanxi province, Ling had worked through the CYL centrally till he was appointed into the key administrative position as director of the Central Research Department, reporting directly to the Central Committee and in effect into the Politburo, undertaking critically important policy research work and briefing. Fiercely publicity-shy (he had told Xinhua news agency reporters during one visit at the side of his master in the early 2000s to 'not mention me'), he was made chief of Hu Jintao's office in the mid 2000s, and then chief of the General Office of the CPC Central Committee from 2007 to 2012, a hugely influential position that had been critical in the ascent of former leaders like Qiao Shi, Wen Jiabao and Zeng Qinghong. In this position in charge of the daily affairs of the Central Committee Ling had also been expected to play a pivotal role in preparatory work for the Eighteenth Party Congress. The untimely death of his son, Ling Gu, in such mysterious and scandalous circumstances meant that at a critical juncture, when intense deal making and negotiation were likely to start, Ling was effectively a marked man. The final revelation in the *South Morning Post* in September 2012 that the driver was indeed his son meant that he had to be sidelined to the less important United Front Department. A person critical to Hu's influence had been weakened. And Hu's failure to emulate Jiang Zemin in getting one of his main allies onto the full Politburo was only final evidence that the Eighteenth Party Congress result, when it finally materialised, was, amongst many things, an open criticism of the 'do nothing, say nothing' Hu era of politics.

WEN JIABAO: THE GOOD GUY OR THE ENEMY WITHIN?

If there has been one person with a reputation as a good guy in modern Chinese politics, then Wen Jiabao was it. Alone of the members of the Seventeenth Party Congress, he had spoken out about the need for hard political reforms, particularly after 2009. From summer 2010 he had mentioned political reform no fewer than seven times, from a meeting at Shenzhen to celebrate 30 years of the reform and opening-up process on 20 August, to an interview with CNN's Fareed Zakaria on 4 October. In each one he had talked of the need for political, as well as economic and social, change.[21] 'I believe I and all Chinese people have such a conviction that China will make continuous progress, and the people's wishes and needs for democracy and freedom are irreversible,' he had stated to Zakaria, '[...] this political party should act in accordance with the constitution and the law'.[22] Wen was careful in his talk to appeal for political cover to the memory of Deng Xiaoping, and made sure that his comments were long on rhetoric, but short on specifics. Even so, these were far more directly reformist in tone than anything else being said by a leader in China over this period. Fellow Politburo member at the time, Wu Bangguo, was, in fact, directly working against this reformist language in the 'Five Noes' he had been promoting over 2009 and 2010 (see Chapter 5).

Wen's avuncular image is as a major political and public-relations asset. A lot of this skilful management of his image is down to the real mastermind behind the CNN interview, the head of the official Chinese news agency, Xinhua – Lu Wei – who at least according to one account was effectively acting as Wen's publicity guru. That the premier had a keen interest in his image was clear from earlier in his time in office. More than his other colleagues, he showed a far sharper instinct for the dynamics of the new communication channels in a China being reshaped and changed by social media.[23]

This might be due to the fact that Wen had a shallow Party base from which to operate and therefore needed this sort of public support to compensate and shore up his position. But there was a possible deeper reason, and a less benign and more crudely political one, for his great interest in reformist language and in strong public image making. Wen had created, in his leadership of the government structures and the ministries centrally at the State Council, an empire of his own, and one that was particularly important because of the protection it offered him for a problem already alluded to before – the immense corruption of his family, and in particular of his wife, Zhang Peili. Zhang had attracted attention from early on in Wen's time in power for her involvement in diamond and luxury goods trading. Never seen in public with her husband, Zhang is pictured only once with him, in a photo in 2011 where they are shown standing in a courtyard setting with Hong Kong businessman Wu Kangmin and his wife.[24] The *New York Times'* masterly dissection later in 2012 of Wen's family's immense interests, which came to over USD 2 billion, offered documentary proof of what was already suspected. The most political reformist leader in the Hu Wen period, at least in his public talks, was also the one whose family appeared to be most out of control. How could Wen propose better governance of this country he was meant to be running when he was clearly unable to control those most immediately connected to him?

Wen's family certainly placed the premier in a position of vulnerability. But Wen was an infamously slippery and effective operator, someone who had been famously portrayed next to Zhao Ziyang in late May 1989 before the Tiananmen Square crackdown and his fall from power, but who had remained in positions of influence. The 1989 picture, far from being of a man who was sticking by his boss till the bitter end, offers another possible interpretation as an operator who was placed there to be Zhao's minder, and who was able to revert to his true master, ambition, once the crisis had passed. The ways in which Li Keqiang, as his heir apparent to the position of premier after 2007, had come within his sphere of influence, acting as his deputy and working closely with him as a vice premier in charge of micro-economy development, showed the transference of political allegiance by Li from Hu to Wen. Wen's awareness of his problems after leaving formal power in 2012 because of his family and their immense wealth meant, at least on this reading, that the

State Council, the organs of governance – despite their subservience to the Party and its guidance and political precedence – became the main ground for his protection. He would want to see the government strengthened, and rule of law ordained by it in the ascendant, precisely because once one translated this from the institutional to the network map of modern China, this was the base and power-area where his future protection needed to come from.[25]

Wen's demand for greater constitutional restraints and law-based behaviour, while it had a pleasing reformist flavour, was also supportive of these network interests in which his family were so embedded. Constitutionalism and rule of law would clearly support ministries and the operations of government, and restrain the behaviour of the Party. Wen's promotion of these, therefore, was directed at Hu, whose leadership was of the Party, not the government.[26] Since 2007, therefore, Wen's political adeptness and skill had ensured that the State Council was strengthened, a further sign of Hu's weakness. For all the arguments about protocol and historical precedents, the fact is that in 2012 it was the leader of the State Council, rather than the National People's Congress, as it had been over the last decade, that had walked out as the second-ranking member of the Politburo.

Criticisms of Wen, despite his general public popularity, have appeared since 2010. The most trenchant was by dissident author Yu Jie, who in a book on Wen that year stated:

> Wen Jiabo and Hu Jintao are like the two sides of a coin. They are on a tandem bike, heading in the same direction. I think they are playing the good-guy–bad-guy routine [...] But they share the same goal, which is to strengthen their power base. I think they have more in common than differences.

Yu continued: '[Wen] is seen as a man of the people and known affectionately as Grandpa Wen. But not everyone believes this image to be a true reflection of the premier's character.'[27]

Contention swirls around Wen. Yu's own treatment is a case in point. After writing 'Wen Jiabao: China's best actor', Yu was placed under house arrest for a year, before fleeing to the US in 2012.[28] Yu claimed to have been stripped naked, burned with cigarettes and tortured while in detention.[29] The felled railways minister Liu Zhijun was also quickly isolated and jettisoned by Wen, who had been associated with him earlier in his career. Wen also worked with Liu on the State Council while he was in office, with responsibility for oversight of Liu's activities while he was accruing many billions of RMB during the high-speed rail construction boom.[30] The picture that emerges of Wen is a complex one. It is of a man who publicly performed so well during the Wenquan earthquake in 2008 and the snow storms that year during the Spring Festival that stranded so many people, but who also at the same time protects his family and their immense accrual of wealth. Wen's story is illustrative of the Hu and Wen period and its internal contradictions and issues generally. Far from being a harmonious period, despite all the loud public declarations of its leaders the finale of the decade showed that Hu and Wen were often working at cross purposes and with precious little harmony. The result of this was to produce profound public cynicism and a lack of any idealism by which to mobilise elites and society for change.

THE RESURRECTION OF JIANG ZEMIN

On 4 July 2011, in the new social media jungle that now straddles virtual space across China, a rumour started to take root. Jiang Zemin, former leader and president, one of the great figures of modern Chinese political history, had died. The evidence for this was heavy police presence around his compound in Shanghai. *Time* magazine on 6 July supplied a provisional eulogy:

> Perhaps most significantly in an autocratic nation, Jiang knew when to let go. At the end of his terms as President,

> Communist Party General Secretary, and Central Military
> Commission chief, Jiang handed over the reins to Hu Jintao,
> avoiding the public tussles that had plagued previous leader-
> ship transitions in China. Even as his possible passing creates
> an Internet furor, Jiang will still be remembered as a man
> who knew how to make a graceful exit.[31]

This was to prove a somewhat hauntingly bold prediction, and one
that would be thoroughly disproved. The Hong Kong station that
had gone public on his death had to retract when it was clear he was
still alive. His reappearance for the first time in public on 8 October
that same year at a Party meeting in the Great Hall of the People
in Beijing to mark the centenary of the revolution that ended the
Qing dynasty was final proof that Jiang had either never been dead,
or, in the acid words of some Weibo users, had been resurrected.
Even for the vast squads of conspiracy theory specialists inside and
outside China, the 'Jiang' that sat down unsteadily at this meeting
in October had the air of reality about him. Unlike the case of Bo
Xilai's wife Gu Kailai, there was no chance of claiming a body double doing service here.

Jiang Zemin made a far more dramatic comeback as the road
towards the leadership transition of 2012 proceeded. In hind-
sight, there were always signs that his position in the firmament
of Chinese elite political activity was a highly privileged one. He
was, in the words of one description, 'the great emperor'.[32] His use
of language even after he had retired was interpreted as indicating
that he still regarded himself, and was regarded by many within the
elite, as important, someone whose speech acts carried an edict-like
nature. As 'core of the third Party leadership' in official discourse,
Jiang was able in his public utterances to talk to an audience he
described as 'comrades in the Party and especially leadership cadres'.[33] This grand, patriarchal language linguistically indicated a
hierarchy, even if it was hard to pin down Jiang's position within
this structure. What his case did, and does, show, is that it is very

hard to withdraw from the top leadership position in the CPC as it is currently configured in China. Too many owed him debts, respect and allegiance in his long career before. Even if he wanted to, he was not to be so easily left alone.

Describing his somewhat nebulous function after 2004 when he finally retired from his last formal position of leadership (or 2005 if one includes Party secretaryship of the Central Military Commission) has proved tricky. Emperor is one term, though this does little justice to the somewhat more circumscribed terrain he had to work in. A more modernist way of looking at him is as a sort of retired chairman of the board of directors of a company, in which he still holds a significant share. That the Communist Party has some striking similarities to a company that is directed at seeking shareholder profit will be covered later. In this framework, however, the key thing to bear in mind is that the Eighteenth Party Congress offered the last chance for Jiang to get his people in place for another generation of leaders. It was Bo Xilai's threat to the networks around Jiang that he had built up so painstakingly over the years that perhaps explains why Jiang was reportedly so supportive of his complete, quick dismissal from all positions of influence.

Prolonging their political influence through the active promotion of people linked to them so that they stood a chance of attaining high office in the new leadership was a battle also worth fighting to figures like Zhu Rongji, Jiang's premier. Zhu was someone who had kept a remarkably low profile since his retirement in 2003, but who re-emerged around 2011 through the publication of his speeches, which had enjoyed great popularity. He had also made widely reported appearances at places like Qinghua University. Former Premier Li Peng, disliked domestically and internationally by those that remembered him for what was viewed as his harsh role in the 1989 crushing of students (what were less well remembered were his more supportive roles, in bringing China into the WTO, and in being a key implementer of the deeper economic reforms from 1992), also started vaguely to reappear along the edges of political activity, with a diary of aching banality from his period in power issued under his name in Hong Kong in 2010. Zeng Qinghong's activities were also important.

BO XILAI'S FALL: OPENING
THE DOOR TO THE OLD MEN

The 'Gang of Old Men', as they were called in some commentary, were given space in which to start operating again when the catastrophe of Bo Xilai occurred. The events around Bo's demise present particularly tricky interpretive and analytic challenges because they pull in several different directions. The issue about which most ink has been spilt was of course that of the salacious details of his wife's involvement with the death of Neil Heywood; the fleeing of his security deputy Wang Lijun to a foreign consulate; and the various details that emerged through this of his personal life and the behaviour of his son, Bo Guagua, and other associates.

There is another dimension that has been woven into this, which involves the political threat that he reportedly posed. In this, he was the promoter of a specific set of pro-poverty-relief, popularist policies that were to assist and aid the less well-off – those who had lost out in the great Hu Jintao society being constructed, in which the rich had grown richer and the poor had remained stuck in a trap. The phrase used for this constellation of policies was the 'Chongqing Model', and it had managed to attract ardent followers once Bo had moved to the city to direct it in 2007, with British think-tanker Mark Leonard a particularly noisy promoter in his *What Does China Think?* book in 2008. Governance and administrative reform in Chongqing all seemed to be happening, though it was hard to apply many measures to this. The city province still had large areas of entrenched poverty among those who worked there, and a high level of environmental degradation. Bo was a visible political personality in a terrain dominated by greyness, however, and so his charisma attracted foreign visitors and international acclaim, even as it evidently deeply irritated the two people he could least afford to alienate – Wen and Hu.

This new model for pro-poor housing subsidies and better access to social welfare was also cover for something else about Bo that figured in the overall narrative of his fall – and that was his network of inherited patronage and political support through his father, Bo Yibo, one of the Eight Immortals of the CPC. Less commented on during all of Bo's travails was that Bo Yibo's role in the development of modern Chinese history is a slightly uneasy one. While an ally of Deng Xiaoping up to a point, he had played a highly active role in the fall of Hu Yaobang in 1987, and in the removal from office of Zhao Ziyang and the treatment of students in 1989. Bo Xilai himself always seemed to carry this complicated shadow with him, with tales of his life in the CR divided between his roles of victim and victimiser.[34] A schoolmate of his while in Beijing had noted his good manner and courtesy in the early 1970s. Others linked him with the radical Red Guard student movements of the time. All that could be safely said is that of the great Party-founding families, along with the Deng family, his were amongst the highest profile.

Putting the personal with the political in Bo's case led to explosive outcomes. That this happened at such a sensitive time with an imminent leadership transition only added to the combustibility. Accounts after his fall talk of Chongqing's being run like a private fiefdom under him, and of his actively attempting to replace Xi Jinping as supreme leader in Beijing. But there was also a whispered narrative of a hugely popular and compassionate leader who was at least trying to do something. The campaigns he was publicly linked to captured this ambiguity. The 'Red Song' movement was either a brave attempt at emotional mobilisation for a population revolted and disengaged from politics, or a dangerous opportunistic dabbling with the demons of the CR (Wen Jiabao's line of attack in March 2012 when finally he indirectly and publicly denounced Bo). The 'strike hard' campaign against the mafia he pushed from

2010 was either a noble effort to take on some of the most unscrupulous criminals in society and clean it up, or, according to lawyers and some of its collateral victims, a festival of illegality and violence in which for every criminal caught there were a dozen innocent people who were given rough justice.

One of the striking issues over the leadership transition process was that there seemed to be no real debate about policy. The Party corporately wanted to present an outward image of utter unity, calmness and continuity. And yet the open letter sent to Wen Jiabao by 1600 intellectuals attacking him for over-liberal support for non-State companies mentioned in Chapter 1, and the clash between Wu Bangguo and his 'Five Noes' with Wen and his democratic-friendly language, showed that in fact beneath the surface there were often profound division and argument over both how to assess and prioritise, and then how to address future challenges. Bo raised this in an argument with fellow elite politician Wang Yang. Of course, there was no public debate as such. But in Chongqing, a place where Wang Yang had been Party secretary before Bo, and in Guangdong, the place where Wang was Party boss from 2007 to 2012, this issue of how to divide the new wealth in Chinese society alluded to a split within the Party over the most critical issue of all – economic policy.

DIVIDING THE CAKE

The clash between Wang Yang and Bo Xilai was presented as an elemental one. Wang Yang had a starkly different background from Bo. Born in Anhui, the same province in which Li Keqiang was growing up, his father had died before he was a teenager. He started work at the age of 17 in 1972 in a local food factory before attending the Central Party School in Beijing from 1979 to 1980. In the 1980s he was involved in leadership positions in the Anhui local CYL, working on propaganda and education before promotion while still under the age of 40 to the level of deputy governor of the province in 1993. In 1999 he went to work in Beijing in what was then called the State DRC (it was changed in the early 2000s to the National DRC), the powerful central ministry in charge of implementation of China's Five Year Plans. In 2005, however, he was made Party secretary of Chongqing, before elevation to the Politburo in 2007 and a move to Guangdong to serve as Party secretary there.

In his path through provincial and national power, Wang Yang gained the reputation of being independent minded, someone willing to talk about policy issues outside the usually somewhat sterile formulations of the Hu and Wen period. In this environment, his critics had accused him of 'being someone who likes to come up with theories opposed to the CPC'.[35] His great strength, however, lay in his rich administrative experience and abilities.[36] As shown in his handling of the Wukan incident of 2011, Wang was able, in Guangdong, to handle major incidents of unrest well.

While in Guangdong he promoted a number of campaigns that ran parallel to those of Bo in Chongqing, but occupied a different political terrain, and appealed to a different strand of thinking in the CPC. He strongly promoted the idea that the province 'needed to find its own path'.[37] He had asked officials under him in mid 2011 to be daring and to take the imprecation of the early reform period to 'liberate thinking' seriously. In particular he had urged cadres not to live on their achievements in the past, indulging themselves and becoming complacent.[38] A keen user of his iPad, Wang had been active in engaging, through new social media, with the opinions and ideas posted on the internet. He had also praised the Hong Kong system of governance where civil society and other groups were able to do some of the work traditionally, but often inefficiently, undertaken by government entities in China.[39] This idea of the communities managing their own affairs, and of the government being by and for the people, appeared in a context in which, over the period of the early 2010s, the Twelfth Five Year Plan, starting in 2011, contained much discussion of social management and resources to go into this. But as the assessment of

Hu Jintao's period in office already given made clear, this amount
of stress on social management could be interpreted as evidence
of the general inability of the leading politicians to make tough
decisions about how best to govern a society with such a dynamic
and fast-changing economy in a more efficient way that avoided
all this administrative intervention. In many ways, China in the
late Hu era looked like a country with a modern economy that
was still wrestling with structures of governance and administration borrowed from the Soviet Union in the middle of the previous century. Instead of these expensive regimes of coercion and
control, therefore, Wang seemed interested, in his much repeated
slogan of 'Happy Guangdong', in the idea of society and people
having a greater say in governance issues and being served by the
government, rather than managed by it. This argued against the
fundamental, hierarchical dynamics of power in contemporary
China, where government was often prescriptive, rule-enforcing
and centralised, and brooked no opposition.[40]

Wang Yang had opposition to some of his more free-wheel-
ing ideas not just in the central government, but also from his
own governor, Huang Huahua, who had expressed dissent from
his supposed political superior.[41] Perhaps the most powerful of
Wang's statements, and the one that reached sharply towards Bo,
was the idea that the Party in and of itself had no God-given right
to power. It could not, just by being the Party, bring benefits and
happiness to people.[42] The idea of power being the Party's by right
rather than by being earned was a subversive one. In Wang's framework, therefore, the Party had to base its legitimacy on continuing
performance, social relevancy, efficiency and public support. There
was nothing ontologically in itself or in the way that it had come
to power and maintained that power that meant the Party had to
be in power. All was based on performance, and all could be taken
away if the Party failed in this.[43] This could be read as an attack
on those who occupied positions in the Party through blood linkages with key figures in the past, creating a hereditary aristocracy.

People, in fact, like Bo. It hearkened back to the campaigns in the CR over four decades earlier, in which revolutionary ability and prowess were shown to belong to someone through inheritance. Wang Yang was placing his finger on one of the most sensitive issues for the contemporary CPC – that it was forever seeking elites to lead it, and that those elites had a habit of being formed around the core founding fathers and their direct family networks. How could a modern party, presiding over such a vast and fast-changing economy, rely on this sort of semi-monarchic system?

Over the middle part of 2011, a strange discussion of the 'division of the cake' appeared in some Chinese media, alluding to the different economic outlooks of Wang in his new position in Guangdong, and Bo. It was given a particular edge because of the fact that Wang was Bo's predecessor in Chongqing. The new eye-catching campaigns that Bo was leading in the city were in some ways interpreted as a covert critique of the previous occupant of the Party leadership there. To add piquancy, Wang, born in 1955, still had plenty of time to be promoted even if he failed in 2012. For Bo, six years older, time was no longer on his side. In July of 2011, Bo declared that the cake needed to be cut first, then made bigger. For Wang, the priority was to grow the cake and enlarge it before dividing it up. Encoded in this were messages about attitudes both held towards how much they should tolerate increased economic and social inequality even while growth rates were good. Bo, in his social housing campaigns, had made it clear he wanted to act sooner rather than later to close this gap, using some of the wealth being created to bring about social welfare and better provision of public goods, and using these as the means of pulling the extremes of the wealthy and the poor together. For Wang, however, it was a case of still going for growth no matter what, and letting society get richer before any heavy welfare provision and more radical policies could be brought in.[44]

The political and personal competition between Bo and Wang grew in intensity over 2011. But what nascent policy debate there had been while Bo was at liberty ended with his dramatic fall. This event dominated most of 2012, until the Congress itself put personalities and the battles between them, together with their associated machinations, at the forefront again and pushed what little policy discussion there was deep into the background. The questions simply became who would be winners and losers after Bo's demise, and how would a selection choice be made.

PRIDE AND PROCESS

Two conversations made a big impression on me in the course of 2012, as the Bo issue and the collateral from it were being worked through the system in China, showing how much into uncharted waters the Party was getting as it tried to effect this 'once-in-a-generation leadership change' (as the Western media started to call it). During a talk in Brussels in the middle of the year on the leadership transition, a leading official from the Party School in Beijing stated reassuringly that consultations had already been completed on who would constitute the approximately 3,000 members of the Party Congress that would then assemble later in the year to make the decision on who the new leaders would be. His declaration was simply that everything in 2012 would be done mostly as it had been in 2007.

But another conversation a few weeks later was less clear-cut. At an informal dinner with Chinese academics and officials visiting Europe, I observed them start a fierce, albeit polite, debate on exactly how the voting would be done. 'I don't understand,' said one, 'what happens after the Central Committee is elected. Are we saying that once that is decided, then the Central Committee votes in the Politburo, and then they go into session and vote in a Standing Committee?' Discussion followed for several minutes. It was clear that even the best-informed insiders who were in some ways involved with the whole process did not quite know what was happening.

Looking at literature produced by Party experts about the mechanics of how this process was due to work is not helpful. Li Junru, former vice president of the Central Party School, and one of contemporary China's leading Marxist theorists, issued a book 'for all those who want to know more about the Communist Party of China' in English in 2011. Chapter 3 of this book discusses the 'operating mechanism of the CPC'. In this, Li states:

> As for the selection of major leading cadres, the procedure begins with Party conferences or cadre conferences at the same level, at which candidates are nominated by secret ballot. Then the organization department talk to the voters one by one to find out the qualities and capabilities of the nominees. The candidates are decided on according to the comprehensive result of the ballot and the talks.[45]

The idea of a ballot and then talks is perhaps the key here. Casting a vote in a secret ballot is only halfway to getting someone elected. There also have to be 'discussions'. And the room for these 'discussions', in which delegates were debated with and harmoniously helped to reach the right conclusion, was at the heart of the transitional leadership process from 2011 onwards.

In fact, within this decision-making process, there were a whole number of different pressure points and sources of influence. There was the 'Gang of Old Men' who had been brought in more closely because of the severe wobble that had occurred around the fall of Bo Xilai. There were the meetings, reported throughout 2011 and 2012, of families who had a strong interest in ensuring their financial and political interests would be preserved when the winning candidates emerged. There were the participants and contenders themselves, some of whom were retiring but needed to make sure their legacy and their patronage networks were in good shape after they had done, and some, like Bo Xilai had been and Wang Yang still was, who had a chance of being elevated. The least important in this intra-elite hub of activity and discussion and negotiation, most of it done covertly and out of sight, were the actual members of the Communist Party itself, and the broader society the Party was meant to be serving.

One of the crucial issues was to decide how many would be on the Standing Committee. Historically, membership had ranged from five to nine members. There were no constitutional restrictions. Before 1992, there were five members. From 1992 to 2002 this had become seven members. Then it had increased under Hu and Wen to nine. There were good arguments to see it grow further, up to ten or 11 (though strangely, the Politburo Standing Committee membership had never been an even number). These were based on ideas about the core function of this body being to create consensus in the political heart of a society by putting key representatives of Party, government and society together, and needing therefore to embrace a larger membership in order to achieve this. Speculation through 2010 pointed to a Politburo that would maintain this balance, institutionalising a process that had occurred organically where the separate positions in the Standing Committee had come to be associated with particular responsibilities, ranging from Party discipline, to ideology, to microeconomics.[46]

What was most striking when looking at the key contenders for promotion before the fall of Bo was how small the pool of eligible people was. Those that had the relevant senior provincial and national ministerial leadership experience, and then had strong enough patronage and support links in the Party and government, were probably no more than a dozen. There was little likelihood that anyone this time would be promoted from outside the full Politburo direct into Standing Committee. This had been done with Xi and Li in 2007, but its justification then had been to set up leadership succession five years afterwards. Such a consideration did not figure in 2012. The most likely candidates were already in the full Politburo, meaning the list of real contenders could be got by taking away those due to retire from this group and seeing who was left. As these came to a small number, in order to resolve the various conflicts between some being brought into the Standing Committee and some left out, why not make them all members and expand the size?

This was to prove too neat and straightforward. Throughout 2012, and particularly after Bo had been removed from contention, lists appeared of possible configurations for the final line-up. Some of these had nine names, a few had 11. Only in the middle of the year did rumours start to surface of a Politburo reduced in size down to seven. The argument for this was that, at nine, the leading group had been unable to make any significant decisions beyond economic ones. There was a need for a group of people who could at least come to some hard conclusions without being caught in permanent gridlock.

As the formal process for deciding how the Congress of late 2012 would be constituted was occurring, there was a parallel lobbying campaign. This was mostly easily and vividly traced in the meetings of elite families through 2011 into 2012 – key tribal groups that had huge and self-evident interests at stake in the eventual outcomes of the leadership transition. One of the most striking of these occurred on 6 October 2011, ostensibly to commemorate the 35th anniversary of the smashing of the Gang of Four, the group of radical leaders around Mao Zedong's wife who had been blamed after his death for the CR and placed in jail. Meeting at the China World Hotel in Beijing, with a mixture of well-known scholars, they had been exercised by the issues of inequality under Hu and Wen, the widening gap between the countryside and the cities, corruption, inequality in education, public trust, problems in the environment and resources, and general issues of social justice. The report of the meeting from one attendee afterwards was that 'China is now coming to a highly dangerous period.' Descendants of former elite leaders like General Ye Jianying, Hu Yaobang, Hua Guofeng (former Party chairman) and Li Xiannian (former Politburo member and resident) were present. Their conclusion was that reform was needed urgently, not in the economic realm, but the political.[47] In addition to the meetings of second generation members of revolutionary families there were also a series of prominent intellectuals like journalist Hu Shuli, who participated in seminars discussing the challenges facing China over this period, all of which were aimed at influencing the process of selecting new leaders.

COUNTING THE VOTES

Arriving at a final line-up after canvassing the opinions of the 82-million-strong membership of the Party in order to get 2,270 delegates was always going to be an epic quest. As some indication of how tough even the administration of this was one might look at the case of a single province. This process was top-down and bottom-up, involving different procedures. An official in Xinjiang speaking in late 2011 said that this involved 25 steps in order to get to the final 2,270, an increase of 50 delegates over the Seventeenth Party Congress. A total of 40 election units were involved, from provinces to municipalities, special administrative regions like Hong Kong, the army, the central Party and other entities. Jiangsu province, as an example, had a list of 37,000 eligible candidates, from whom a shortlist of 90 was finally produced. On 20 March 2012 the particulars of these 90 were sent to Beijing to be investigated. Ten days later, an approved list of 84 candidates was issued from Beijing to Jiangsu, finally coming down to 79 on 21 April. After consultations and discussions with other democratic parties, the All China Workers Union and non-Party members, at a meeting also attended by members of the local United Front and the Party Organisation Department, an election was held in Jiangsu on 14 May, in the provincial capital of Nanjing, at which the local Congress then voted 70 from the 79 by secret ballot.[48] These were the delegates from Jiangsu who attended the final Congress in November.

However effective in terms of intra-Party democracy this was as an administrative process, the idea that delegates were being sent to Beijing to produce unexpected consequences was soon scotched by the fact that it was clear the real negotiations were occurring in the reconvened Beidaihe retreat, held at the end of August 2012. Beidaihe had been the location for political and military super-elite retreats during the late Maoist period, through the Deng years and into Jiang Zemin's tenure as Party head. It was the scene of some of the great factional intrigues and fights of the late CR, with a villa by the seaside in which Marshal Lin Biao had reportedly stayed with his wife, the hugely ambitious Ye Qun, and where he had per- haps worked on the plans to assassinate Mao and seize power – a scheme that was imputed to him in the vilification campaign after his death in a plane crash in Mongolia in 1971 while reportedly fleeing to the Soviet Union.

About three hours' drive east from Beijing, in Hebei province on the north-eastern coast, Beidaihe maintains the same air of dis- arming sleepiness typical of so many seaside provincial centres the world over. In the early 2000s, Hu Jintao had stopped the cus- tom of these curious collective retreats as part of a superficial move to show clear space between his leadership style and that of Jiang Zemin. But with the reappearance of Jiang and the Gang of Old Men after Bo Xilai's fall in August 2012, the Beidaihe summer retreat was held again. And from this meeting rumours and reports started to emanate of 'consultations', the content and nature of which was never fully disclosed, but which implied that the old generation headed by Jiang were trawling through lists of possible Standing Committees, contemplating who might finally be placed in the leadership.

Observers at the time were quick to point out that the Communist Party, presented as a force at the vanguard of moder- nity in China, shared, in the selection of its leaders at least, some parallels with a much older and more traditional organisation – the Catholic Church. There were multiple ironies here. The

Catholic Church and the Party had been at loggerheads with each other since the establishment of the country in 1949. The need for Roman Catholics to obey the higher authority of the pope in Rome, and the recognition, set out by Saint Augustine over 1,500 years before, of an allegiance to the State only in material terms, but to the Church in spiritual ones, was something the Party never accepted, particular in its more zealously atheistic period up to the early 1980s. Even in reform China, however, the Catholic Church was regarded with suspicion, and an indigenous Patriotic Catholic Church was set up which stood as a counterweight to the banned Roman one, appointing its own priests and bishops. Despite this, and the Roman Catholic Church's diplomatic recognition of the Republic of China on Taiwan rather than the People's Republic, there was respect in some circles of the CPC for the longevity of the Church, its ideological cohesiveness and its moral standing. These were things the CPC itself wished to emulate. In the 1990s and early 2000s, Party School thinkers had studied the leadership and organisation of the Church, seeking ideas for what they might be able to use in their own battle to survive longer than the minuscule 74 years that the Communist Party of the Soviet Union had managed. 'Each of these unelected elites,' wrote international editor of the *Sydney Morning Herald*, Peter Hartcher, on 12 March 2013, 'relies on an historical mandate to exclusive powers. One claims power in the name of God, the other in the name of the proletariat.' And both, Hartcher went on, referring to the resignation of Pope Benedict in February 2013 and the convening of a convention of Cardinals to appoint his successor, 'meet at times of acute crisis'.[49] The parallels were deeper. Both had highly opaque means of finally deciding who their leader was. The Beidaihe meeting of 2012, in that sense, functioned like the innermost box of this decision-making process, the place where the consensus right at the top was established, which then had to meet up with the opinions of the lower levels of the Party and the other vested interests and inputs from all directions that now flowed into this.

Like a vast game of trumps, provisional decisions made along the way were bit-by-bit trumped by higher-value cards, till the final and largest-value cards were laid, settling the outcome. These were held by the grand old former leaders who, while they had no formal positions at all from which to make this decision, were the ones with the most valuable political capital.

Writing in the *South China Morning Post* on 16 August 2012, Shi Jingtao, the correspondent based in Beijing, stated that:

> the secretive party conclave in the beach resort of Beidaihe is widely believed to have come to an end [...] Although state media and mainland officials have remained tight-lipped about the existence of such a meeting [...] analysts said all signs pointed to the conclusion of this year's seaside gathering, where the most important personnel and policy issues were expected to be finalised ahead of the 18th party congress this autumn.

During the meeting, 'the nation's top incumbent and retired leaders had reached a broad consensus on the central government's future leadership, through behind-the-scene negotiations'.[50] From this meeting, news started to circulate of a seven-strong Politburo Standing Committee.

THE FINAL LEG: NOVEMBER 2012

The enormous variable of the fall of Bo and the ways in which it had cast a shadow throughout 2012 meant that speculation rose to fever pitch in September. There was no set date by which a Party Congress needed to be held except that it had to happen before the end of the five-year limit in 2012. Historically, congresses had occurred throughout the year, from April (the Ninth, in 1969) to July (the First, in 1921) to November (for example the Sixteenth, in 2002). But since the regularisation of Party processes from the late

1970s, there had been a tradition that had been stuck to to ensure that they happened mostly in October, and only exceptionally in November.

In 2012, a great deal was exposed about how little still the dynamics of elite politics in China are understood – possibly because of the huge number of individual variables, and the highly dynamic and largely unregulated way in which negotiations and deals are made before outcomes are arrived at. In the next two chapters, I will tackle this by simply taking the final seven who won through and looking closely at the routes by which they came to power. Before 15 November, when all finally became clear, there was still uncertainty as to whether the Standing Committee would comprise seven, nine, eleven or some other number of people. There was wide speculation about who would be on this final group, and lists were produced with dizzying regularity right up to 15 November, with widely different names figuring on them. Some even suggested that the Congress might, exceptionally, be delayed; that Hu and Wen would stay on (there was no constitutional restraint preventing them doing so); and that the whole process might be finished off when things calmed down, a few months or even a year or so hence. Arguments abounded about whether Hu would follow the precedent of Jiang and remain as head of the Central Military Commission for a year or two, or whether he would relinquish all posts. The only widely accepted fact was that when all was finally done, Xi Jinping had to be appointed Party boss. The disruption of his not doing so now was too great.

Nerves were frayed by a series of odd events in 2012. Xi Jinping 'disappeared' for a fortnight in early September, cancelling meetings with visiting US secretary of State, Hillary Clinton, and a number of other dignitaries from Singapore and Denmark. The lack of a precise explanation led to suggestions ranging from Xi having had a heart attack, to injuring himself in a swimming pool incident, to suffering from injury after an assassination attempt. As Australian

analyst Ryan Manuel pointed out, 'Xi's absence was his third fort-
night-long disappearance from public view this year.' And indeed,
in early August, just before the time of Xi's 'disappearance', only
two serving Politburo Standing Committee members were actually
sighted publicly from 31 July to 9 August – Wen Jiabao on the 1st
and, ironically, Xi on the 5th.[51] Manuel went on:

> The recent hubbub over Xi's disappearance says as much
> about our analysis of China as it does about the Chinese
> regime [...] Our hunt for the 'next Gorbachev' means we
> focus on how a new individual at the top could bring great
> change. But Beijing focuses intently on preventing another
> Gorbachev. And we inevitably end up disappointed.[52]

The issue of the opaqueness of the Chinese political system giving a
field day to speculation and wishful thinking amongst observers is
a long-standing one.

The announcement at the seventh plenary session of the
Seventeenth Central Committee of the CPC in October was the
first sign that at last things were going to happen. The plenary session was the full meeting of the serving Central Committee full
and alternate members. Its main function was in being the final
step formally announcing 8 November as the date when the Party
Congress would be held. Rumours of block bookings of hotels in
Beijing had been correct. Finally the 2,270 delegates, painstakingly selected from across the country, were now able to descend
on Beijing and start to listen to work reports, investigations and
discussions. That this was a highly staged, theatrical event was
no surprise. On the first day of the Congress, Hu Jintao gave his
last report, during which he displayed his usual sweep of rhetorical flourishes and ideological formulations. 'Taking people as the
key', 'peaceful development', 'creating a beautiful China', 'firmly
marching on the path of socialism with Chinese characteristics'
– all got a look in, as did the phrases most closely associated with

him: 'harmonious society' and 'scientific development'.[53] With that over, he stepped down and the formal deliberations began. Only on 15 November was the final line-up prepared. Journalists stuffed into the Great Hall of the People in central Beijing, waiting in anticipation to see who and how many might come out. Some spotted marks on the carpet on the stage that suggested seven or nine places were specified. It was to this sort of barren hunting for clues that people had been reduced after the ups and downs, false leads and blind alleys of the last few months. The moment for the press announcement slipped past the designated hour of 11. This only raised the pitch further. Was there some problem? Afterwards, people claimed that a final decision makers' meeting had ended in argument over who was to go where, with former grandees involved. Such a sign of indecision in what was meant to have been a highly structured, deliberate process was the final irony. At last, the seven men appeared. The most tricky part of the leadership succession, the Party elite lineup, had been concluded. The old men who had been leaders over a decade before were, the moment the seven were in clear public view, judged winners, and one of them – the resurrected Jiang Zemin – was linked closely with at least five of those staring back at the flashing cameras. That at least was the immediate reaction. The next chapter will interrogate this a little deeper and will ask – now we know the men who won out and can understand a bit more about their path to the Politburo – in what way we can make political sense of them, and how we can create a better framework and narrative to explain how they got there. How can we avoid seeking what we wish to find, rather than seeing what is actually clearly before our eyes? That will be the task set out in the rest of this book. And to achieve that, we have to come down to the level of the personal, of the individual life stories and inner dynamics of people who are often working very hard to avoid any details about their personalities or biographies beyond the barest outlines being known at all.

EPILOGUE

A journalist who was attending the 2012 Congress in Beijing told me when we met up just before its climax on 15 November that she had observed the remarkable disconnect between the 2,270 delegates assembled in the Great Hall of the People and its various meeting rooms each day and the pulse and rhythm of the rest of the city going on around them. Once one penetrated the security cordons and police checks, she said, one left a world of chaotic traffic movements and bustling people coming to and fro, and went into a sort of hushed sanctuary, where thick carpets cushioned the sound of footfalls, and meetings were held in reverent silence.

Her observation of the delegates was telling. Evidently, from the way they dressed and behaved they were extremely wealthy. While they were supposedly drawn from all walks of life, assembled to create the idea that they were truly representative of a diverse society and able to reflect its wishes in selecting a new elite that they would have input on deciding (an idea, as I have shown above, that is perhaps highly questionable, seeing as it was probably 99 per cent decided weeks before the meeting had even been called), in many ways they looked, spoke and, in the journalist's words, even smelled, of wealth and the power that wealth was able to accrue in modern China.

Like the description used in *The Fat Years*, the infamous best-selling novel by Chan Koonchung about the new wealthy of China that had been issued first in Hong Kong and then abroad a few years earlier, the Party Congress delegates of 2012 seemed overwhelmed in their public appearance by a sense of self-satisfaction.[54] They were, after all, in the elite club of clubs, flattered by the regime into believing that they were having input into a leadership core that would propel the world's second largest economy over the coming decade, possibly to a time when it would replace the United States to become the world's number one. This happiness sat oddly in a context in which large numbers of people in the rest of the country were in daily ferment and turmoil, with riots, disagreements, clashes between officials and people's groups, and the continuation of the Hu strategy of solving political stagnation with security overspend. That the Congress delegates made this sort of impression on a firsthand observer raises questions about how politics is done in modern China, and what relationship the governing elite has to society more broadly. The whole series of events of 2012 seemed to show that decision making in the country was still the preserve of a small group of people operating in highly opaque ways.

There was an implicit political justification for this. In Hu and Wen's China, the most precious thing in the Party was consensus. For all the faults of their period in power that have been written about in the first chapter, they managed to maintain stability in a political organisation that was vast, diverse and far more prone to historic divisions than people now remember. The greatest threat to this Party unity in their eyes was not the ill wishes of ideological opponents outside the country, but more probably a reversion to leftism (this will be discussed later), to a nostalgic Maoist utopianism that had been practised up to 1976 with such devastating and tragic outcomes, running from the great famines in the early 1960s to the intra-elite agony and self-destruction of the CR. While much official narrative of history promoted by the authorities in contemporary China can still, often with some justification, impute many of the causes for the country's past woes and tragedies to colonial outsiders who visited humiliation upon the country from the middle of the nineteenth century onwards, what is often much harder to stomach is the fact that the Party itself, self-appointed saviour and liberator of the Chinese, also visited calamities on the people it was meant to protect and take to a better life. That resentful thought, while repressed, lurks in so much of the critical domestic internal discourse about the Party and its moral right to rule.

This hard-won consensus was maintained in Hu's period in office even during the fall of Bo, when there was a brief chance that backers like powerful security chief Zhou Yongkang might support him. A top-level Party schism at this moment would have been potentially devastating. As it was, even over the fall of a figure as publicly appealing to some as Bo, the Party maintained its unified line. Some argued that this consensus was reached through the Politburo itself being an entity in which the different voices in society somehow got a call in – from the Party, SOEs, non-State companies, and the United Front and other forces in society in the Chinese People's Political Consultative Conference whose chair sat on the Politburo, and provinces and other non-central voices through the National People's Congress. The Politburo somehow had to distil representatives of all these into one functioning body, demonstrating that it had the right to say it was truly representative of the 'people' and the masses, and that it was hearing, listening to and learning from them. But there were dissenting voices who argued for a darker interpretation – that the Politburo was a brute declaration of raw power, that the very process by which the Eighteenth Congress had been decided was explicit evidence of this raw power. In the end its membership consisted of a group of people who had managed to build significant enough alliances in their areas of society and politics to be able to win a seat and beat off potential opponents.

Bo Xilai's most interesting aspect, in all of this, was not so much his Party links and his own princeling status, but the way in which he was conducting politics and campaigning in ways that resembled how a Western politician might operate. Politics in contemporary China had become the pastime of a small group who were able to conduct their negotiations and manoeuvres in a mini universe of their own. There were symptoms of this in the way that the Party elite spoke in a strange internal dialect that differed starkly from the language of the general populace, operating with tightly controlled rituals and administrative performance. These questions of language in particular will be addressed in greater depth in Chapter 5. Bo Xilai was disruptive to many of his fellow elite because of the uncomfortable ease by which he was able to

reach across to a public constituency for support, and to appeal to
'the people' emotionally, rather than just through their pockets and
material life standards. That he did this using the old symbolic gifts
of Maoist political mobilisation only added to the problems he
posed. His popularity was shown in some of the public, and highly
risky, demonstrations of support after his fall. Bo 'did politics', and
was campaigning for higher office in a context in which this sort of
emotional mobilisation and tactical manoeuvring for support outside the normal elites were evidently disliked. There was clearly a
profoundly political dimension to his fall, which went beyond the
supposed crimes of his wife and the salacious details of his private
life and corruption when he was felled. Bo's case shows the real
problems of mobilisation and doing politics in present-day China,
which is still recovering from the highly disruptive charismatic
leadership of Mao almost 40 years before. Bo's threat may well have
finally been managed during 2012 and into 2013, but the questions it raised – of how elite leaders appeal to a vast and complex
population, and mobilise them behind specific campaigns in which
there are winners and losers and hard choices have to be made –
were valid ones. This challenge awaits the group of people decided
upon in a process involving a tiny group of key decision makers
who were the final winners in the Eighteenth Congress leadership
transition – the seven members of the Standing Committee of the
Politburo that appeared on 15 November 2012. It is to them that
we now turn.

3

THE NEW EMPEROR: XI JINPING

As they stood facing the world after their delayed arrival on a winter morning in 2012, to a person who had seen nothing of the journey taken to get to this point these people would have looked physically remarkably similar to each other. They wore the same Western-style suits, with the same uniform black hair, and they looked around the same age. They were people of the same ethnicity, and they were all male.

Looking a little closer, one would have seen some small clues to potential differences. One of them added a tiny dash of colour, with a red tie instead of the darker colours sported by the others lined beside him. One of them smiled more broadly, and wore glasses, and stood next to the more portly one at the centre who had led the whole group out, and seemed to have more of a swagger. It was he, and he alone, who spoke. 'Good day, ladies, gentlemen, and friends,' he started off:

> Sorry to have kept you waiting. I am very happy to meet with you, friends of the press [...]
>
> Here, let me introduce to you my colleagues, the other six Standing Committee members.
>
> They are: Comrade Li Keqiang, Comrade Zhang Dejiang, Comrade Yu Zhengsheng, Comrade Liu Yunshan, Comrade Wang Qishan, and Comrade Zhang Gaoli.

He went on:

> During the civilisation and development process of more than
> 5,000 years, the Chinese nation has made an indelible contri-
> bution to the civilisation and advancement of mankind.
>
> In the modern era, our nation experienced constant hard-
> ship and difficulties. The Chinese nation reached the most
> dangerous period. Since then, countless people with lofty
> ideals to realise the great revival of the Chinese nation rose
> to resist and fight, but failed one time after another.
>
> Since the founding of the CPC, we have united and led
> the people to advance and struggle tenaciously, transforming
> the impoverished and backward Old China into the New
> China that has become prosperous and strong gradually. The
> great revival of the Chinese nation has demonstrated unprec-
> edented bright prospects [...]
>
> Our people love life and expect better education, more
> stable jobs, better income, more reliable social security, med-
> ical care of a higher standard, more comfortable living con-
> ditions, and a more beautiful environment.
>
> They hope that their children can grow up better, work
> better and live better. People's yearning for a good and beau-
> tiful life is the goal for us to strive for.

This was standard rhetoric, which could have fallen from the mouth
of his predecessor Hu Jintao. But then the mood darkened:

> In the new situation, our party faces many severe challenges,
> and there are many pressing problems within the party that
> need to be resolved, especially problems such as corruption
> and bribe-taking by some party members and cadres, being
> out of touch with the people, placing undue emphasis on for-
> mality and bureaucracy must be addressed with great effort.
>
> The whole party must be vigilant.

The metal itself must be hard to be turned into iron. Our responsibility is to work with all comrades in the party to be resolute in ensuring that the party supervises its own conduct; enforces strict discipline; effectively deals with the prominent issues within the party; earnestly improves the party's work style and maintains close ties with the people. So that our party will always be the firm leadership core for advancing the cause of socialism with Chinese characteristics.[1]

Finally he thanked everyone and the brief meeting was over. No questions were taken. There was no fanfare other than this meeting, and no celebratory actions. In many ways, a skilled reader of body language might even have detected relief in the seven men who had finally emerged.

Press and expert commentary over the next few days remarked on Xi's easier style of speaking, and responded favourably to what was seen as his directness. As I will show later, anyone who had looked at what Xi had said and written in his three-decades-long political career beforehand should not have been surprised that he chose this trope. Since the early 1990s, corruption and the need for the Party to assume a moral as well as an economic leadership were common motifs he had come back to, even up to the eve of the Congress in his speeches to the Party School, of which he was president. But Xi's moral language, as I will also show, needs to be located in a particular context. And that context was framed by the very way in which the Party as a collection of interests, individuals and ideas had been able to execute this very strange transition.

Were China a multi-party democracy, then there would have been a campaign in which candidates spoke, engaged and set out their ideas. There would have been fierce competition, much of it out in the open, as people from different parties or from different interest groups challenged each other for position. The PRC over 2012 had engaged in something rather different. Robert A. Caro, in the fourth volume of his masterly multi-volume biography of

American president Lyndon Johnson, has written that power not only corrupts but also reveals:

> When a man is climbing, trying to persuade others to give him power, concealment is necessary; to hide traits that might make others reluctant to give him power, to hide also what he wants to do with power; if men realized the traits or realized the aims they might refuse to give him what he wants. But as a man obtains more power, camouflage is less necessary. The curtain begins to rise. The revealing begins.[2]

This is a powerful insight into the role of concealment and subterfuge in politics. In the Chinese system, where one party has a monopoly on power, these qualities operate according to different dynamics than in a democracy, but they are still important. The career of Hu Jintao is illustrative here. In many ways, he never ceased to conceal, leaving many who observed him closely as confused about him at the end of his time as they were when he started. The criticisms of him outlined in the last chapter argued that, for a decade at the top, he had done nothing and ventured nothing. Under him China had grown rich and complacent, and that was all. Hu's continuous concealment of his personal opinions and vision despite being, at least in terms of formal positions, the most powerful man in the country, was puzzling. Perhaps this betrayed the fact that he never really had much secure power to begin with. He never had the space truly to reveal himself, and was surrounded by constraints and restrictions on his action. The modern role of the Party itself, and how it acts, are also important to factor in here. It has become, as Singapore-based Party expert Yongnian Zheng phrased it, an 'organizational emperor', increasingly restricting the space for individual politicians to make any real difference.[3] The Party acts in corporate ways, increasingly suppressing the powers of individuals because of the terror of having another Mao visited on the country, forcing its contemporary leaders to be subsumed in some grander collective purpose. In this context, the very question of someone like Bo Xilai promoting and pushing themselves forward is unsettling and distasteful, and threatens this hard-won order. It was this potential threat, rather than his claimed corruption and the failings of his own and his family's personal morality, that were his real crimes.

The transition of leadership therefore involved repressed, concealed and covert competition between different individuals and the networks around them. It was undertaken with great opacity. This gave the final moments culminating with the winners of this process walking out on 15 November an oddly flat air of a campaign ending that, in many ways, had never really taken place. For years before, gradual, calculated moves were made to steer the transition and to ensure that it happened smoothly. Questions of policy outlook of new leaders and of legitimacy of the process by which they were appointed amongst a wider constituency than the tiny band of political elite involved at the core were never raised. That was too risky and disruptive. The events on 15 November were presented as a triumphal moment for the Party collectively, with no particular celebratory voice from any of those who emerged as apparent winners. Such individual celebration when it was the Party's victory collectively was inappropriate. In many ways, the less profile this whole process had publicly and in the media, the better for the Party.

Xi had also stated in his brief comments on 15 November, after introducing his colleagues on the Politburo, that 'You have known them well.' As I will show, however, the people he had brought before the world as the new elite of elites of the political leadership in China were figures who had, institutionally and politically, been extremely good in one specific area, and that was to remain as little known as possible. Zhang Gaoli was a taciturn apparatchik from the State oil industry whose greatest claim to fame was succeeding in pumping out immense levels of GDP growth wherever he had been, and who in his few public comments had boasted of the need to say less and do more. Zhang Dejiang was known mostly from his brief period of study on the DPRK – the only member of the group to have studied abroad. Yu Zhengsheng was best known for his father's being romantically linked very early on to Mao Zedong's wife, Jiang Qing. Wang Qishan had some profile from his former leadership of the US China Strategic High Level Dialogue, where he had engaged with President Obama and Secretary Hillary Clinton effectively. Liu Yunshan was almost wholly unknown, although analysts had seen him being integral to the repressive press, media laws and clampdowns of the last few years as the 'pro-stability' campaign had deepened. Xi and Li were the two great stars in this firmament, both with careers in the provinces that had shown a little about them. But these leaders had shown a capacity for self-concealment and for managing to keep a low profile that stood starkly at odds with the noisy self-promotion of Bo Xilai.

As I will seek to show, when we look at each of these figures a little more closely we do detect stories of some kind of inner journey, allowing us to glimpse a little of the lives they have concealed. Xi offers the most, because the narrative of his journey towards the top has been written about and studied more extensively than the others. But they too also offer insights into the nature of the remarkable world in which they live through the deals they have had to make, the debts they have accrued and the networks they had built around them: and at the core of this the lives they have lived and the ideals they have tried – or, more often than not, compromised over and failed – to live up to. The more one stares at these seven figures, and sees them as representative and symbolic figures that have emerged from a process in which so much has had to be concealed and controlled, the more one can build out from them to a whole society around them. In that sense, they offer, finally, the 'single unmoving point' in the firmament of modern Chinese politics that can help one at least get some traction on the complex, dynamic, confusing society around them. This is why the man who is at the heart of this leadership, Xi Jinping, is so important to understand.

XI STOOPS TO CONQUER

The tools to understanding elite figures that I will use in this and the next chapter will be the biographies we have of them, and the words they have used in their careers prior to being on the Standing Committee. These will help in understanding the two crucial areas where we have to get under their skin; their networks, and their ideological position. In the materialistic, dialectic system of modern China, ideology helps with the network, and the network is built through ideological management and campaigning. Xi is a figure about which there is much knowledge.

This is partly because, from the moment he appeared in 2007 as the most likely successor to Hu Jintao, the Party propagandists had an interest in reinforcing his political position with a suitable narrative, a life story that helped with elite and public, and, to some extent, international acceptance of this figure. The one question that anyone on 15 November watching the events in the Great Hall of the People unfold, if they were dispassionate observers, was why, of all the 84 million members of the Party, of the 2,270 members of the 'high-level cadre' band, of the 350 members of the Central Committee and of the 14 or so eligible members of the Politburo as it was constituted in the Seventeenth Congress from 2007 to 2012, was Xi the chosen one? This was not a fatuous question. In 1997, at the Fifteenth Party Congress, Xi had failed to make it as a full member of the 167-strong Central Committee, coming last in a ballot for membership. He was only able to serve as an alternate.[4] How was it that in the space of a decade, the man who, when asked whether he would ever be the top leader of China in 2002, had reportedly said 'Are you trying to give me a fright?',[5] ended up as the Party leader, the chair of the Central Military Commission, and the president?

One of the great clues to understanding Xi is not that he is a 'princeling'. The first chapter sought to show that this is a hugely contentious and ill-defined term. The more specific and meaningful question about him is what sort of assets and help he gains from his

family links in ways that evidently did not help for Bo Xilai and his
equally sterling Party-elite family networks. Xi's father, Xi Zhongxun,
while important as a figure in the history of the country from its
foundation in 1949, was nowhere near as well known as Bo Xilai's
father, Bo Yibo, nor a raft of other figures. What political assets and
advantages did Xi Zhongxun's life story give to his son, and, perhaps
more importantly, how was Xi able to deploy and gain benefit from
these? Why was Xi the one who finally came out on top?

Xi Zhongxun has one of the most uncomplicated and attractive
narratives of CPC senior military leaders of the revolutionary period
before 1949 who subsequently became political figures in the Mao
and Deng era. Felled as an 'anti Mao, anti Party element, a careerist
and schemer' at a Party meeting in August 1962, Xi was accused of
covertly supporting Gao Gang, one of the early opponents of Mao
and someone who was felled in 1953.[6] His real crime, however, was
associating with and claiming support for Marshall Peng Dehuai.
Peng was minister of defence in 1959 when he had directly challenged Mao Zedong at the Lushan conference that year about his
economic policies, and had pointed out the devastating hardship they
were causing in rural areas. Peng was quickly removed from office,
isolated, placed in internal exile and then, during the CR from 1966,
brutally persecuted. He died as a result of this maltreatment in 1974.
His warnings, however, were proven correct, with subsequent revela-
tions about the devastating famines that had blighted China from
1958 to 1962. The attack on Xi Zhongxun was spearheaded by Mao
Zedong's security head and chief hatchet man, Kang Sheng. Things
were made worse because he occupied the sensitive, key role as head
of the Propaganda Department from 1953 to 1954, and then secretary general of the State Council from 1954, the latter in particular
a position that carried great weight because of the coordination of
central ministries it entailed. All of this gave his enemies plenty of
ammunition when he was put in the firing line. After the suspension
of his positions, he was sent to Luoyang in the central province of
Henan for a decade after 1962, working in a factory.

That Xi Zhongxun was sidelined during the build-up to the CR and its early phases, sitting out his time in relative obscurity, has proved an enormous asset to his son. Xi Zhongxun was almost unique amongst leaders of his generation in never being associated in any shape or form with leftists. Leftism was the great illness of Chinese political life after 1949, festering at the heart of the most destructive post-1949 movements, from the Great Leap Forward of 1958, to the disastrous central economic policy that caused the famines from 1958 to 1962, to the CR itself. Leftism was behind the purges that occurred from the fall of opponent of Mao, Gao Gang, in 1953–4, to the purging of subsequent waves of leaders and intellectuals from the Anti-Rightist campaign of 1957 onwards. The control and restraint of this extreme form of Chinese politics was one of the great achievements of Deng Xiaoping, who established a system where sporadic reversions to leftism in the form of spiritual pollution clampdowns were short and controlled, their social damage way less than from similar campaigns under Mao.[7] Xi Zhongxun had no association with any of the Maoist class rectification campaigns except as a victim of one of them. His isolation in the CR meant that his sons, and in particular Jinping, were never able to join a Red Guard rebellious group because of their bad class-background label.[8] This is in stark contrast to Bo Xilai, who was dogged in his past by claims about his radical behaviour in the CR period, despite ending up finally in jail in the early 1970s.[9] Xi Jinping's biography in this period is a blander, more benign one. He was one of the many millions of 'sent-down' youths, so called from their being sent in a form of internal exile to work in the countryside. He was largely based in Shaanxi province. This experience of hardship seems to be authentic, and gives the presentation of his life path a level of complexity, even in official media. He was, as one description puts it, 'a mixture of peasant and princeling', and this fact captures much of the contradictoriness of the experiences of the country he now leads.[10]

The experience of the CR is an uneasy one for the political elite in China from the fourth and fifth generations. For almost all of them, it has presented complexities and conflicts about how they account for their actions then. Were they victims or victimisers, activists or somehow incapacitated? The CR decade touched almost everyone, at least in the cities. It divided society, setting groups across the country against each other. This divisiveness was one of the great issues that Deng Xiaoping and his colleagues had to deal with after Mao's death and the return of more stable politics. Many of the newly returned leaders had to work with people they had been pitched against in the internecine wars of this period. During the subsequent leadership of Jiang and Hu, they too had to demonstrate that they were unconnected to the greater excesses of that time. The one certainty is that Chinese with any memory of the period after 1966 have been profoundly formed by the unique events back then. As historian of modern China Richard Kraus wrote:

China's Great Proletarian Cultural Revolution shook the politics of China and the world between 1966 and 1976. It dominated every aspect of Chinese life; families were separated, careers upended, education interrupted and striking political initiatives attempted amid a backdrop of chaos, new beginnings and the settling of old scores.

This history is not over, as Kraus goes on to explain, for the CR continues to be an unsettling memory even to a China now richer, stronger and more confident, for the simple reason that 'the movement remains contentious for its radicalism, its ambitions and its impact upon almost a billion lives'. The CR was 'violent, yet it was also a source of inspiration and social experiment'. This ambiguity means balanced treatment of it by modern historians within China offers great challenges. Its events sit in the memories of those who directly lived through it in unsettling ways. This partly explains the reticence with which the period is now treated.[11]

This reticence is shown in the fact that the only time elite leaders from the time of Hu and Wen, or of Xi and Li, refer to the CR

is in a highly circumscribed way.[12] Wen Jiabao is the most prominent of these. Speaking during the period when Bo Xilai was being
eased from power at the National People's Congress on 14 March
2012, he stated that:

> Now reforms in China have come to a critical stage, without
> a successful political reform, it is impossible for China to
> fully institute economic reform and the gains we have made
> in these areas may be lost, and new problems that popped up
> in the Chinese society will not be fundamentally resolved,
> and such historical tragedies as the Cultural Revolution may
> happen again in China.[13]

Bo's dabbling with the red heritage of the CR period was seen as one
of his most provocative, daring acts.[14] The consensus position over
the last three decades is based on the resolution on Party history
issued in 1981. There, the judgement was a simple one: 'The "cultural revolution", which lasted from May 1966 to October 1976,
was responsible for the most severe setback and the heaviest losses
suffered by the Party, the State and the people since the founding of
the People's Republic.' It was a tragedy and a disaster.[15]

The fourth generation of leaders around Hu and Wen can be
seen in some ways as an unlucky generation because of their loss of
education possibilities during this era when so much tertiary and
primary education was disrupted by mass mobilisation, particularly
in its earliest and most violent phase. But Xi's generation also sneak
within the experiences of this period, despite being younger. Xi himself was to enjoy no formal education until his arrival at Qinghua
University in 1975 to study Engineering for four years. His Ph.D.,
which he received in 2002, also from Qinghua University (which
will be looked at later), has been attacked by some as an 'outsourced'
piece of work by someone who did not even have a master's degree.
Despite the lack of explicit references to the CR experience by many
of them, however, the particular challenges and collective memories

of the period belonging to the sent-down youths is a striking badge of identification for this whole generation. That Xi's father was wholly remote from this movement, and only returned to political life at the recommencement of the 'good times' in 1980, has been an asset for Xi. In what little is presented in the official literature of the country's history at this time, Xi and his family are untainted with the vicious internal fights of the period. They were well out of it.

The other great asset to his son of Xi Zhongxun's story was his service as Party leader of Guangdong province at the very start of the economic reforms ushered in after 1978. Guangdong, where he occupied key leadership positions up to the level of first Party secretary from 1978 to 1981, has become hallowed territory in the historiography of the Deng era in modern China. It is regarded as a privileged place, the crucible of reforms through the establishment of Special Economic Zones (SEZs) from 1980, the location at the vanguard of the Party's rebranding and reorientation after Mao's death where Socialist marketisation succeeded. Xi's role at the dawn of this period when most was at risk meant that, till the day of his death in 2002, he was accorded immense respect. This respect transcended his apparent demotion in 1987 after he supported Hu Yaobang during the latter's removal as Party head nationally.[16] It even outlasted the reported criticisms he made of the treatment of students in the 1989 uprising (though hard evidence of these comments is difficult to trace – the most one can confidently say is that once more Xi Zhongxun was absent when controversial deeds were ordered by the leadership in Beijing at that time, and for that reason he was never tarred with their bad consequences). Having retired to Shenzhen, a place whose stratospheric economic success he had nurtured, Xi was accorded distinguished status, visiting Beijing as an honoured guest under the patronage of Jiang Zemin's right-hand man Zeng Qinghong in 1999 during the fiftieth anniversary of the Party's rise to power. It is safe to say that post 1949, with all the myriad ups and downs of political fortunes, and the concomitant changes of allegiance and positions that this involved for so many

of the political and military elite, there are few more straightfor-
wardly benign personal tales than Xi's. Xi Zhongxun was untainted
by participation in the procession of campaigns that harmed the
reputations of others, but associated only with more positive events
and issues. He was a man with few enemies. This inheritance of the
evident good standing of his father across a broad spectrum of leaders in the Party meant that almost from the day Xi Jinping became
the most politically active in his family and started work as a secretary to a military leader, he was to enjoy immense political capital
and help. That he was smart enough not to labour this, and ensured
that those who came across him during the years of his rise through
the leadership in the province of Fujian – where he was to spend 16
years – knew little about his famous father, was advantageous.[17] But
he was a significant enough member of the family-elite Communist
clan to merit paramount leader Deng Xiaoping's making a special
effort to visit Xiamen, the city where Xi was mayor in 1984.[18] Xi
Jinping has gone out of his way to do nothing to betray the memory
of his father. In a society still largely patriarchal and filial, this is an
immense advantage. It plays well to conservatives, who like to see
support for family values and respect for the elders; but even to the
more liberal, links to Xi Zhongxun are good ones because of his lack
of involvement with previous divisive campaigns under Mao.

FIRST STEPS ON THE PATH TO BEIJING

We can trace life events and the ways in which these have opti-
mised and increased Xi's networks from the moment he graduated
from Qinghua University right at the start of the reform process in
1979. At a time when his future close colleague, Li Keqiang, was
flirting with more radical ideas in Beijing University linked to the
Democracy Wall movement, which exploded over the winter of
that year, Xi went to work as the private secretary of Geng Biao, a
military leader in the Central Military Commission, the topmost
body in charge of the all-important army. Geng, one of the major

leaders of the Chinese Communist military forces in their struggle for power, had been in charge of the forces that secured the critical city of Zhangjiakou in Hebei Province near Beijing in 1945, and the capture of Taiyuan in neighbouring Shanxi province in the central part of China in 1948. A member of the PRC's diplomatic structures after 1949, he rose to be vice premier and a member of the Military Commission Standing Committee, a position he occupied when Xi worked for him. As Geng's private secretary, Xi was joining the select group of confidants and assistants to the core elite, the kind of jobs that had proved to be hugely helpful for the careers of figures like Wen Jiabao. Had Xi stayed in this position he would no doubt have progressed to senior military leadership in the years ahead. But in 1982 Xi made the decision to depart Beijing and the army headquarters for a civilian job in Zhengding, Hebei province, as deputy Party secretary on the local committee. A year later he was Party secretary.

If Hu Jintao's formative core administrative experiences happened in the remote north-western province of Gansu, an arid, backward area that still ranks as one of the country's poorest areas, then Xi Jinping earned his spurs in Fujian. His transfer from Hebei to the great coastal province from June 1985 was a hugely significant step. Without the breadth of economic and personnel management challenges and political experiences that Xi got in his provincial career, he would not have been eligible for elite leadership later.[19] As Singapore-based analyst Bo Zhiyue put it, the simple fact is that from the 1980s the road to the highest levels of Party leadership in Beijing lay through the provinces. Careers of people who had largely risen while working solely in Beijing like Wen Jiabao were the exceptions that proved the rule. Xi's 16 years in Fujian were to be seminal experiences. While there he was to work as mayor of a major city that was also designated an SEZ, Xiamen, and then as Party secretary of Ningde prefecture and Fuzhou city, finally reaching the level of provincial deputy Party leadership and the position of governor.

One of the trademarks of Xi in the future was to be heavy occurrence in his public language of attacks on corruption. This usually occurs in an abstract context, as it did in his first words as national Party leader in November 2012, quoted at the start of this chapter. But even in 1988, while newly appointed as Ningde prefecture Party secretary, Xi had started to refer to the need to combat corruption. In 1989 there was a particular point to this. The turbulence in Beijing in May and June during the Tiananmen Square uprising had sent ripples out to over 260 cities across the country. Largely an urban phenomenon, it had unsettled the Party leadership enough for them to send troops into the square in the centre of the city on the night and morning of 3–4 June. Crackdowns had occurred throughout the country, and even in Fujian local leaders had to make an appropriate response. For Xi, according to one account, the issue of corruption had been at the heart of the cause of the uprising. In his own area since 1982, local officials had managed to build themselves 7,392 private houses. A relatively small local elite had manipulated and exploited their official positions for huge gain.[20] That year he is recorded as commenting publicly on this issue of Party responsibility and the need for clean officials. 'It's a problem of who is letting down whom,' he stated. Building houses on stolen land and with no legal right 'destroys the Party power and its structure, lets down people, and weakens the powers of the Party to be able to govern the country'. This was a case of 'cadres attacking their own interests' by behaving in this way. News of Xi's harsh words on corruption even got coverage in the national *People's Daily*, which sent a reporter to do an article on the campaign in 1990.[21] Xi's own assessment of his two years in the prefecture was not modest. He had, he said, 'liberated thought, cultivated a cadre of good officials, dealt with poverty and developed the local economy through exploiting its natural attributes'.[22] But even this early on, Xi's language about corruption and the real meaning that lay at its heart was an issue. Xi moved on to senior levels of leadership in the city of Fuzhou and then in the province as a whole. Ningde subsequently suffered much more profound issues of corruption as China grew richer. In 2005, a raft of local leaders were tried on charges of huge graft and embezzlement of State funds. One, Li Rongfei, leader of a local county, was sentenced to death. His crimes were tracked back over a decade.[23] The brute reality is that for all Xi's talk early on, the structural issue of corruption locally had not changed. His self-assessment in 1990 of his achievements in the province and the reinforcement of this by national media had been wide of the mark. Was this noble-sounding campaign something truly ambitious, guided by a vision of the moral leadership of the Party, or was it led solely by the imperatives at the heart of Xi's own career?

Xi's promotion to Party secretary of the major industrial and commercial city of Fuzhou in 1990 was critical in giving him access to figures like Jiang Zemin, who had just become national Party leader in Beijing, and his advisor Zeng Qinghong. One of the campaigns that Xi promoted in his time in the city was to 'close the gap with the people'. But probably more important was his reading of the significance of Deng Xiaoping's southern tour in 1992, a moment when the strategic priority of the Party to take economic development as its key task was reaffirmed after the period of confusion following June 1989. The easiest route to building up fast GDP for the city and for the province as a whole was to open more deeply to its closest developed economy and its most active investor and technical partner, the island of Taiwan off the coast, which had enjoyed de facto independence from the mainland since 1949 despite Beijing's still regarding it as an inalienable part of China's territory. Throughout the early 1990s, a number of deals were signed between Taiwanese companies and entities in Fujian, making the island one of the largest inward investors, and creating in Fujian in particular a massive production centre for goods that were processed and exported as part of the acceleration of the Chinese economy from 1992.

One of the great events that dominated Fujian at the end of the 1990s, and one that illuminated the dark corners that had now appeared in a China experiencing breakneck growth, greater openness to investment, and a legal and governance system that were starting to show signs of being under immense pressure, was the case of Lai Changxing. Lai was a businessman who, through his Yuanhua company, had managed to set up a vast smuggling ring running into hundreds of millions – one that implicated customs officials, local leaders and business people across the elite spectrum. At the time of his exposure in 1999, press coverage inside and outside China dwelt on the salacious aspects of his buying of officials, particularly his infamous red mansion, a modern-day pleasure palace for those in his control who went there to gamble, have sex and do deals.[24] But for observers of this scandal, one of the more striking facts was that of all the senior leaders in the province at the time, right up to the level of the serving Party secretary, Jia Qinglin, a man who went on to be a Politburo Standing Committee member, Xi was the only one who was untouched.[25]

KEEPING IT *OUT* OF THE FAMILY

That one of the most spectacular scandals in modern Chinese history did leave Xi unaffected may strike cynics as only a sign of good political manipulation and avoidance strategy by someone who had been underestimated. Even so, reports of Xi saying early in his career, and then repeating it often, that 'if you want to get rich, don't go into politics',[26] deserve more attention here. In a world of what Fei Xiaotong called 'elastic networks', family ones, and most particularly direct family ones, were some of the strongest and most durable. In the CR, perhaps the most shocking acts had been by children denouncing their parents simply because this was regarded as unthinkable and against the whole tenor of Chinese society. The power of this bad memory still leaves a nasty taste for some to this day. Xi's comment that going into politics is not a path to riches seems to be the opposite of what is actually the case in contemporary China. It is precisely to get access to the most unimaginable levels of wealth that people do go into politics. Xi's case helps us see that reality is a bit more complex. One of the key skills that has helped Xi in becoming Party leader, beyond patronage and network building, has been management of his relatives. And in a country where refusing the demands of these members of the closest of close networks is one of the toughest issues, it is here that we can see something of Xi's inner values and world.

Xi's attitude towards the management of his relatives is one of the areas where the more abstract, general language he has deployed against corruption starts to have sharper definition. Xi is quoted speaking in a telephone conference in 2004 about the need to 'control and manage your spouse, children, relatives, friends, and people under you'.[27] Even as late as 2011, Xi Zhongxun's widow, Qi Xin, had summoned a family meeting in Beijing to tell relatives that they had to be prudent in their business dealings.[28] Xi himself simply avoided family involvement in any business while he was in Fujian. In the few months when he was in Shanghai he asked his younger brother Xi Yuanping to get out of the city and not to undertake any more commercial dealings there.[29] In this context, the Bloomberg reports in 2012 of his sisters' property deals in Hong Kong and elsewhere were a hard blow.[30] For all Xi's words and his evident efforts over the years, the simple fact, as the cases of Wen Jiabao and Bo Xilai show, is that family bonds are the firmest and the hardest to control. Here temptation is too easy, and too great.

The Bloomberg report on Xi's family conceded that no direct link could be found from either Xi or his wife, Peng Liyuan, to business interests. In a sense, however, that wasn't the issue. Bloomberg had proved that Xi was in the same uneasy position as other leaders in the centre. He was an extremely powerful figure who said nice-sounding things about the need to act well in public life. But he was still dogged by suspicion about how some of his contacts had grown wealthy, particularly his relatives and those believed to be his friends. Was their link with him a source of wealth? Xi might say he was not interested in money, nor motivated to act venally. The key thing was not his behaviour, but those linked to him and how they acted.[31]

From 2002, Xi was Party secretary of the private-sector boom province of Zhejiang, and linked with strong development policies there. His real emergence as front runner for future national leadership came when he was made Party leader of Shanghai in 2007, after Chen Liangyu, the former Party boss of the city, was felled for corruption and removed from power. His brief tenure in the city was a stepping stone.

XI'S ASSETS

Making a provisional assessment of why, in the end, Xi was elevated to become Hu Jintao's successor, and the key figure in the fifth generation of CPC leadership in China, involves recognising elements that were simply good fortune, and then issues that we can say had some strategic design and assisted him. The falls of Chen Liangyu and of Bo Xilai belong to the former. Even the most purblind conspiracy theorists would be hard pressed to come up with much evidence that these events, while they eventually benefited Xi, were somehow managed and provoked by him. The response Xi showed to the fall of Bo Xilai is the most instructive. Xi was clearly someone who gained much from Bo's removal. A potentially disruptive rival for ultimate power had disappeared, making the field less competitive. Even so, Bo and Xi were not obvious rivals, and what evidence of their interaction there is shows that at least in public they maintained a cordial harmony. Their experiences of the CR were similar in their harshness, but dissimilar in what they show about the characters of the two. Xi was out of Beijing, never a Red Guard and largely inactive. Bo was reportedly highly active, to the point of becoming an 'anti-reactionary' group member so zealous he ended up in jail.[32] Both were to have brief unsuccessful first marriages, both were to remarry, both carried good military links because of their backgrounds with their fathers, both were chosen over their siblings to pursue political careers, and both then spent years in provincial leadership positions before working in central leadership posts.

Xi Jinping demonstrated this closeness to Bo by being one of the troupe of senior leaders who went down to Chongqing while Bo was leader there, visiting in early December 2010 after his appointment as deputy of the Central Military Commission – one of the strongest signals that he was indeed on his way to being Hu's replacement. 'While top central leaders including President Hu and Premier Wen have refrained from commenting on Chongqing's Maoist exploits, Xi Jinping heaped lavish praise on the city's achievements during his two day visit,' Hong Kong commentator Willy Lam wrote at the time. Quoting Xinhua official news releases, Lam continued:

> The former party secretary of Shanghai, [Xi] added [... that] singing the praises of the party's 'red' heirlooms was 'essential to propagating lofty ideals and establishing core socialist values in society'. Moreover, Xi seconded Chongqing's myriad social security policies, especially its renowned subsidized housing schemes. 'Chongqing's public housing is a virtuous policy, a benevolent effort and positive exploration,' Xi said.[33]

After such a ringing endorsement, it is unsurprising that Xi kept silent once news of Bo's claimed misdeeds surfaced. Nor was there any reaction from him one way or the other when Bo was removed from power. Whether this was a sign that some of the critics of Xi were right when they talked about his passivity,[34] or evidence of more trenchant criticism that he was politically inept and out of his depth,[35] the reality was that with Bo gone, Xi's claim to the final crown grew even stronger. All that one can say is that he did not blow his good fortune. In politics, inside and outside China, one of the greatest skills is knowing not just when to be active, but when to do nothing.

Xi has a diverse range of supportive networks in the Party and in society generally, some of which were inherited, some acquired in the last four decades. The range of these connections is almost uniquely broad. One of the most important but least understood comes from living in the countryside very early in his career, something that is played up in accounts of his background. Unlike Jiang and Hu, he has an authentic record, at least in the five years from 1969, of living in a rural area.[36] Of all the connections that modern Chinese elite politicians wish to lay claim to, this one is amongst the hardest in view of their largely urban backgrounds and careers. That makes it a great political asset, even in the second decade of the twenty-first century, when half the population live in what are classified as rural areas. Xi's networks spread through those he inherited from his father; to those he acquired while working in his military position; and then in the country, prefecture, provincial and national entities from 1979 onwards. Fujian and Zhejiang, and the brief stay in Shanghai, gave him links not only to powerful local business interests, but also to provincial political and social elites who would be supportive of his future success. In a sense, cultivating positive relations with him was like investing in a good prospect that showed promise of one day paying back rich dividends.[37] He has proved a sound investment. The issue now is how he repays some of these debts accrued from earlier support.

Beyond the symbolical and practical value of linkages with these groups, like Hu Jintao before him Xi has a powerful top-level patronage network. For Hu, the lead players were Deng Xiaoping, Hu Yaobang, and head of the Organisation Department in the 1980s, Song Ping. Each of these was very supportive in his early career. For Xi, similarly helpful patrons have been Jiang Zemin, Zeng Qinghong and Jia Qinglin. Unlike Hu, he has some links into the military, with people like Liu Yuan, an outspoken general and commissar of the academy of military sciences, and son of former President Liu Shaoqi amongst his elite network.[38] The area where his networks are most shallow is in the CYL, and amongst intellectuals and academic elites, despite his leadership of the Party School from 2007. In the era of the networked leadership, therefore, Xi can be said to enjoy the most extensive range amongst his peers. The converse of this is that, again like Hu, his negative network, those who would count as potential enemies and opponents, appears to be shallow. Unlike Bo he had not acquired a figure as powerful as Wen Jiabao as an antagonist. Bo's problems of 'negative support' in the Party was shown by the fact that no one was willing to move to protect or speak up for him when he started to experience problems in early 2012. This meant that figures like Wen who were clearly unhappy about him had the space actively to contribute to his removal – something they would have found far harder had there been larger constituencies of support in the Party elite.

Xi's final skill is to have made no particular entrenched alliances with any of these networks. As with Bo, his allegiances beyond his closest family have come and gone. In whatever groups and networks one can observe him to have operated, either at the centre, or in the provinces, he has created an aloofness that means while his network has become extensive, he cannot be easily pigeonholed. The liquidity and elasticity of his allegiances, centred on himself, are strikingly close to the descriptions of social and, in particular, Chinese social behaviour outlined in the first chapter in the words of Fei Xiaotong.[39] For Hu Jintao, the famously sarcastic question in 2002 when he arrived at full power was 'Who is Hu?' The answer to this question never really became clear. For Xi, it might be easier to ask 'Who does Xi belong to?' The answer is everyone, and therefore no one.

THE INNER LIFE

Talking of the private lives of modern Chinese elite leaders is fraught with peril. The opacity that dominates areas related to even the most public aspects of political and social life thickens, in the more intimate zones of life, into a smog as deep as a Beijing winter. Wen Jiabao is never seen with his wife. The date when Hu Jintao's father died is unknown. Liu Yunshan and Zhang Dejiang's family situation, as far as their spouses go, is largely a mystery. As we will see with this younger generation of leaders, this trend to total clampdown on matters around their private lives is in many respects worsening. The family is a source of strength, but also, as Bo's case proves, a source of attack and potential weakness, and that risk means that information about it must be kept to the minimum.

Modern Chinese leaders live in a world in which almost everything is political. Their every act is calculated, the subject of regimes of assessment and control. In their march towards the centre of this power terrain the zones of freedom and release from this sort of restraint and control dwindle to the point where they disappear. For Xi, the question of his having any kinds of friendship acquired in a life before politics, of intimacies and personal interests that have endured and transcend this later political existence, is a complex one. This can be understood by looking at his relationship with his first wife, Ling Ling, daughter of a diplomat, Ke Hua. Ke Hua had served in the Chinese embassy in London. His original name had been Lin Dechang, and he was a native of Guangdong. He had served in senior positions in the Ministry of Foreign Affairs, then in as ambassador to the UK from 1978 until 1983 at the key moment when the issue of the sovereignty of Hong Kong was raised. He remained involved with the Hong Kong issue up to 1995. Ling Ling was married to Xi in the early 1980s, though dates are unclear. So too is the reason for their separation. Some blame his interest in his second wife, Peng – and some the simple fact that Ling Ling wished to study in the UK, causing them to separate amicably. It is odd that Xi shares having a brief first marriage with Bo Xilai, along with the fact that their first wives both reportedly ended up in Hong Kong. Unlike Xi, however, Bo had a son from his first marriage.[40]

Xi married Peng Liyuan, a celebrated singer from Beijing, in September 1987, when he was 34 and she was a decade younger. Their courtship had reportedly been brief. Their careers also unfolded in different places. Peng remained in Beijing, concentrating on her singing career, and Xi in Fujian. They were physically in the same place relatively infrequently.[41] A daughter, Xi Mingze, was born in 1992. Rumours of their estrangement have surfaced over the years, and in some ways they resemble the ultimate US power

124   THE NEW EMPERORS

couple, the Clintons, both trying to marry ambition and intimacy. Unlike the Clintons, however, Xi's private life is untainted by any public reports of mistresses or intimate liaisons. And with immense pragmatism, even if they had experienced problems, from 2007 and Xi's elevation, Peng Liyuan forsook her starring role in the annual CCTV Chinese New Year concert and maintained a lower profile.

Licentious gossip and speculation about the private lives of elite leaders has been a mainstay of Chinese political life since the era of Mao. His multiple marriages, and the sometimes remarkable brutality with which he treated his wives, became linked to rumours afterwards of his having a semi-imperial-style harem. Prurient interest in the inner world of these remote and god-like leaders manifested itself in subliminal gossip about their love lives, something that often came across as a relatively low-risk and seemingly unpolitical way of in fact making pointed criticisms of their moral and therefore leadership qualities. Deng remained mostly immune to this, and Jiang suffered only from rumours emanating from Hong Kong that he was linked with another famous singer, Song Zuying. Hu was once more largely left alone, the prospect of his having any kind of carnal urges off-putting enough for even the hardiest aficionado of tittle-tattle to indulge in speculation. Xi has moved into this oddly problematic zone. As heir to the former leaders, he has to live up to certain publicly desired standards of personal behaviour, but in an atmosphere pervaded by Victorian-era levels of hypocrisy.

Around him, there are no overt signs of deep links of friendship with particular figures. Even less than Hu, he has no clear administrative or academic allies. The aloofness in terms of close identification with specific networks mentioned above is reflected in his personal life. This is not to discount the possibility that he may well have many rewarding and close friendships that are not suspected or known about. Names that figure in this inner circle include ex-Shanghai security chief Ding Xuexiang, and policy research deputy director in the Central Committee, He Yiting. Reports that Xi's long-time secretary Zhong Shaojun accompanied him to the launch of the Shenzhou Ten space mission surfaced in early June 2013. The Central Party School vice principal Li Shulei is also said to be in his inner circle, as is Xi's university bunkmate Chen Xi, who was also moved in early 2013 to the Organisation Department as a deputy secretary. But the precise nature of these relationships and their real purchase on Xi and meaning to him is unclear.

Thinking of Xi's inner world also allows us to reflect a little about his personal style, and the language that he uses, something that gained plaudits during his brief performance on 15 November 2012. His style then was seen as more direct and more down to earth, less littered with the awful slogans and long memes of Hu in his pomp. Xi actually sounded like a human being rather than a political automaton. This more approachable style and direct mode of expression, however, may mean very little. As the discussion of the ideology and belief system of this leadership will show in the final chapter, Xi has camped out consistently through his career on the safest possible territory of abstractly attacking corruption, appealing to the moral mandate of the Party and leaving specifics well alone. There is very little that one could object to in the language he uses, but nor are there any signs of someone who is willing to take risks, to spell out more difficult options, and to deploy their rhetorical gifts to mobilise and challenge their audience. As Xi is aloof and isolated in many ways amidst his wide array of networks, so there is also an aloofness in his language, despite its surface animation. In many ways, the political zone of China after the Maoist period has seen the slow restriction and reduction of this sense of the personal in leadership language and created something that is more generic. This again will be looked at in greater detail in the final chapter.

4

THE LAWYER: PREMIER LI KEQIANG

Li Keqiang can consider himself unlucky. Described in 2001 by Cheng Li of Brookings Institute, Washington, as a 'rising star', he was slated more persistently as the likeliest successor to Hu up till 2007.[1] Li has impressed those who have met him with his intelligence and his smooth operating style. He was one of the first leaders to meet AIDS sufferers, a disease that has attracted particular stigma in China over the last two decades, and the handling of which is something that Li himself has been closely associated with.[2] Three aspects of his career stand out. The first is his legal background, which makes him the first ever member of the Standing Committee of the Politburo in Chinese history to be legally trained. The second is his management of crisis. Unlike Xi, he has managed far tougher and more contentious provinces – Liaoning and Henan. Both threw difficult challenges at him. He allows us to understand how important the management of crises is in contemporary Chinese politics and society, but also what the role of these are and how they occur. Finally, he seems to come from a humble, grassroots background, like his mentor Hu Jintao. But once more, looking harder at his patronage and family links one sees something a little more complicated. The nature of his networks is different from Xi's, but it would be wrong to claim that he did not start off with some inherited and acquired networks. These will be figured out later in this chapter.

Perhaps the highest-profile incident after Li Keqiang was appointed to the Standing Committee of the Politburo in October 2007 that made people focus on him was the visit he made in August 2011 to Hong Kong. During his speech to the students, Li had talked of '100 years of Hong Kong University, of cultural accumulation [...] training so many personnel', following this with the grand statement that 'this was for the glory of Hong Kong and a great contribution to the motherland'.[3] In his speech, he suddenly broke into English, declaring that 'The University of Hong Kong was used to be for China and the World' (*sic*), continuing in English for two minutes.[4] Even this use of a few words of English, particularly in Hong Kong, was controversial. Critics inside and outside China wondered why it was that in a place that had been run by the British until 1997, Li would use the language of the oppressors. Did this betray some secret admiration in him for the old colonial masters? Had he some latent cultural cringe, a fatal strain of self-doubt and lack of confidence that meant he belonged to those Chinese accused of looking up to the old, loathed masters?[5] Interpretations like this in various levels of disguise swirled around in cyberspace to and fro across the Great Firewall of China.

The bigger news was more about the extraordinary amounts of security that surrounded Li as he went to and from the university. The local commissioner for police in Hong Kong had guaranteed lock down, with a sterile area around the visiting vice premier (as he was at that time) that meant three students who tried to reach through to him were manhandled and taken into custody. A major demonstration against what was perceived as suppression of freedom of speech was held two days later. In some ways, one of Li's highest-profile visits 'abroad' (Hong Kong is a special administrative region, which has its own currency, law courts, administration and overseas representation, at least till 2047) showed the partly comical, partly serious side of how remote and sensitive Chinese elite leaders are. Some of this was probably down to nervousness accrued from hosting past leaders. Jiang Zemin had lost his temper at prying journalists in Hong Kong while on a visit there in 2000, lecturing them about the tough battles he had been through, wagging his finger at the cameras and being rewarded for this by becoming an immediate early internet sensation. These kinds of experience were all read by potential hosts as showing that Beijing top-level leaders needed to be handled with the softest of soft kid gloves.[6]

DEMOCRACY WALL

Li's birthplace was in Anhui, the central province, which is ancestral home to Hu Jintao. In 2011, Zhang Jinghua, a biographer of Li who visited his home county, Diyuan, found that local people's memories of their famous son were ambiguous. According to one relative quoted in the book, 'We all wish him well, but Li Keqiang has not really done anything for us. His world is better than ours, at least seen from here.'[7] Born in 1955, he had been a brigade worker in a commune in Fengyuan county, Anhui, from the age of 19 to 21, right at the end of the CR. In 1976, only 21 years old, he joined the Communist Party, and from 1976 to 1978 worked as a Party official in the local commune. A clear sign of how highly his abilities were rated was the award, once formal courses restarted at the universities, of a place to study Law at Beijing University. While aspersions have been cast and questions asked about precisely how Xi Jinping managed to make it into the elite Qinghua University (he had, for a start, been what was called at the time an agricultural and industrial brigade member; members had no reason to take the national entrance exam but were admitted to courses directly with the approval of their work unit, something very much regarded as a soft option), there is little doubt that Li went through the formal examination system and relied on his own abilities to get into Beijing.[8]

Li's period at Beijing University covered the era of the 'Democracy Wall' movement, a period of free expression and thawing politics in the aftermath of Mao Zedong's death in September 1976 and the fall of the Gang of Four, who were largely blamed for the ills that had happened over the previous decade. As the Party considered deepening commitment to the Four Modernisations of industry, technology, agriculture and national defence – something prefigured as early as 1963 and then again in 1975 but never fully implemented because of hardline leftist fears of embracing elements of capitalism too much – in the winter of 1978 and the early part of 1979 students freshly back at university started to spread their wings, placing big-character posters on a long wall in the Xidan western district of Beijing (the Democracy Wall no longer exists, and has been somewhat symbolically replaced by an immense shopping district). Wei Jingsheng, the most celebrated of the participants, was repaid for his demands for a fifth modernisation, democracy, by lengthy prison spells that kept him incarcerated until 1998 when he was sent into exile in the United States. The clampdown on the students mandated by Deng Xiaoping was harsh and effective. By the spring of 1979 hopes for political reform and liberalisation were dashed.

Wang Juntao was one of the earliest activists, and involved in the Tiananmen Square protests in April 1976 a few weeks after Zhou Enlai had died. He was linked with the Democracy Wall movement, and had been a colleague of Li's at Beijing University over this period. Speaking years later, Wang said that 'Li at university really couldn't stand bureaucracy and bureaucratism.'[9] Perhaps this inspired Li to consider studying in the US after his graduation, but fatefully he stayed in Beijing and started his political career in the CYL at almost exactly the time that Hu Jintao returned from his long period in Gansu to take up national leadership of the League. Rumours of Li's links to more radical liberal thinkers in the Democracy Wall era have surfaced since 2007, but it is hard to find much content to these. Nor do they have much bearing on Li's latter career. That he translated the English lawyer Lord Denning's works in the 1980s means no more than that he practised translation on a legal text that had a bearing on his academic background. We know nothing about whether he approved or disapproved of the contents.

There is better evidence of Li's interests and intellectual approach as a thinker. Unlike any of his predecessors, he has left a written trail of his academic development in articles he authored or co-authored from his graduation onwards. His *Computerisation of Legal Affairs*, written in collaboration with a renowned legal scholar, Gong Xiangrui, was published in 1983, as part of a series in the *Institute of Social System Engineering* magazine, named *The Excellent Governance and Social System Engineering in Worldization* [*sic*] *Times*. Two years before, just at the end of his undergraduate career in Beijing, he wrote an article for the same series, 'On the control process of the legal system'. Both were impenetrably technical to non-specialists, the second in particular a tabulated discussion of governance tools, legal social structures and legal observation behaviour.[10] Li also subsequently completed a master's degree that formed the basis of what was to become his doctorate in 1991. Part of this was published in the *Journal of Social Science* that year. It was mainly concerned with the development of rural economy, and in particular the dynamic role of Town and Village Enterprises after 1978. For his Ph.D. he had transferred to the Economics department, completing this in Beijing in the 1990s under Li Yining, the highly regarded Western-trained professor of Economics.[11] The fifth generation of leaders in China have been described as the best educated, with the greatest number of postgraduate degrees, and with two key leaders, Li and Xi, who have doctorates. The intellectual content of their doctorates will be looked at later. But the fact that they have this level of education and the way it shows a trend towards more academically and technically prepared leadership is significant. For Mao, Deng and their generation, university was a luxury enjoyed by the tiniest of tiny elites. Leaders were almost wholly from military backgrounds. Jiang's generation were technocrats trained either domestically or in the Soviet Union. Hu Jintao and Wen Jiabao still belonged to this strand of technocratic leadership, serving in Politburos where everyone had graduated from university, the overwhelming majority having studied Engineering, or hard sciences. With the Xi and Li generation we see much more diversity, with Ph.Ds, and training from Economics to Social and Political Science. In that sense the academic backgrounds of the Chinese leadership elite are becoming a little more similar to those of liberal democracies. The era of the technocrats seems to be drawing to a close.

From 1983, Li was an official rising through the ranks of the national CYL. He served at the Central Party School and then from 1985 to 1993 as secretary in the CYL Central Committee and Secretariat. After gaining his Ph.D. he worked from 1993 to 1998 as the first secretary of the CYL Central Committee and Secretariat, and president of the China Youth University for Political Science in Beijing, before serving from 1998 to 2004 as first deputy Party secretary, then governor, then full Party secretary of Henan province. From 2004 to 2007 he was Party secretary of Liaoning province.

WHY EVERYONE HATES HENAN

In the last two decades, provincial leadership has become increasingly important in proving the ability to become a national leader. Of the current elite leaders of China, as of 2013, all but one (Liu Yunshan) has experience in running provinces. This is the common characteristic between them. Their actions and behaviours in these places show what they are really capable of and can be used to judge them. Across China, there is great diversity in the economic level and social cohesion of specific provinces. Being Party head of Jiangsu is different from leading Inner Mongolia or Tibet. The dynamics of the internal economies of these places are different, sometimes radically so. The per capita GDP of a province-level entity like Shanghai, which comes directly under the central leadership, is rising to levels on a par with middle-income countries, reaching to around USD 12,000. In Gansu it is barely up to half this. The central government collects most taxes and then disburses them. The wealthy coastal provinces – places like Zhejiang and Fujian where Xi Jinping had spent so much of his career – are net contributors, whereas places like Tibet rely on large subsidies from the central government.[12] Healthcare, education, the legal system, the ease of doing business: all vary across each of these 31 provinces, autonomous regions and municipalities directly under the government.

Henan ranks as one of the toughest. In his discussion of the province, journalist Jonathan Watts, in his work on China's environment, asked tartly 'Why do so many people hate Henan?'[13] Its population is amongst the highest of all the provinces, its environmental problems amongst the most severe. Henanese are amongst China's most active internal migrants, and they experience prejudice across the country. Site to some of the most ancient landmarks of former dynasties, Henan is also now a place where social unrest is particularly sharp. On 14 December 2012 a knife attacker injured 22 children in Chengpeng village in the province. A few months before there had been strikes in electrical factories in Xinxiang, with 3,000 walking out over working conditions. Foxconn, a Taiwanese-owned company, experienced strikes in its plant in the provincial capital of Zhengzhou only a few days before. On 30 October 2011, there were violent protests after a car driven by a policeman who was reportedly drunk killed five people in Zhengzhou. Such phenomena are not new. Henan has been a place of restiveness and contention for many decades.

Henan is neither one of the poorest nor the richest of provinces. It comes in the great middle swathe across central China – the hard-to-govern places that also include Hebei, Hubei and Hunan. Those that manage to rule well here can probably do so anywhere. Citizens are reaching levels where they are more assertive, more vocal, and where there is enough wealth for people to compete fiercely with each other. Courts are burdened with complaints and cases that they have neither the infrastructure nor the capacity to deal with. In provinces like this, the Party stands above the government, the legal system and the law enforcers as a sort of final arbiter, and its privileged position means that it and its key office holders are almost permanently under siege by people wanting to get their attention, and to recruit them to their purpose. In a system so densely networked, support from the tiny band of upper-level Party leaders provincially, and particularly from the Party secretary himself, is a massive 'circuit breaker'. They function as the prime mediator between the centre and the province, and their role is often critical in getting funds, political support and elite attention.

Paying attention to the role of the Party secretary in provinces in modern China is also helpful in better understanding the dynamics of the country internally. Party secretaries are often outsiders. They come on their way from somewhere, hoping if they do well to head somewhere else. This is a staging post on their career. The one thing they don't want is a calamity to occur that will mark their future careers and means their patrons and their networks weaken on them when promotion opportunities come. In such an environment, proactive policies are less important than management and crisis control. That there will almost always be crises because of the dynamism and fast change occurring economically in the society around them is unavoidable. Often, these crises are simply because the modes of governance and administration have failed to keep up with what is happening elsewhere in society. Hu Jintao's national policy was simply to clamp down on these multiple occurrences of contention and unrest wherever they occurred across China, particular after the series of politically highly sensitive uprisings in Tibet, Xinjiang and then Inner Mongolia from 2008. From these years, support for the internal security agents ranging from the Ministry of State Security, the People's Armed Police, and the Ministry of Public Security increased. Figures released at the National People's Congress in 2011 showed China spent a billion US dollars more on internal security than on national defense in 2010. By 2011, its figures had leaped up to USD 111 billion on internal security, and USD 5 billion less on national defence. China was spending greater amounts on protecting itself from enemies within than on those from outside. This was truly the price tag of the Hu and Wen 'pro-stability' strategy.

A SOCIETY IN PERMANENT STATES OF EMERGENCY

Crises occur day by day and province by province in contemporary China. They are part of the landscape. It is not a case at the moment of attacking their root cause, though as the last chapter will show that is something the new leaders have to think about. It is more about handling protests so they don't become full riots, doing so by diffusing crowds, brokering deals and dispersing the energy they unleash. The overwhelming objective is to avoid their escalating to the point where they even threaten national security itself. Chinese leaders are often described as having a strong sense of history. Hu Jintao and Jiang Zemin insistently repeated the mantra of '5,000 years of civilisation'. This means they are aware of the counter-history, where dynasties were undone by local unrest that got out of control, contaminating the whole body politic and ending up toppling governments nationally. The Xinhai rebellion in 1911 that felled the 264-year-old Qing dynasty; the rebellion by the Manchus from 1642 to 1644 that toppled the Ming dynasty; and the roots of the Ming itself in the rebellion by a former beggar, Zhu Yuanzhang, in 1368 are examples. Statistics on social unrest were collected from the late 1990s into 2005 by the National Statistics Bureau, and famously showed steep rises from a few thousand to over 88,000. Their collation ceased after arguments about what they truly showed, since unrest or mass incidents as they were technically called ranged from a few people shouting angry slogans at officials outside government buildings to immense riots similar to that which convulsed Wukan in Guandong province in late 2011.

Even so, credible figures like Yu Jianrong of the Chinese Academy of Social Science were willing to state that in 2009 alone there had been over 90,000 incidents.[14] Such estimates only shot up later, with Sun Liping at Qinghua University claiming over 120,000 in 2011. The impact of these on the careers of officials could be dramatic. According to research by Christian Godel and Lynette Ong, management of unrest has been impeded by the simple fact that in the cadre evaluation system, by which officials get promoted or demoted, economic growth is a hard target and something that they have to succeed at, but providing social cohesion is a 'soft' and less important one. For ambitious officials, therefore, unrest is an impediment to growth, and has to be stopped, no matter by what means, even if that entails use of State violence.[15] In the play-off between social cohesion and low growth, or high growth and contention that can then be managed, the latter in this system always wins.

Li Keqiang's record of crisis management is both a strength and a weakness. One criticism of him is that he has no real creativity, and no particular originality. He is a problem solver and manager of thorny issues.[16] These are not qualities to be sniffed at. The two issues where he has shown his real abilities are in the blood crisis in Henan, and the fires in Liaoning. 'The East is red' was the anthem of Maoism, sung almost constantly in the CR decade. In the original it had been:

> The East is red, the sun rises up
> China has given rise to Mao Zedong.
> He works for the people,
> He is the great saviour of the people.

In a new setting by 'netizens' in 2011, this became:

> The East is red, the sun rises,
> China has given birth to Li Keqiang.

He plans handling accidents for the people,

He is the great king of disasters.

Li Keqiang, Li Keqiang, he is leading the way in selling blood,

In order to construct a new China

Leading us moving forward.

Without Li Keqiang, how could we be liberated from disaster?'[17]

The contaminated-blood scandal in Henan was something that Li inherited. According to veteran journalist John Gittings writing in the *Guardian* in 2001, Henan in particular was a centre of commercial operations in the early-to-mid 1990s, where 'bloodheads' went around buying blood from farmers and rural dwellers, extracting the plasma and then returning the blood to the donors. They used wholly unhygienic methods, largely oblivious to – or worse, ignorant of – the risk of AIDS. Part of this was due to the government's insistence at the time, overtly and covertly, that AIDS was a foreign disease and that the only way it was going to spread in China was through foreigners. 'In Henan, unlike elsewhere, the blood buying was organised not only by entrepreneurs but by the province's health department.' As many as half a million people became infected with HIV because of these joint actions of local government and business people. 'The provincial health department's blood collection scheme was also driven by a fierce desire to make money. An anonymous document [...] describes how the department was "caught up in the get-rich craze".'[18] The spread of the contamination was almost certainly made worse by the cover-up of the local government when it became clear how serious the plasma economy problem had become. Only the efforts from 1996 of a retired local doctor and member of the province's People's Congress, Gao Yaojie, raised any public awareness of the issue. Initial plaudits in the early 2000s for her work on the problem were replaced in 2007 by escalating harassment, a period under house arrest and finally exile to the United States two years later.

The contaminated blood scandal touched on a number of areas of governance challenges in a mid-level province like Henan in contemporary China. Firstly, it showed collusion between local authority and business interests, and a lack of scruple about how they protected each other. Secondly, it showed that the initial response by officials when the scandal became public was denial, cover-up and harassment. Thirdly, it showed the lack of any proper system of accountability and crisis management. Throughout the latter part of this phase, Li Keqiang was in senior positions in Henan, as deputy Party secretary, acting governor, governor and finally Party boss. While the blood collection stations that had caused the problem were stopped as early as March 1995, the real issue for the leaders later that decade and early the next, and the one that Dr Gao focused on, was the treatment of the victims. In 2007, *The Economist* recorded that:

> victims and activists say that not a single official has been punished for his [*sic*] role in the plasma trade [...] Many victims and activists resent Li Changchun, then Henan's Communist Party chief [and subsequently from 2007 to 2012 member of the Politburo responsible for propaganda] for not intervening sooner. They also blame Li Keqiang, his successor in Henan, first as provincial governor and then as party chief, for allowing the cover-up.

Particular villages became known as 'death' spots because of the incidence of fatalities as the decade wore on. The *Economist* article cited Shuangmiao, where 500 out of a population of 3,000 people in the village contracted HIV and 200 died.[19] If these reports are accurate, Li Keqiang's behaviour showed he was a faithful practitioner of the Hu line of clamping down for the sake of stability, offering compensation to the noisiest complainants, enforcing news blackouts and isolating particular places to ensure that they did not start publicising their plight. In that sense, the fallout of the AIDS disaster in Henan shows 'pro-stability' measures in practice.

Li's time in Henan and then in Liaoning from 2004 was also marked by high-profile disasters. According to Cheng Li:

> In April 1999, two months after he was appointed governor of Henan, a fire at a furniture factory in Nanyang took the lives of 19 people. In March 2000, a fire in a movie theatre in Jiaozuo killed 74 people. Nine months later, another fire in a dance club in Luoyang killed 309 people, which was the second deadliest fire in PRC history. Some people in Henan gave Li the nickname 'the governor with three fires'.

In Liaoning, what Cheng Li calls 'the bad luck' continued: 'Within two months after he was appointed Liaoning Party secretary, a gas explosion ripped through the Sunjiawan coal mine in the province, killing 214 miners.'[20] On 5 July 2007 there was more 'bad luck', with an explosion in Tian Ying karaoke hall and bath house, Tianshifu Town, Liaoning.

There was less bad luck for Li in the one area where he could not fail – and that was economic growth. Liaoning's economy boomed, its exports rose dramatically and its GDP jumped by over 14 per cent in 2007. These were the figures that mattered, rather than the grim statistics of fatalities from accidents. The Henan blood scandal was an inherited problem, and in any case lapped close to the power base of Li Changchun, someone already on the Politburo by 2002. The younger Li's fall was not in the elder Li's interests, as far as this problem goes. Mine accidents in boom-time China were becoming horribly common, with stories of non-existent safety standards and perilous disregard for even the most basic health and safety regime pushing fatalities up to the thousands.[21] Blaming one official for this was not likely to change things. This was a systemic problem arising from lack of implementation of regulations and collusion between businesses, and government and other bodies. In some cases the problems arose from lone-wolf actors who were acting from their own sense of anger and injustice and were next to impossible to catch before they acted.

The bottom line is that crisis management has become part of the day-to-day job description for leaders of the new modernising China. In this area they deal with collateral arising from the breakneck gallop towards modernity that the Party was leading society along. In such a dynamic situation crisis is to be expected, and their management is the key thing. Avoidance is a luxury for more peaceful, quieter times, when society calms down and has the wealth and leisure to deal with its causes rather than pacification. That Li dealt with crisis with no big fallout was a plus that stood in his political favour. Grim though it was to say it openly, the officials with prospects never let a crisis happen without trying to put it to good use. The officials who were sucked into an issue were the ones whose shelf life shortened dramatically. Wang Lequan, Party secretary in Xinjiang in 2009, is an example of this, his removal from the province back to Beijing probably caused by the fact the Centre was forced to intervene to tidy things up after the riots in July and had lost confidence in him.

THE FAMILY LI

While Xi comes across as the master of aloofness and of drifting within the liquid networks of Chinese contemporary elite society, Li is easier to locate. He 'belongs' to Anhui more easily as a birthplace because he seems to have existing family links there, however complaining they are – unlike Xi, the location of whose family in his early years was disrupted for political reasons, and who drifted from Beijing to Shaanxi and then back to Beijing with no real sense of there being a specific bond with any place. This 'placelessness' links back to an earlier period of revolutionary leadership, and figures like Deng Xiaoping who, from the moment he left his birth place in Sichuan at the age of 16, never returned. The link of Chinese leaders to specific places and their perceived attributes, the sorts of values these localities embody and the image they have is a little studied area. But Li spent his life up to his early twenties in Anhui, and in that sense can be said to have been formed by his time there.

Li also has a different sort of relationship to his wife, Cheng Hong, if only because he has only been married once, and because she seems to have at least impacted on him through teaching, or inspiring him to study, English. Cheng entered the PLA University of Foreign Languages in Henan in 1977, and after completing a master's at Qinghua University in the early 1980s went to Brown University in the US. In 2013, she was a professor in the Foreign Languages department of the Capital University of Economics and Business. Cheng seems to have only ever been interested in research and teaching, and has a distinguished publication list in American literature in China.[22] The two married in 1983 after meeting through friends when Li was starting out his career in the CYL. They have one daughter, who was reportedly in the US before being recalled to China in 2013.

Through his marriage, Li Keqiang also inherits elite connections and relations. His case highlights issues with the concept of princelings. Princelings as a term attempts to give definition and clarity to a way in which former Party elite leadership are able to preserve their material and political influences and interests through the careers of their children and grandchildren, usually by their taking up political office. But as the first chapter argued, princelings is still an imprecise term and covers a bewildering range of relationships and ranks. It gives the impression of pointing at a relatively tight-knit and self-contained group. In fact, this group can be surprisingly widespread. Those that become princelings through marriage throw up a host of issues, particularly because these links can be so powerful and useful for men who marry the daughters of elite former leaders because of the male-dominated nature of elite Chinese politics.

Li Keqiang seems to be someone who comes from an archetypal grassroots background. Glancing at his official biography, he looks like a carbon copy of Hu Jintao, the only difference being that he is 13 years younger. But whereas Hu genuinely had no family links, directly or through marriage, to any kind of former leaders of any rank (his father was reportedly a lowly tea merchant, and therefore a member of the despised petit bourgeois class), Li, through his wife, has inherited a network, and one that comes close to his own interests. His father-in-law, Cheng Jinrui, was a senior official in the CYL, active even in the CR in Henan, where he was head of the Student Alliance office, and a senior official in Beijing from 1982 in the State Development and Planning Commission, responsible for managing cross-ministerial and provincial implementation of the Five Year Plans. In 1986, he was appointed an advisor to a small group in the planning commission dealing with impoverished areas. In these positions, his contacts, reputation and networks had huge use for his son-in-law.[23]

Li has also been able to leverage and supplement these acquired family networks (something he shares with one other figure to be looked at later, Wang Qishan) by building up a group of close aides and allies around him. Chapter 1 described the manner in which the State Council has become its own particular entity for vested interest, and a foundation for protection in particular for Wen Jiabao. Li has managed to extend his patronage links to the famously slippery and agile former premier, despite his first great patron being Hu Jintao. As one analyst put it, 'Without Wen Jiabao's support, Li Keqiang could never bring his own people in to the central ministries and State council.'[24] Many of these were contacts Li worked with in his years in the CYL. You Quan is one such person; an executive deputy secretary general of the Standing Committee of the State Council under Wen Jiabao, elected to the Central Committee in 2012, it was You Quan who worked most closely with Li after his appointment as vice premier on the State Council in 2007, and became Li's right-hand man.[25] Another with whom Li has close relations is Xu Xianping, appointed a vice minister of the National DRC in 2009, but someone with whom Li worked closely during Xu's time as a local leader of the Hunan branch of the CYL from the 1980s into the early 2000s, when Li was directing things from the centre. Li is also close to Zhou Qiang, who ended up as Party secretary of Hunan from 2010, but who had been working there from 2006 as acting governor, then governor. It was Zhou who managed to get Xu Xianping elevated to national position in Beijing in 2009. This marshalling of supportive forces around Li up to his final elevation offers some evidence of his talent as a network builder.

The bonding experience of provincial senior leadership is perhaps underestimated, largely because it cannot be encapsulated as neatly as something like membership of the CYL network or the Oil group. People have talked of the Shanghai group a lot, and even more recently of a Shaanxi band, or a Guangdong band. But there are shifting levels of traction and adhesiveness across the provincial roles that specific figures go to, and trying to make any clear structure from the rank of people, their political skill, the networks they have already taken with them and their fortunes when they get to a place would be next to impossible. All one can do is note that provinces are places where many leaders have to spend much of their time, and that their achievements there are very important for their future promotion. In these outposts, they are placed amongst alien networks (the vast majority of senior Party leaders in provinces are not locals), somehow having to make meaningful working relations with the people they find there. Such leaders, airlifted in, as it were, into these situations, are often permanently under siege, trying to deal with day-to-day crises and manage these in ways that do not alienate the business, tribal and political loyalties that are ranged around them, were there before they came into their office and will be there after they leave. For these leaders, embarking on high-risk campaigns to clean out the local stables of vested interest and corruption would make them even more isolated and exposed. Their isolation works both against and for them – they can show, as Xi did in Fujian with the Yuanhua smuggling scandal in the late 1990s, great skills in avoiding trouble spots and not getting dragged down when the real crises come. But it can also make them vulnerable when they need to call on support for implementing particular measures. In this condition of permanent exposure, elite leaders in their provincial careers build up deep networks. It is here where they often create their most lasting and meaningful links. But these connections are diverse, disparate, hard to tabulate easily, and they change from person to person. For Li, at least, his life in Henan and then Liaoning gave him valuable and enduring bonds. Having these is useful on returning to the centre and to the life of national politics there.

LI: A SECOND SUN IN THE SKY

Li also differs from his earliest mentor Hu Jintao in another area – his style of speech and his communicative ability. Unlike Hu, Li is not a wooden public orator, and while he is no Winston Churchill in his rhetorical ability, he is certainly a more expressive figure. He is also someone more comfortable operating in an international setting than Hu. His early career dealing with law, his English language abilities, his appearance on forums like Davos at the World Economic Forum where he spoke in 2010, all suggest someone who is more at ease dealing with the outside world than his mentor. Unlike Xi, too, on the issue of Bo Xilai, even from 2009 Li was more wary of endorsing his campaigns, perhaps taking his lead from his new patron, Wen Jiabao. In particular, he made no statements supportive of Bo's 'Red Song' movement.[26]

Li's manner of public expression and his English abilities have gathered plaudits. These have allowed him to be interpreted as a potential reformer, someone who understands the critical importance of the rule of law in developing China, and to link this with the imperative for political changes. A report of his speech in 2010 by *Forbes* magazine typifies this sort of adulation: 'China's Li Keqiang,' it stated on 28 June, 'cuts the polished, poised figure of the world leader he is about to become [...] China's headliner in Davos delivered a flawless summary of China's five year plan to deliver sustainable long-term growth.'[27] But more dissonant voices point to something different: 'Look at his record,' one unnamed senior executive interviewed by the *Financial Times* stated in March 2013, 'and you will know he has a serious problem with execution'.[28]

Li's academic training was initially in law, but his postgraduate work was mostly in economics. Whether he has the instinctive understanding of Chinese economic dynamics that Zhu Rongji had, or even that of his new colleague on the Politburo Standing Committee, the hugely respected Wang Qishan, is another matter. And Li's understanding and appreciation of law may lie a long way from that of Western leaders. Excitement about his intellectual and academic background, and his international outlook, only masks how little is really known about what he really does believe, and whether, even if he had a profound belief in the need to implement rule of law in such a way that it might challenge some of the modes of behaviour of the Party, he would have the political basis and talents to start moving in this direction. Li is spoken of as someone who is a problem solver, but not a policy initiator – someone who is competent, but not creative. In this area at least, he does share the true qualities of Hu Jintao.

Like Wen Jiabao, Li had reportedly also drawn inspiration from the less well-known work of a great classical thinker. Wen Jiabao, according to some reports, was a fan of *The Theory of Moral Sentiments*, a work of moral philosophy by the father of modern economics, Adam Smith. While *The Wealth of Nations* has long been translated into Chinese and referred to in debates about the operations of a market in Beijing, Smith's less well-known work was a surprising choice, wrestling with issues of emotions, rationality and the internal governance of the self. That someone as busy as Wen even had time to read at all was surprising, but it fitted with his nicely cultivated image as a modern-day Chinese public intellectual. Strangely enough, in 2012 rumours abounded of Li and his circle studying Alexis de Tocqueville's work on the revolution in France, *L'Ancien Régime et la Révolution* – a book less well known than his famous analysis of the revolution in America.

There was politically a highly purposeful message promoted from the mention of this book, however:

> Li Keqiang [...] has started recommending to his colleagues that they read Alexis de Tocqueville's [work because] some Chinese academics see it as a warning – de Tocqueville blamed the 1789 French revolution in part on the fact that the bourgeoisie inspired envy among the masses while the nobles elicited scorn.[29]

The book seemed to show that 'the French revolution was one of rising expectations that could not be met', and in this way had parallels with China, where poverty was largely under control and the real battles in society were from people who simply wanted more of the good things they had already started to get.[30]

Bold, risk-taking creativity and originality of thought were not what were perhaps most needed in a premier, and head of the executive arms of government nationally, when faced with immense structural challenges in a society also undergoing the tough journey to middle-income status by 2020. Steady, patient application was perhaps more important; Li Keqiang's most important skill was probably to do as he had done before – manage crises, deal with them in a way that stopped them becoming overwhelming. Only one of the many hundreds of violent clashes that happened in China each day needed to catch fire and spread from its local base to other communities, other groups, other alliances, for the whole system to be under attack. The premier's position, the one that Li Keqiang finally reached, is primarily China's disaster-manager-in-chief. It is to him that the issues others cannot solve come. Only when these become so overwhelming that intervention from the military or the people's armed police is necessary does the Party secretary become necessary – as happened in Tibet and Xinjiang in 2008 and 2009, the latter forcing Hu Jintao to make a humiliating exit from the G8 meeting in Italy to return home and issue direct orders to the security services to intervene. From this point of view, the value of Li's provincial career in the chaotically dynamic spaces of Henan and Liaoning makes sense. Far from being bad luck, his chance to handle hard issues there was precisely the training he needed for his final, toughest job.

EPILOGUE: THE BOND OF BEING SENT-DOWN YOUTHS

The CR, as most research on the events that happened in China after 1966 shows, was not uniform. Spanning a decade and manifesting itself in different ways across the whole country, it inevitably affected those it touched in markedly diverse ways. The Hu and Wen generation and the Xi and Li ones illustrate this. Hu and Wen were already graduates and on the Party leadership ladder when the 'ten years of turbulence' started. For them the main impact was in the vicious factional struggles that convulsed the universities they were attending in Beijing at the time. Xi was barely an adolescent when 1966 came; Li was not even a teenager. It was the latter phase of the CR that had impact on them. By this time, despite Mao's intentions, the movement had become almost institutionalised with set patterns of social mobilisation and their associated campaigns. One of the best known examples was the phenomenon of the 'sent-down youths', or the youth brigades, consisting of largely urban, often elite children and teenagers who were sent out to the rural areas to contribute to fermenting revolution and to ensure they never lost their engagement with the rural part of the country, its life and challenges. This was considered a fundamental ingredient of their revolutionary development.

For the generation occupying the uppermost Party and government positions in China in the early twenty-first century, the memory of this era of rural experience and training is one that is specific to them. Along with the particularities of provincial experience for leaders outlined earlier in this chapter, rural experience was also a moment for the formation of close bonds, of similar world views, and of shared experiences and intimacies, though in this case ones that started earlier and that, for this reason, would have a longer-lasting impact and be highly formative. Again, scientifically tabulating this is not easy. None of the elite leaders written about in this book directly refers to their experiences during the latter years of the CR in any great detail. Indeed, in some ways referring to the time directly has become taboo. But for all their diversity and differences, the vast majority of leaders born from 1950 to 1960 in China, those that are now in the key positions across the country, have something in common at one of the most crucial periods in the development of anyone's life – late teens and early twenties. They share memories of the final Maoist campaigns to develop the country, forge a revolutionary spirit, attack capitalism and make the countryside the source of the nation's strength and wealth.

Factionalism cannot easily capture the bonds and links that are made during these moments unique to a particular society or to a person's individual experiences. People were sent to different contexts and into areas across the country in China at this period. Where they went they made their own networks and forged links that they then carried away with them when they left. The period of being sent-down youths, however, gave the leaders of this generation, and those alongside them of the same age range across society, a similarity at least in parts of their life experiences. And this was the basis for a shared language with each other, and a joint vocabulary that had some meaning in creating cohesion amongst them later.

5

THE STARS AROUND THE TWO SUNS: THE OTHER FIVE

If Xi and Li are like two suns in the sky, then ranged around them are five lesser lights. Working out the reasons for why these are where they are has proved tough. Excited talk before late 2012 looked forward to a balanced band of liberals and reformers. Some of the names who eventually made it through had long been on people's lists – Wang Qishan, Zhang Gaoli, Zhang Dejiang. But others, like Liu Yunshan and Yu Zhengsheng, were big surprises. What were the abilities and skills that brought these people into the inner sanctum of power, and what political rationale might be defined behind all this? In what ways had they gained support from across the decision-making elite of the Party in order to be elevated? This chapter will address these questions.

A Politburo in modern China is about creating political balance. It has to show Party-elite consensus across the spectrum of views, institutional interests and special groups in society. People are on it because they represent important constituencies and are supported by them. They are there as people, with their networks and links. But they are also there representing particular political standpoints. It is partly on the basis of these that they have been successful in gaining elevation, and for this reason that, when the five colleagues presented themselves to the world alongside Xi and Li in November 2012, the outside world had the final and most important clue to what the country's strategic direction would be in the coming five years. Most commentators regarded the line-up as risk-averse, based on age, and full of people whose outlook was highly conservative. But looking at these seven men, one had also to remember something about the things around them that were not visible that day: the networks of supporters, of people who had invested in them, supported them, helped them to be where they were in the phoney campaign the Party had been engaged with over the last few months and years. This was never a proper open competition but a process of slow moves, accruals of influence and power, and final decisions on who was able to bring the most into the circle.

A first glance would have seen seven men of a certain age, similar in appearance, in the ways they dressed and even in their body language. They were all, to a man, officials, promoted after long and distinguished careers in the Party. But there was another dimension in which they could be viewed. Wang Qishan did not even join the CPC till he was in his 30s, after working in the Shaanxi History Museum in Xian and the Chinese Academy of Social Sciences in Beijing. Zhang Dejiang had studied abroad in North Korea in the late 1970s when it was still regarded as economically more successful than China. Liu Yunshan had written under the pseudonym Liu Cai in the early part of his career while a Xinhua journalist in the 1980s in Inner Mongolia. Yu Zhengsheng had a brother who had absconded to the United States as an intelligence official in the 1980s, creating an immense scandal from which Yu was regarded at the time as unlikely to recover. Zhang Gaoli had served as an executive in a State oil company for nearly two decades before moving to government. The last thing anyone might think looking at the 15 November 2012 line-up was diversity – but that was what could be found in their careers after a little enquiry. In this chapter, I will look at the paths that the other five beside Li and Xi made to get where they were on that day. There was also a shared linkage between some of them that was less auspicious. The brute fact is that most people would have said, a year before, that for some their appearance on the stage that day was extremely unlikely. This chapter will try to work out how it was they had finally managed to win through.

JOKER IN THE PACK: WANG QISHAN

On 9 March 2009, at the National People's Congress being held in Beijing, Xiang Wenbo, the president of major Chinese machinery maker Sany, asked the then premier, Wang Qishan, if he might have some financial support to expand overseas. It was, as *The Wall Street Journal* commented, a reasonable request in view of the fact that at that time China was in possession of USD 2 trillion in foreign reserves (a figure that subsequently rose to USD 3.5 trillion by 2013). Wang's response was to the point:

> 'Are you sure of your managerial skills?,' Mr Wang asked, according to the China News Service. 'Have you analyzed the corporate culture differences between the two parties? Do you understand how to deal with unions and their relations with management in the country [where your target company is based]?' He finished with, 'If you don't know your target and yourselves well, your ambition really scares me.'[1]

A joke afterwards asked whether people in France should start learning to speak Hunanese in order to accommodate investors like Mr Xiang. But Wang Qishan had a serious point. While the rest of the world was urging China to go on an immense buying spree in order to help out in the recession setting in over 2007 and into 2008, Wang's words typified the feeling of caution in Beijing. Earlier mini spending sprees had mixed results. Chinese investment through TCL into Thomsons, the television manufacturer in France, exemplified this, with the Chinese company struggling with bad debt and poor technology, and hitting union and other legal issues once they had bought the French partner. Political impediments in the US had derailed planned high-profile investments in the telecoms and energy sector there. And some investments made by the newly established China Investment Corporation (CIC) in 2007 had led to significant enough losses for it to attract the ire and indignation of netizens in China. As one diplomat said to me in 2009, 'Our government seems very good at wasting our money on loss-making projects abroad.'[2]

As senior-ranking Chinese representative on the Strategic and Economic Dialogue with the United States from its formal establishment in 2009 after President Obama took office (it replaced the former Strategic Dialogue, which had been set up under President George W. Bush), Wang was one of the highest-profile and internationally best-regarded of Chinese national leaders. Pictures of him holding a basketball next to President Obama in the Oval Office at the White House typified his accessible image. Wang has been described as the most westernised and the most individualistic of the current leadership.[3] The sharp wit he betrayed in the sentences to Xiang of Sany quoted above typifies this. And his background is an interesting one. He came late to politics, and like politicians who were late starters in the West he has a hinterland.

Wang was born in 1948, in Qingdao, Shandong province – though his family were originally from Tianzhen, Shanxi province – into a family of intellectuals (his father had graduated from Qinghua University).[4] Around 1956, the family moved to Beijing, where his father worked as a senior engineer in the town planning department of the Ministry of Construction. From the age of eight, Wang studied at the 35th middle school in the capital.[5] He was a youth pioneer, like Xi, although he was already in his late teens when the CR started. From 1969, he belonged to a sent-down youth group in the neighbouring Shaanxi province, working on a commune in the great historic revolutionary base of the Party, Yan'an. From 1971 to 1979, he worked in the provincial museum in

Xian, Shaanxi, during the period when the first Terracotta Warriors were discovered. In the mid 1970s, he also undertook a history degree at the Northwest University in Xian. He is, therefore, the first formally trained historian ever to have served on the Politburo Standing Committee, and typifies the shift in leadership academic backgrounds from hard sciences to humanity subjects.

During the early years of the economic reform period after 1978, Wang moved to Beijing to work in the Chinese Academy of Social Sciences Modern History section, specialising in the Republican period (1911–49). His move to Beijing is connected to his marriage to Yao Mingshan, the daughter of one of the key economists in the early years of the Communist Party, Yao Yilin. Yao Yilin had served in Beijing as head of the Ministry of Commerce from 1960 until he was felled in the CR. Close to Premier Zhou Enlai, he was reappointed minister of commerce in 1973, and became deputy prime minister in 1978. During the 1980s he was director of the State Planning Commission and a full member of the Politburo from 1985. Yao was therefore a great patron to have through marriage. Wang's relationship with Yao Mingshan has been described as 'a political one', and the two have never had children, although they have adopted a daughter.[6]

Wang has shown great adaptability in his career. Never formally trained as an economist, he started to concentrate most in this area from 1982. He was Party secretary of an agricultural policy office and development office in the State Council from 1982 to 1986, leveraging off his father-in-law's great links in this area. But it was clear he had real ability and was not solely reliant on patronage. He was regarded by his peers as open-minded, hard-working and highly accomplished intellectually. Yao Yilin adopted a hard line during the 1989 period against the student rebellion, siding with those in the inner circle of decision makers that urged removal of Zhao Ziyang and a crackdown on the protestors. At this time Wang was still in Beijing, working in a State-run agricultural investment bank and then in the People's Construction Bank. The banking and finance sector was remarkably liberal and unconstrained in the 1980s, with much bottom-up experimentation along the lines that had occurred in rural China after agricultural reforms in the early part of the decade. All of this stopped after 1989 as a result of the crackdown on the June rebellion and the subsequent soul-searching about its causes. Wang was therefore working in a sector that was undergoing greater regulation and political control over this key period. He was to continue his career in the State bank finance sector in Beijing till 1997, when he was transferred to Guangdong, first to serve on the provincial Party committee and then to be deputy governor. From 2000, he was brought back to Beijing to be head of the Economic Structure Reform Office in the State Council for two years. From 2002 to 2003 he was Party secretary of the island province of Hainan in the south of China, and from 2003 to 2004 deputy Party secretary and mayor of Beijing, where he headed the organising committee for the preparation of the Beijing 2008 Olympics.

Wang's return to Beijing was also connected to his skills as a crisis manager. In 2003, the Severe Acute Respiratory Syndrome (SARS) crisis broke out. What began as a flu epidemic in the south of the country, spreading from Hong Kong and other parts of Asia, ominously grew into a widespread health threat in which numbers of fatalities started to rise exponentially. The authorities in one of the key hot spots for the disease, Guangdong, were accused of implementing a cover-up, but it was the officials in Beijing, and in particular the then mayor and the minister of public health – accused of fobbing off the public with poor information in order to save the government's face – who were forced to resign in April 2003. Wang was brought in by the new national leadership of Hu and Wen, signifying how regarded he was as a crisis manager. Massive public awareness campaigns and quarantine measures were introduced. Beijing became like a ghost town in the spring of 2003. But the disease was contained, and finally eradicated. What threatened to grow into a major pandemic had been managed.

Wang was appointed a member of the Politburo in 2007, and a vice premier the following year. Over this period he was regarded as the most impressive and authoritative voice within the elite leadership on economic matters. He enjoyed the support and patronage of a key figure from a former leadership period, Zhu Rongji. According to a cable from the US embassy in Singapore in 2009, leaked to Wikileaks in 2010, he had also impressed the former prime minister of Singapore, Lee Kuan Yew. Yew told the then US deputy secretary of State, James Steinberg, that Wang was 'an exceptional talent', continuing that he was:

> very assured and efficient. Wang handled SARS superbly when he was in Hainan. He excelled in coordinating the Beijing Olympics. Li Keqiang may not get the Premiership and the Party is looking for a way to keep Wang on past his 65th birthday until he is 70. [Mentor Minister] Lee said he had first met Wang back in the 1990s but had not forgotten their meeting. This time when they met, Wang told Lee he had reviewed the records of all Lee's meeting [sic] with Chinese leaders going back to the days of Deng Xiaoping to see how Lee's thinking had developed. Wang told Lee he respects him as a consistent man.[7]

Wang's skills at flattering the ever-eager Lee's ego shine through here. But the lines about his perhaps being considered for the premiership above Li Keqiang were worrying, because they hinted at a potential future elite clash between the two. Even more ominous for Li was the fact that other reports showed that just as Wang early in his career could endear himself to his father-in-law, extract maximum political support and gain the patronage of someone as hardnosed as Zhu Rongji, so he was also able to forge a good link with Xi Jinping. This was mostly based on their links to the province of Shaanxi, where they had both spent formative years of their lives in the 1970s. While Wang was a pioneer volunteer in the commune in

Yan'an from 1969, Xi Jinping, five years his junior, was steeling the revolutionary mettle in his soul a mere 60 km away in Yanchuan. It is unknown if the two even met each other then, but this common experience has helped them create a close relationship.[8] Such closeness might have prompted Li to be uneasy.

Rumours of Li's fortunes slipping started intensifying when Xi was elevated above him in 2007. One strand of speculation at the time of the Seventeenth Party Congress was that Li had been given a far tougher portfolio than Xi, with responsibility for the economy and for hard policy areas like health and education where challenges and arguments amongst the decision-making elite were much likelier. A major misstep by Li here and competitors like Wang Qishan were well placed to capitalise. An assessment from an analyst in Hong Kong in 2011 put it bluntly: 'Objectively, Wang Qishan's ability and his style are far, far superior to Li Keqiang's.'[9] To cap it all, Wang Qishan communicated in the same earthy, straightforward language as one of his mentors, Zhu Rongji. Here was a man who described himself as a 'peasant', who was infamous for his addiction to smoking, despite being cooped up on most of his visits abroad in ultra-plush, ultra-expensive and ultra-non-smoking VVIP suites in which he had become adept at finding spaces to light up that did not bring sprinkler water from the extinguisher systems clattering down on him, and whose marriage had aroused the same speculation of being more political than personal as Yu Zhengsheng's.[10] Such idiosyncrasies meant that there was always guessing about his prospects and intentions, especially after the fall of Bo in 2012.

This speculation was terminated before the Eighteenth Party Congress had even ended, when it was announced on 14 November that Wang had been appointed head of the Central Commission for Discipline Inspection (CCDI). Bo Zhiyue, an eminent analyst of elite Chinese politics based in Singapore, expressed the surprise felt by many at this move: 'This is going to be a huge waste of his strength in dealing with economic, financial matters and foreign affairs,' he stated in an interview on the day the announcement was made, 'He's a banker who's going to be in charge of disciplinary affairs. It's a mismatch between his true talent and his assignment.'[11] But politically, at least, the appointment cleared the way for Li, and meant that a potentially threatening challenger to leadership on economic issues would be fully occupied with trying to manage, or even clean up, parts of the Party.

There may have even been a bigger strategic reason beyond the purely personal for why Wang was put in this place. Precisely to whom in the networks of vested interest and powerful loyalties amongst groups and individuals did Wang belong? Like Zhu Rongji, he had pursued a maverick path – museum worker, history graduate, specialist in Republican-era history at a research institute, State planner, banker, provincial leader, then economic planner again. He had been in provinces like Hainan and Guangdong for relatively short periods. His family links to Party aristocracy were acquired through marriage rather than directly his own. There was no easy clan he could be linked to. With an adopted child, too, his most immediate family figured in none of the horror stories about the new generation of greedy children of elite leaders, disgracing their parents by growing obscenely rich. The most one could say when looking objectively at this career was precisely what Lee Kuan Yew had observed in 2009 – that he was immensely competent as an administrator and crisis manager. And the crisis facing the Party in 2012 when he was appointed was precisely in the area of intra-Party governance and the control of corruption. Stimulating economic growth was easy compared to trying to rein in the vast amount of larceny and embezzlement that was going on in the worlds of the various political and business elites across the country, and the links they had made with each other to protect and enrich themselves.

Corruption was perceived by many in the Party and society more widely as reaching crisis levels throughout the 2000s. In this context, a figure like Wang with a track record of good administrative implementation comes across as precisely the right choice to lead the fight to tackle this. Corruption by officials eats at the moral authority of the Party, and the problems it poses to stable rule and public support because of this have figured heavily in the speeches of leaders throughout the first and second decades of the twenty-first century. But China's corruption is particularly hard to grapple with because it involves dealing with a huge paradox, something scholar Andrew Wedeman has called 'a tale of two Chinas'. On the one hand, there is the tale of the China that has experienced an economic miracle, growing at an average rate of nearly 9 per cent from 1979 to 2010. But the second tale involves a China that faces worsening corruption, a place where economic crime cases rose from 9,000 in 1980 to 77,000 by the end of the decade. 'By 2000,' Wedeman notes, 'the regime was indicting over 2,500 senior officials a year', up from 190 in 1988. 'Bribe size, albeit crudely measured, grew at an explosive pace, jumping from 4,000 RMB in 1984 to 54,000 RMB ten years later, then almost tripling to 140,000 RMB in 1998 and doubling again to 272,000 RMB in 2005.'[12] Yet despite this, China's economy continued to boom. Wedeman's own explanation for this paradox was that the Party addressed perceptions of corruption by acting against the worst and therefore most symbolic cases, and that this kept the problem just about under control. It also meant that corruption was 'not an *a priori* barrier to growth' as it had been in smaller economies that had developed into kleptocracies.[13] China's size, the rapidity of growth and the diversity of its productivity meant that, uniquely, immense corruption went hand in hand with enough growth to keep other people in society mobilised.

This was the complex situation that Wang was put in charge of in late 2012. He had his work cut out. There were rumours that on his very first day in charge of the CCDI he ordered his key officials to write an outline of what they thought their key responsibilities were with no reference to the Party manuals and rule books. This showed how hands-on he intended to be. The crisis of corruption and how it figures, as much as an issue of moral threat to the Party as a systemic source of potential instability and social anger, will figure in the final chapter in the discussion of the ideological and intellectual worlds of China's fifth-generation leaders.

One other attribute that Wang shares with Xi is an aloofness from any specific single cohesive network and a sense that he has accrued no vast political debts or profoundly binding ties to specific people that he could not easily free himself from on his journey to the Standing Committee. Some of his networks were gained through marriage, but others were accrued during his career, largely spent after his mid thirties in the centre in the domains of history and then economics. This combination of useful connections and political capital gained through marriage enhanced by those based on a reputation won through demonstrating intellectual and administrative ability puts him in opposition, at least superficially, to Yu Zhengsheng, who inherited a remarkable series of links and connections through his father, meaning he was less reliant on those gained through demonstrating ability.

THE BIG BROTHER OF THE ELITE: YU ZHENGSHENG

Yu Zhengsheng is as profoundly a part of Party royalty as either Xi Jinping or the imprisoned Bo Xilai. His father, Yu Qiwei, was a senior leader in the early decades of the CPC as it came to power. Through his father, Yu Zhengsheng can be connected to the family of Deng Xiaoping, to whom he is very close, and whom, in many ways, he represents on the Eighteenth Party Congress Standing Committee almost like a board member represents key shareholders in a family business that has now gone public.[14] Yu Qiwei was a leader of the 'December 9th' student movement held in Beijing in 1935, demanding nationalist government resistance to Japanese colonisation and aggression. While living in the 1930s in Qingdao, he was the lover of Li Yunhe, whom he had introduced to the Party, sponsoring her membership application. Li Yunhe later changed her name to Jiang

Qing and married Mao Zedong in 1937. Under his assumed name of Huang Jing, Yu became mayor of Tianjin in the early 1950s before moving to Beijing to become a Ministry of Industry leader. During the first anti-rightist campaign in 1958 Huang was labelled a counter-revolutionary and moved to Guangzhou. He died there at the age of 46 in unclear circumstances.[15]

Yu Zhengsheng inherited more from his father than just good links with the Deng family. In the 1950s, while minister of industry, Huang came into contact with a very young cadre starting out his career in Shanghai municipality, working in the electrical machinery section of the First Ministry of Machine Building. In 1953, this young engineer, the 26-year-old Jiang Zemin, was assisting an electronics expert from Czechoslovakia whose good work was so appreciated that Minister Huang invited him at the end of the project to Beijing to a banquet at the Quanjude duck restaurant, a place that still exists to this day. Young Jiang was also in attendance, recalling over half a century later that he had 'never eaten such a good tasting duck'. Jiang was subsequently to meet Huang again in 1956, when he returned from the Soviet Union after a period studying there and was assigned to Changchun Automobile Factory in north-east Jilin province. During an inspection tour to the factory by Huang, according at least to Jiang's later testimony, the two sat talking one evening from 7 till 11.[16] It is unsurprising therefore that Huang's son Zhengsheng has inherited a good connection with Jiang and is seen as one of his allies.

Yu's great links do not end with his father. His mother, Fan Jin, was a deputy mayor of Beijing before the CR, and president of the *Beijing Daily*, joining the Chinese People's Political Consultative Conference after the end of the CR period. On his wife's side too he is profoundly linked to the founding CPC elite. Zhang Zhikai, whom he got to know while studying in Harbin at the Institute of Military Engineering there, is the daughter of Zhang Zhenhuan, a native of Beijing born in 1915 and a close ally of his father, whom he had got to know as a student leader in the December

9th movement. A military leader in the Red Army from 1936, he was subsequently to enjoy a distinguished career both in the south of the country and in the famous Eighth Route Army where he was a political commissar. After 1949, Zhang became a leader in the Marxist Leninist College in Beijing and was involved in the planning, development and testing of an atomic bomb, something successfully accomplished in 1964. Placed in jail during the CR as a traitor and spy, he was released in 1973, rehabilitated in the late 1970s and died in 1994.[17]

For all these stellar links, Yu has not had an enviable life. His father died when he was only an adolescent. Huang's romantic past links with the vindictive Jiang Qing, however, meant that when the CR came and she was able to exercise some power one of her first priorities was to strike at those who knew something of her complex past. Death may have made Huang beyond reach, but his widow Fan was slammed in jail as a member of the Peng Zhen clique (Peng Zhen was at the time mayor of Beijing). The impact of this turbulence on Yu's sister Huisheng was profound, with her reportedly so humiliated by the treatment of the family that she suffered a breakdown and committed suicide.[18] Yu himself was sent from Harbin to Zhangjiakou in Hebei province in 1968 to work in a wireless factory. He stayed there seven years till 1975 when he was able to return to Beijing and work in the Electronics Ministry, maintaining close links with Jiang Zemin, who was also active in this area.

Like Xi Jinping, Yu has spoken directly of the CR and the impact of that time on him. 'Six or seven of my relatives died in that movement,' he has said ruefully, also noting that the ways in which campaigns were undertaken in the CR to cleanse the ranks and dig out enemies were 'inappropriate' and should never be used again. These bitter personal memories explain the ambiguity in Yu's description of Mao Zedong as someone about whom 'the judgement and attitude of the Party are basically correct', a figure worthy of respect because of 'the influence of his works and thought on people', but who had used the wrong route for social change.[19]

Highly qualified language like this about the founding father of the regime hints at a powerful anger at the impact that Mao's movement had on Yu's close family and Yu himself.

Yu's career was based initially in the electrical engineering State-owned apparatus and bureaucracy, deepening the link with Jiang Zemin until 1984, before he became a leader in the China Foundation for Disabled Persons, a group closely linked to Deng Pufang, Deng Xiaoping's son. From 1985 to 1997 Yu worked in Shandong, first in the city of Yantai, and then in Qingdao. Over this period he moved into the same world of networks as Li Wei, the best known of China's mistresses discussed in Chapter 1, with whom he has been linked. From 1998 to 2000, he was a deputy minister and then minister of construction in Beijing, and then, from 2001 to 2007, Party secretary of Hubei. From 2007 he served as Party secretary of Shanghai.

Yu Zhengsheng had one great liability when he came up in speculation about contenders for central leadership in 2012. Despite the fact that he combined the highest possible provincial and central ministerial experience, culminating with five years in Shanghai, and had deep Party-elite links, there was the delicate matter of his brother, Yu Qiangsheng, to factor in. Qiangsheng was a bureau chief in the Ministry of State Security who defected to the US in 1985. Amongst other things, this brother's defection exposed Larry Wu-tai Chin, a Chinese spy working for the Central Intelligence Agency. Chin tragically committed suicide after being apprehended in Virginia in 1986 on the basis of Yu's information.[20] Qiangsheng himself disappeared in the 1990s, reportedly assassinated in Latin America. That Zhengsheng was able to rebuild his position after a scandal of this magnitude shows great instincts for survival. As veteran Beijing-based journalist Benjamin Lim has stated: 'The resurgence of Yu [...] shows that even in modern-day, market-driven China, political staying power can depend largely on good old-fashioned Party connections.'[21] The links with Jiang and Deng were the most potent here.

Yu's image is of an old-style elder brother who has seen it all and will be a source of stabilising wisdom on the Eighteenth Congress Standing Committee. He has clear patronage and obligation links to surviving family members of elite figures from the past, particularly the Dengs. But he also has at least some successful implementation record. In Shanghai, where he replaced Xi Jinping after his brief tenure there, Yu was handed stewardship of the vast World Expo to be held in the city three years after his arrival, a global event with a projected 70 million visitors. Preparation for this gargantuan festival involved digging up half the city, building a showground on the north and south sides of the Huangpu River, and putting in new subway lines, bridges and roads. The security of the event became a priority for a leadership in Beijing increasingly nervous after uprisings in Tibet in 2008 and Xinjiang in 2009. The city was largely in lockdown on the night of the grand opening ceremony in May 2010. Shanghai's six-month Expo, however, was generally judged a success, with the planned visitor numbers exceeded and the multiple billions spent on the preparation regarded as worth it. What was less impressive was Yu's management of a huge fire in the city on 15 November, only days after the Expo had ended, in which 58 people died, and the case of Yang Jia, a 28-year-old from Beijing, whose anger at being fined by Shanghai police for riding an unlicensed bicycle in 2007 caused him to set off a Molotov cocktail and attack police a year later on the heavily symbolic date of the founding of the CPC. Angry attacks on figures of authority in China have become increasingly common, but the sting in the tale for Yu was that Yang was portrayed by many on the internet as a modern-day folk hero simply standing up for his rights after being unjustly picked on by bullying officials.

Provincial leaders have as their key jobs the positive function of supporting economic growth and the negative one of preventing disasters. The 15 November fire in particular, with its high death toll, was a big black mark on Yu's crisis management record. A further accident on the subway line 10 in the city the next year, which led to another 271 being injured, 20 seriously, also highlighted problems. Yu's ability to survive the impact of these shows that, at critical moments, just as it had after his brother's defection in 1985, focusing on deploying all your political capital and patronage networks to protect your career is a major priority. From this angle at least, Yu's ability for ensuring that no matter what problems he has come across, their impact in his career has been containable, is irrefutable.

Yu has himself reportedly spoken about the motives of those who might come out to offer criticisms of how Party officials act. Recalling his time in Hubei, and a conversation he had with a local official about those that were always offering advice and criticisms, Yu said:

> There are four kinds here you need to draw a distinction between. The first are those who really want to take part in monitoring the work of the Party and the government, and this is supportive. The second are those who want to monitor but in fact have no experience and are biased, and there is little you can do about that except just let it go. The third are those who just want to attract attention to themselves, which is no big deal as far as I can see. The fourth are those who want to topple the Party from power, and are looking to establish Western-style systems.[22]

Yu's fourth category are the true 'enemy within' and need the most vigilance and attack.

In keeping with his technocratic background and his conservative image, Yu has been resolutely consistent in speaking about the inappropriateness of trying to introduce multi-party democracy into China. Speaking at the 90th anniversary celebrations of the foundation of the CPC in Shanghai in 2011, he was blunt:

> Some comrades feel we can sort all our problems out with multi-party democracy. Is that really so? Look at Taiwan.

Mainland China is vastly more complex compared to Taiwan. If China was to become a multi-party democracy it would end up as a political battleground, a place where ambitious people run riot for their own power interests, and separatists can carve up the place.[23]

Such words sound like papally infallible edicts by a high priest of one-party permanence. This is perhaps not so surprising. Of all the Eighteenth Party Standing Committee members, Yu has the most complex relationship to the Party. He has gained almost all he has through it – but he and his family have also suffered so much at its hands. In his life story, therefore, he represents in miniature the contradictions of the last six decades of Party rule. He comes across as someone who has been a victor and a victim. That the Party is almost all his life is shown through the sense that his marriage is also, like Wang Qishan's, a political one, a marrying of clans. This has given rise to the stories of his links to figures like Li Wei. He has no children, and nor have his family been linked to major corruption stories.

MASTER OF GDP: ZHANG GAOLI

The almost complete lack of evidence of any kind of cultural hinterland around Yu is duplicated in the figure of Zhang Gaoli. At least the undercurrents implied by Yu's links with figures like the lover businesswoman Li Wei gives some colour. With Zhang, there is a uniform greyness. If the CPC top-level leadership has consistently stated that it regards its key objective since 1978 as producing economic growth, then Zhang Gaoli embodies this in one person. Wherever he has enjoyed leadership positions provincially he has been able to deliver high levels of growth to such an extent that he has been called the 'master of GDP'. Like Yu, however, he has a patchy history with disaster management and, also like Yu, a clear relationship with previous president of China Jiang Zemin, though one acquired later in his political career and through naked pragmatism rather than clan ties.

The simple characteristic of Zhang that sets him apart from the other members of the super elite is the modesty of his background. Born in Fujian in 1946, he lost his father before the age of ten. Entering Xiamen University in 1965, he specialised in Economics and Statistics, joining Maoming Oil Company in 1970, where he worked in a number of positions for 17 years. While based in Guangdong he attracted the attention of Liang Lingguang – also a native of the same area of Fujian where Zhang had been born and brought up – Party secretary of Guangdong from 1983 and governor when Zhang was working there. Through this patronage link, Zhang Gaoli transferred to the local economic planning committee, becoming in 1988, at the age of 42, the deputy governor of the province, a position he served in till being appointed Party secretary of Shenzhen at the end of 1997.

Shenzhen is one of the great sacred sites of post-reform-and-opening-up China, the hallowed turf on which the first SEZ that re-engaged with capitalism was founded and where markets were reintroduced into China after 1978. As such, Party leadership of the city is a high-profile job. Here, a leader is in charge of a place somewhere at the forefront of the Chinese economy, a 'Wild West' where the population is hugely mobile, and where innovation happens so fast that, as Thomas Campanella said in his book about modern Chinese city-planning and architecture, it has 'humiliated vision'.[24] Shenzhen's growth in the 1980s famously exceeded 40 per cent a year. By 1997, things had quietened down though the city was given a new spurt of energy by receiving authorisation to produce goods not just for the international market, but also for the domestic one. Only five years before, the great architect of the reform-and-opening-up process, Deng Xiaoping, had descended on the city during this southern tour, making clipped remarks for his daughter Deng Rong to inscribe. These were interpreted as a full commitment to the process begun in the 1980s, despite the shock of the 1989 uprising. Let people continue to grow wealthier, let the Socialism with Chinese characteristics give ideological cover to pragmatic acceptance of the market, and continue the full-on gallop towards the most raw capitalism the world had ever seen.

By the time Zhang Gaoli had arrived in Shenzhen to be Party leader, much of the wealth making had been achieved. But the city had clear problems. Mobility meant everyone who was there was an outsider. The sleepy backwater of the late 1970s that one can see in photos taken at the time had been swept away. It was a city now of chancers, dreamers and middle men: migrant workers, those on the make, and the winners and losers of the reform process. Businessmen were busy with making their fortunes, the karaoke parlours heaved with officials and their contacts doing illicit deals, and the signs of brash visible wealth were everywhere. But there was also a clear underclass – the vulnerable who had precious few if any rights, and the most shallow networks to protect them, who came from elsewhere in China to work in the factories, often for soul-destroying long hours and the most minimal remuneration. The Dickensian atmosphere of the city struck many that visited, with the only difference between it and Victorian London being the lack of cold, frosty winters.

Zhang Gaoli, as Party head, was associated with two moves during his time in Shenzhen. The first was to create a hi-tech zone. Already it was clear that now its companies were able to sell goods to the internal market a process was in train where the vast unde-veloped domestic market of the country was going to open up fully. Already, even in the deepest western regions of the country, there were scientific zones, districts that tried, with varying degrees of success, to ape what had been done in Shenzhen and the other SEZs. Eventually, these would offer competition to Shenzhen. They would never enjoy its amazing location next to Hong Kong with its great logistic links. But they could offer the most potent and dangerous competition of all – cheaper costs. The future of Shenzhen had to be investing in industries that were further up the value chain. Being a hub for finishing off partly processed imported goods with local cheap labour was only going to work for the short term. Moving into high-value-added goods was the future path. The hi-tech zone that Zhang Gaoli got authorisation to establish was the first step to achieving this.

The second policy he supported was environmental protection. This is more contentious. The city had been built at breakneck speed, with only a second thought given to urban planning. Skyscrapers were knocked up at the rate of a storey a day, some of them collapsing because of the poor quality of the materials used. One famous shopping precinct with over 700 units was almost unusable because it had no transport links and existed in a no-man's land surrounded by bypass roads and tunnels. The manufacturing and industry in the city had taken a terrible toll on the natural environment. Water was polluted, there were barely any green spaces and the city looked like a concrete jungle, parts of it dominated by smog-producing factories in which armies of people lived in shanty towns. Zhang Gaoli supported campaigns to create a garden city, a place with at least some woodland, somewhere that wanted to experiment with new methods of urban environmental protection.[25] It was a nice aspiration, but as visitors to Shenzhen even today will note, there is still a long way to go.

The other benefit the city would give Zhang, though it was something he could not have appreciated at the time, was a clear link to Xi Jinping. Xi Jinping's elderly father, Xi Zhongxun, lived there. His hugely respected military and Party background meant that Zhang was solicitous of him, and made sure he was looked after well. It was to prove an excellent future investment. This solicitude over old retired cadres was a feature that occurred again when Zhang had moved to Shandong in the north, the place where Yu Zhengsheng had recently served as a senior official. On Labour Day, 1 May 2006, he hosted the already 'retired' Jiang Zemin, who was visiting Mount Tai, one of the great sites in the province. A photo of the visit has an almost imperial air, the elderly and immobile former President Jiang dressed in a dark, thick coat, a hood over his head, with a swarm of younger men holding him on a sort of bier carrying him into a gateway. Walking just behind the bier, directing everyone and ensuring the former president was looked after properly, was a self-effacing Zhang.[26]

From 2001 to 2007, Zhang was based in Shandong, first as deputy Party secretary and governor, then as Party secretary replacing Wu Guanzheng, who was promoted to the Sixteenth Politburo Standing Committee in 2002 and made head in the same year of the CCDI. Wu's departure offered a great opportunity for Zhang: one in which he was able to mobilise his business networks from his years in Guangdong and Shenzhen, and his links through his birth in Fujian, to get companies interested in coming and investing in the coastal province further north.[27] This was a campaign he undertook with ruthless efficiency, drawing on connections he had made to businesses in Hong Kong and Taiwan, and further afield in Japan and South Korea. One of the most prominent of these was the father of his own son-in-law, a businessman originally from Zhang's native area in Fujian but now based in Hong Kong, Li Xianyi, who was nicknamed the 'King of Windows' and was chair of the Xinyi Glass Company, listed in Hong Kong in 2005.[28] The net effect of this was that, by 2006, after three years of accelerating growth, the province managed over 15 per cent GDP increase in the first half of the year, running Guangdong a close second nationally.

Zhang Gaoli's close links with Jiang meant that he was rumoured to be someone Hu Jintao regarded with coolness. But his extraordinary success at simply pumping out GDP growth and posting staggering increases meant that this mattered little. In 2007, he was given the city of Tianjin to be Party secretary of, a place only an hour's train journey from Beijing and, for this reason, of immense economic and strategic importance. Tianjin is the home to a huge port, the logistics entry point for the capital, but also a nascent financial services centre, vying with Shanghai, despite its newness to this sector. From his first year in Tianjin, Zhang once more started to produce huge GDP results; the 'Tianjin Model' was a less noisy phenomenon than the Chongqing one, which was emerging under Bo Xilai in the south-west, but it was underpinned by results that were easier to demonstrate. The two simple objectives it strove for were high-end productivity and high salaries. Zhang himself is a poor communicator, and someone who evidently disliked appearing in interviews or any kind of public event. Part of this may have been due to his suffering from a skin complaint, which means that he is immensely sensitive about how his photo is taken.[29] But some of it was also from a business-like air he cultivated, perhaps from his time in the oil sector. Dismissing the idea of a Tianjin model when asked about this in 2012, he simply stated that Tianjin 'didn't have some sort of model, there was no development model, and speaking like this was not appropriate'.[30] Instead, the main thing was to 'serve the people, let the people get some real benefits. If the people say you're good, then that's really good.'[31] His own style may have helped the city in dealing with a reputation before 2007 of having a local corruption problem. Between 2006 and 2007, a series of officials were removed from their positions in the city on embezzlement charges, including the Higher Court president, Zhang Baifeng, and Song Pingshun, chair of the local Chinese People's Political Consultative Conference (CPPCC). Li Baojin, the former chief prosecutor for the municipality, was also dismissed a year before for 'severe breaches of discipline'. Song was to commit suicide after being questioned about links with Wu Changshun, former head of Tianjin's police. Pi Qiansheng, head of the Binhai new development area, was also removed and replaced.[32] This depth of local vested interest and cosy mutual protection and help was something an outsider like Zhang was meant to break up. Sometimes it is not just the networks that you can create that are important, but also the ones you are able to destroy. Zhang was evidently highly capable at both.

ZHANG DEJIANG: THE FIXER

One of the ironies of elite leadership in the PRC is that Standing
Committee representatives have, over the years, become increasingly better educated, far less military, but also increasingly paro-
chial. Mao Zedong's worst nightmare, as Frank Pieke, in a book
on Party schools pointed out, was 'a ruling elite who worship[ped]
book learning and formal educational qualifications' rather than
'first-hand revolutionary experience and direct involvement in the
life and work of China's toiling masses'.[33] The first group of revolutionary leaders, from Zhou Enlai to Deng Xiaoping, worked and
lived abroad for a number of years before returning to China to
continue their political careers. Those from Jiang Zemin's generation tend to have had periods of study in the Soviet Union or its
satellite states. But starting from Hu Jintao and the leaders around
him, from 2002 those in the successive Politburos with any experience of living abroad for more than a few weeks became rarer.
Like many of their counterparts in the West, they gained a certain
credibility domestically from their being almost wholly local actors,
uncontaminated by overlong exposure to the world outside. The
sole exception to this in the Standing Committee of the Eighteenth
Congress was Zhang Dejiang. But the place where he had spent his
time, the DPRK, was the exception that proved the rule.

If Zhang Gaoli is someone who aspires to speak less and do
more, then Zhang Dejiang belongs to the other camp – those
who have been criticised for their love of official language, for the
particularities of Huist discourse with its large memes of rhetorical formulations that straddle across different speeches and have
become almost empty of real content.[34] But Zhang also has two
great strengths – immense experience as a provincial leader, often
in the most difficult circumstances (he had to replace Bo Xilai on
his removal at a moment of crisis in 2012) and a deep pragmatism
that has seen a North Korean-trained economist with a clear commitment to a State-directed economy take charge of China's two

greatest hot spots for private economic development – Zhejiang and Guangdong. Zhang's commitment to the State sector had almost no effect on the continuing healthy growth of the non-State-sector area in the provinces in which he was in charge.

The one area where Zhang is truest to his autocratic, Statist credentials is in his fully signing up to the kinds of repressive policies and measures that Hu Jintao was using more from the centre in Beijing after 2007. In Guangdong he was accused of willingness to use quasi-military-style measures in brutal clampdowns against the rising tide of rights-linked protest movements there.[35] His handling in 2003 of the fallout from the beating to death of Sun Zhigang, a migrant worker at the garment factory in the province, was a particular low point, and something that is still remembered a decade afterwards. Sun was arrested for not carrying his identity papers. According to an administrative regulation dating back to 1982, migrants from outside a province (Sun was from Wuhan) were all required to carry ID. Those who did not have this were to be deported to their hometown. In a China that was close approaching over 200 million people working away from their home base, this was a wholly unworkable law. But the issues raised by Sun's case went deeper. The official account stated that he had been attacked by other inmates in a penitentiary hospital and suffered a heart attack or stroke that then caused his death.[36] For this, 12 people were convicted and sentenced. Sun was better classified as a skilled migrant, however, a university graduate in fashion design, and therefore more likely to assert what he believed were his rights. The more realistic scenario is that his ability to stick up for himself was rewarded with a savage beating by the police and officials to silence him, and this, rather than any unprompted attack by fellow inmates, led to his death. This was the story accepted by Sun's family, and with the help of a local newspaper they managed to get a campaign going that ignited an immense debate and response on the internet, reaching right up to the NPC, which argued for a change in the law on ID papers. The authorities in Guangdong, where Zhang Dejiang was the top person in authority at the time, initially responded to the media report by slamming the editor of the main newspaper in jail. Zhang can therefore be called an early, and enthusiastic, practitioner of the 'pro-stability' measures that were to become even more heavily subscribed to from 2008.

Like the other Zhang on the Politburo Standing Committee, Dejiang comes from a modest background. Born in November 1946 in Taian county, Liaoning, on his own account his grandfather was a farmer, his father a worker, and he lived till the age of 12 in the countryside, then moved to Changchun, the capital of neighbouring Jilin province. The family of nine relied wholly on his father's earnings. After high school in Changchun, he was enrolled in the PLA Art College, but with the onset of the CR he moved instead to Yanbian Korean autonomous region next to the border of the DPRK, working in agriculture in a commune.[37] From 1968 he was part of a youth brigade in Yanbian, and from 1970 to 1972 a Party secretary of the Korean Languages section at Yanbian University (he had entered the Party in January 1971). He stayed in Yanbian till 1978, heading the revolutionary committee (one of the administrative outcomes of the CR), until his period of two years' study overseas at the Kim Il Sung University in Pyongyang. This period, from 1978 to 1980, just as the reform process was starting in Beijing, marks him out as the only leader at the top of the Eighteenth Party Congress who has any experience abroad as a student. He returned to Yanbian University in 1980, working as the deputy president till 1983, when he became deputy Party secretary of Yanji city. In 1986, he finally moved to Beijing where he was a deputy minister at the Ministry of Civil Affairs. From 1990 to 1998, he was deputy Party secretary, then Party secretary of Jilin, the first of his four major provincial positions. From 1998 to 2002 he was Party secretary of Zhejiang, from 2002 to 2007 Party secretary of Guangzhou, and from 2007 vice premier on the Politburo. Only in 2012 did he return to being Party secretary of a provincial centre, in Chongqing. This range of postings, from the north-east, to central coastal China, to the south, and then the south-west, means that Zhang Dejiang is the most richly experienced of fifth-generation leaders in the scope and variety of his provincial leadership record.

Zhang's career, particularly his period in Jilin, allowed him to build a patronage network, despite his modest background and the fact that he was based in the provinces through the 1970s and into the 1980s. Why someone who had been almost wholly based in Yanbian for 15 years might be elevated to head the major province of Zhejiang in 1998 is partly answered by the strong links he built on a visit to Jilin as part of a provincial inspection tour by Jiang Zemin in 1995. The north-east was on the minds of the leadership then, with the issue of what to do about major SOE reform. Zhang's home province of Liaoning, along with Jilin and Heilongjiang, had been labelled 'rust belt areas', heavily dependent on the industrial and manufacturing State companies, which employed hundreds of thousands, and yet were profoundly uncompetitive. Zhang had been linked to Jiang Zemin earlier, when the newly appointed Party secretary had undertaken his first formal visit as head of Party to North Korea in March 1990. The same year, Jiang had gone to Yanbian Korean Autonomous District, where Zhang had just started working, and expressed imperial-style approval: 'Make Yanbian Korean autonomous region a model,'[38] Jiang had written on some calligraphic paper during his visit. Such supportive voices from Beijing meant that Zhang secured promotion at the age of 48 in 1995, when Jiang also descended on Jilin province and declared that 'I am happy to see the leadership in Jilin are all young [...] Your governor and your Party secretary [indicating Zhang] will carry you into the next century.'[39]

Everything about Zhang's background, from where he studied to where he had worked, showed that he should be a full-hearted supporter of State management of the economy. According to Willy Lam, writing in 2006, Zhang 'had handled ideological matters most of his career [...] Zhang's orthodox views about the private sector had cast doubt on his suitability for the Guangdong post.' The title of an article Zhang had written in 2001 in a conservative journal underlines this: 'We must make it clear that private businessmen cannot be enrolled in the Party.'[40]

In fact, in a delicious proof of the separation between the domains of the ideological and the practical worlds in China, it was precisely in 2001 that private business people were allowed to join the Party. Nor does it seem that Zhang's personal views on the non-State sector's role had the slightest impact on how he allowed productivity to grow, either in Zhejiang where, by the end of his tenure, about 60 per cent of the economy was produced by the private sector, or in Guangdong, which was an impossibly complex mix of State and non-State, all combined to pump out the staggering GDP rises over the next decade that would put the place at the top of provincial growth. Finally, and most significant of all, his public words on the non-State sector had no bearing on Jiang Zemin's support for him. In many ways, his rock-solid orthodoxy was precisely what was needed to shut up the more ideological leftists still carping about everything that had happened in China since 1978 (the eminent economists who had written to Wen Jiabao complaining about the China 2030 World Bank and the DRC report mentioned in Chapter 1 fall into this camp), because with a leadership that included someone who was such a publicly open hardliner at least they could see their views were represented in the upper echelons.

Putting someone like Zhang in charge of such vibrant economies was also politically sensible on another level. Like many other elite politicians of his generation in China, Zhang has had to operate in a slightly schizophrenic way. Whatever his ideological beliefs, as a pragmatist he had to accommodate the need to support growth. But he has done this with the justification that it ultimately promotes uncontested one-party rule and preserves stability. On all other social and political issues Zhang has acted as a conservative who is willing to clamp down on rights demands, press freedom and other challenges with great harshness as and when necessary. The *Hong Kong Weekly* in January 2006 talked of what it called six crimes Zhang had committed in his zeal to ensure that stability was asserted at all costs. The SARS cover-up was one, the death of Sun Zhigang another. But there were even worse examples: the crushing of a protest about rights issues against officials in Fanyu Taishi village, with heavy use of the people's armed police that was viewed as disproportionate to the unrest; the Xingning mining disasters, which saw high casualties; and the crackdown on the press as a result of the SARS crisis because of its vengeful style and tone were three other cases. The most serious, however, was the Shanwei massacre, on 6 December 2005, when more than 20 villagers were shot down by paramilitary police. Like so many protests in modern China, this was connected to heavy-handed requisition of land by local officials.[41]

While allowing economic productivity to rise, both in Zhejiang and then in Guangdong, where he was to spend five years, Zhang represents almost perfectly the ambiguity of the modern Chinese leadership – using language that in many ways runs almost completely against the policies they are sanctioning economically, but somehow policing this with the harshest tactics against the social-political contradictions that have arisen from breakneck growth. Zhang's treatment of the *Southern Metropolis Daily* with the brief detentions of its editors was a classic example – taming the appetite of journalists from other investigative newspapers to poke their noses where they were not wanted. Zhang was also willing to construct new patronage networks, with his fulsome support from 2004 for a book on Xi Zhongxun's leadership of Guangdong over two decades earlier. Titled *Xi Zhongxun Governs Guangdong*, this was finally published after several years' work in December 2012. The book had created an opportunity for Zhang to get closer to the Xi family, with his meeting with Xi's mother to discuss the planned contents as early as April 2004.[42]

Zhang Dejiang's wife is a powerful figure in her own right, but also from a modest background. Xin Shusen is a senior leader of the Chinese Construction Bank. She has also been a member of the CPPCC. Two years younger than her husband, she joined the Party in 1976, going to the North East Finance University and graduating in Investment Economics, with a master's degree. Zhang and Xin married at the end of 1977, although they may have known each other at school. They had a daughter in the late 1970s who was born while Zhang was in North Korea. She started working for the Jilin province branch of the Construction Bank in 1983, occupying a series of positions in personnel and management up to that of the head of the Discipline and Inspection Committee of the bank in the early 2000s. While together in the early part of their careers, from Zhang Dejiang's return to Jilin from Beijing in 1990, his wife remained working in the capital. This remained the case throughout Zhang's career in Zhejiang and Guangdong, up till his return to Beijing in 2007.[43]

Zhang Dejiang's career is a wonderful antidote to the notion of factionalism. He has shrewdly chosen a very small number of patrons, an attribute he shares with Zhang Gaoli. He has no powerful central ministry links (having served only four years in the relatively unimportant Ministry of Civil Affairs in the late 1980s), nor any deep family patronage lines, either directly or through his wife. He never worked in Shanghai, never worked in the oil industry, never worked in any capacity with the CYL, nor has he military links. He was able to demonstrate ideological reliability, and an ability to deal with crises, even harshly, if they became difficult. And that has been enough to get him final promotion to the Standing Committee.

THE POLITBURO'S FIRST JOURNALIST: LIU YUNSHAN

Journalists occupy an ambiguous position in modern China. Once upon a time they were disseminators of State ideological guidance and heavily prescriptive messages, and the legions of those who worked for the Xinhua news agency or the *People's Daily* produced thought guidance and were propagators. There were always, however, honourable exceptions – such as the great Liu Binyan, who produced some of China's first real investigative reporting in the 1950s, only to be labelled a rightist and punished. In the last three decades, space has grown for more of this investigative reporting. The immensely courageous Hu Shuli, with first *Caijing* and then *Caixin* magazines, has been a leader here, with some of the reporting from these works already cited. *Southern Weekend* is a further example. Even so, the journalists who work for directly State-supported media are still in the majority.

Many of those, however, have privately complained in the period after 2007 of the increasing restrictions on what they can and cannot report. Their old function as deliverers of wholesome messages to maintain stability has partially returned, with campaigns that make their works carriers of edifying slogans about the need for harmony and balance. This has largely been provoked by the rise of competition from social media, which has made the promotion of State messages more challenging, but also more important. The driver of this campaign has been Liu Yunshan, operating in charge of media and propaganda in the full Politburo since 2007, under the overall control of Li Changchun, the Standing Committee propaganda czar from 2007 to 2012. In this area, demands on the work of journalists have become more restrictive, with an increasingly chaotic game of cat and mouse as journalists and writers try to find creative ways of evading State censors.

On the surface, Liu Yunshan seems a poor choice to be given leadership in the messaging and thought-control area. In the early part of his career he was himself a journalist for the Xinhua news agency, and has therefore left a written record of his earlier positions. But this might also be the reason he has gotten to be where is now. He understands the sector and the people he has to deal with. He once did their jobs. He knows their tricks. That he was so underestimated in the lead-up to 2012, and that so few people rated his chances of promotion, also makes him interesting.

One assessment from 2012 in Hong Kong spelt out his potential starkly: 'Liu Yunshan has no real background supporter, his
work in the propaganda area has been criticised, there are problems he has with corruption, so the chances of him getting into
the Politburo Standing Committee are the hardest to overcome.'
Rather boldly, the assessment concluded: 'He does not have much
hope in comparison to Yu Zhengsheng and Liu Yandong.'[44] This
was also ranged alongside the deadly accusation that he has been
quietly supportive of leftism, with language about 'Mao Zedong
Thought' appearing heavily in material that was officially issued
to mark the 60th anniversary of the establishment of the PRC in
2009. He was also accused of authorising over 125 different monuments, memorial halls and activities celebrating former leaders
in over 75 districts across China until this was banned.[45] Chinese
intellectual and liberal disdain has been high towards Liu. But a
look at his career shows a more complex figure, and someone who,
at least in the early years, has a claim to be the most open-minded
of the Eighteenth Party Congress Standing Committee.

Like Wang Qishan, Liu's ancestral home is Shanxi province,
but he was born in 1947 in Inner Mongolia autonomous region.
This was the destination to which many urban youths were sent
in the CR. It was here, during part of this period, that radical
provincial leadership undertook a particularly vicious purge in the
local Party from 1968, with as many as 22,000 killed and many
tens of thousands injured as a result of purging claimed members
of the Inner Mongolian People's Party, an entity accused at the
time of agitating for reunification with the Republic of Mongolia
across the northern border and aspiring to create a Pan-Mongolian
nation. Senior cadres in the province were removed from power,
many struggled against and some murdered, while others were
exiled or imprisoned. Such a brutal campaign touched the lives of
almost everyone living there. Liu Yunshan was based at the time
of the purges in the Normal [Teachers'] College in the military
garrison city of Jining. Just as the CR was reaching its most violent

stage, with an all-out onslaught on many cadres of Mongolian ethnicity (who at the time made up about a quarter of the population
of the autonomous region) Liu moved in 1968/9 to Tumoteyou
banner (banner is a local term for a country-sized administrative
region), working first in the Bashen School, and then in a commune. He started his formal career in the propaganda administration, working from 1969 to 1975 at the local propaganda bureau.
From 1975 to 1982 he was the Xinhua agricultural and livestock
correspondent, and from 1982 to 1984 the deputy Party secretary of the Inner Mongolian CYL branch. He reverted to propaganda work from 1984 to 1986 as local deputy head of the Inner
Mongolian Propaganda Bureau, and then as head from 1987. He
was Party secretary of Chifeng city in Inner Mongolia till 1993
when he finally transferred to Beijing, becoming a deputy minister
in the central propaganda ministry.

Liu had acquired in this journey only two significant patrons.
The first was Ding Guangen, Politburo Standing Committee member in the 1990s, who had direct control over propaganda. Ding
was a *bête noire* to most liberals in China, someone who was known
to be close to Deng Xiaoping, reportedly through a shared love of
playing bridge. Ding was associated since his return to front-line
Chinese politics under Jiang Zemin in 1992, with tough messages
sent to artistic and media figures. In 1996, he had called together
film industry leaders and told them 'spiritual pollution was threatening to undermine the Socialist values of the Chinese, and that
they needed to start making more patriotic films'.[46] He was also
courted by press mogul Rupert Murdoch in the late 1990s, and
had descended on the UK in 1999 for a formal visit. As a new
official at the British Foreign Office at the time, I remember having
to deal with requests for Mr Ding's entourage to have armed protection (something only accorded to foreign ministers and heads
of State or government), and the prickly issue of how someone
so central to propaganda and ideological work was going to be
received publicy at a time when there was a widespread clampdown

against the Falungong sect. Even from this remote distance, Ding came across as a profoundly unattractive politician.

Liu's other patron was Tian Congming, who had also spent a large part of his early career in Inner Mongolia where he worked initially as a clerk in the political department of the Bayannur banner and then in the Xinhua news agency farming department. It was in this position that he got to know Liu. Tian ended up in the early 2000s as head of Xinhua news agency nationally, but his particular help to Liu was giving him a link to Zhou Hui, the man appointed to be Party secretary of Inner Mongolia when the autonomous region was reunited after a decade-long tripartite division and reduction in 1980. Zhou Hui and Tian supported Liu's study for half a year at the Central Party School in Beijing in the early 1980s, a great accolade at the time.[47] Liu may have had another patron in Hu Jintao, who headed the CYL nationally when Liu was made local leader of the league in Inner Mongolia in 1986.

Liu reportedly had to offer a confession of his work mistakes in late 2009, after a particularly rough patch, when China's soft power campaign, which he had oversight of, was experiencing serious problems: partly though internal issues like the handling of the pro-democracy Charter 08 activists, including Liu Xiaobo, and the ways their stories had been presented in the media abroad, and partly through increased criticism of China's assertiveness and behaviour internationally. In a meeting before other leaders in December that year, Liu accused himself of not doing his best in five main areas: he had not managed his relationship with the current situation well; he had not taken full responsibility in implementing central government policies for propaganda and news; he had not positioned himself correctly because he demanded fame and benefits that severely impacted on leadership team unity; he did not ask for higher personal standards from himself in terms of knowledge and behaviour, so that he kept on making mistakes; and finally he did not discipline people responsible to him using the Party's general standards, and in this way lost control of them.[48] Admission of this staggering menu of faults meant Hu's chief right-hand man at the time, Ling Jihua, was given oversight of the propaganda office work to make sure there were no future foul-ups.

In mitigation, Liu might have tried to argue that his portfolio from 2007 was perhaps the most thankless of all the major ones. In charge of information management and public messaging at a time when changes happened thick and fast, he was constantly caught between a rock and a hard place. The political parameters given by the Hu and Wen leadership of repression rather than any major political changes meant that on the one hand Liu had to take the lead in ensuring that news of uprisings and disasters was managed in such a way that did not reflect badly on the political line of the upper-level leaders, while on the other hand contending with a carnival world of perhaps half a billion new social media users who were ever ready and eager to unleash anger about these sort of events on officials and authority. He also had to deal with the pernicious force of foreign media, forever exploring the rich terrain of China for juicy stories. It is ironic, therefore, that the biggest of these stories, the fall of Bo Xilai, probably brought Liu the most benefit, bringing about a reversal of fortunes for a man who had been so severely criticised both by himself and others. Bo's fall reconfigured the promotion possibilities to such an extent that someone with Liu's abilities to stand fast on hardline issues became more important than more liberal-minded figures.

With Liu, too, factionalism helps little in understanding his success. More than the other colleagues who were also successful in late 2012, Liu was the beneficiary of political changes of fortune and the good winds that they blew his way. His links to the Party Youth League were brief. He had no major link to Jiang Zemin, nor any evident provincial top leadership experience. He had never headed a ministry centrally. His whole career had been in the field of ideology, as a teacher, then a journalist, then a propaganda worker. Perhaps this supplies a key to understanding his importance. Ideology, after all, matters to the fifth-generation leadership,

just as it mattered to all previous generations of the super elite in
the PRC. And in this area, as the final chapter will show, Liu has
unique qualifications.

For the repressive period after 2010, for all the public criticism
and international flak, Liu has proved that striving to control both
the messenger and the message is as politically effective now as it
was in 1949 when the regime was founded. Chen Zhimin, a commentator, has stated that for Liu, personal belief in the messages
he is carrying is not important. What is important is power. 'He is
not someone who doggedly believes in Marxism and Leninism.'[49]
His approach to political messaging is simple. On the one hand,
a back-to-basics campaign over the years from 2009 relentlessly
hammered home news stories of leaders getting close to the people,
with voices given to the 'masses' that fulsomely express their con-
tentment and happiness. An infamous example of this occurred in
late 2010, when Hu Jintao visited a 'normal house' belonging to
Guo Chunping in Beijing. The dialogue proceeded thus:

Hu: When did you move in?
Guo: I've moved in over half a month now.
Hu: Oh, half a month, I see. How big is this apartment?
Guo: It is 45 square metres in all.
Hu: 45, huh. Two rooms?
Guo: Yes, two rooms.
Hu: How much rent are you paying for this apartment?
Guo: I pay RMB 77 each month.
Hu: RMB 77 each month – are you able to cope with the
        rent?
Guo: Yes. Secretary-General, I just wanted to say a big
        thank you to the Party and the government. We are
        so touched to have been given this fabulous apart-
        ment to live in!
Hu: The Party and the government are very concerned
        with the people's daily livelihoods. We've taken up a

> series of measures to further improve your daily lives.
> Well, we're so happy to see that your lives have been
> improved here!
>
> Guo: Thank you! Thank you! Our country is really improv-
> ing day by day. We never dreamed we would be liv-
> ing in such an apartment some day.

Netizens digging afterwards found many holes in this story, and it was removed quickly.[50] But it captures the flavour of propaganda in the Liu period. The second measure was, as Zhang Dejiang had shown in Guangzhou, simply to hassle journalists and bloggers so much that most of them became extremely cautious. This was not a pleasant business. China ranked 163rd in the world in the 'Reporters without frontiers' press freedom index in 2007. By 2011 it had fallen to 174th place. The only countries ranked lower were Iran, Syria, Turkmenistan, the DPRK and Eritrea.[51] Though he would never say it, this was truly a sign of Liu Yunshan's success.

CONFUSION: WHERE IS THE COMMON POINT?

Seeking to find diversity in a group of people that at first glance look like they are cut from the same cloth might seem strange. Superficially the elite running China in the Party from 2012 look like a unified group, representing a homogeneous, single political entity. But the CPC is vast, and nowhere near as united as it seems. It is a collection of many millions of people, promoting and pursuing sometimes highly individual objectives. There are rhetorical and administrative unities, but these often run skin-deep. As an organisation, the Party's flexibility in accommodating these differences has impressed many observers, despite the monochrome image it presents to outsiders.

To tease out these differences, we can see the seven people in the Standing Committee from 2012 in a variety of dimensions. Faction allegiance is the least informative. It shows where they have been, where they have made some links, but beyond that it says little about the content of their lives, the colour of their ambitions, and the ways in which they have been able personally to direct and invest in relationships that are dynamic and changing around them. At most we can build up certain career profiles that have been rewarded by great success. Provincial experience at the top level here seems to be something that gives good returns, though Liu Yunshan is the exception to this. Having immediate links into previously high-ranking family is also helpful – but not helpful enough to save Bo Xilai, and way more complex than simply identifying a neat group of princelings that automatically get to be leaders. Central ministerial experience is not a bad thing, nor is a previous position in the CYL or other arms of Party administration. Crisis management form also helps – but the leaders outlined in this book also have plenty of experience of botching this. Their real skills have been in avoiding this politically sticking on them.

What we wrestle with in looking into the lives and drivers of these leaders is trying to get a deeper sense of how they are as politicians. Factionalism never answers that. It says that they were able to build links with patrons, and up to a point it does illuminate an area where political capital can form. But this is something many other people also try to do. Former leaders of the CPC have always been able to go around being kingmakers and talent spotters. What is more interesting is to work out what it was they saw in the people they decided to support, and how those people rewarded this help with hard work, strategic movements and planning. Jiang Zemin has proved the most active talent spotter, along with Zeng Qinghong. But his career was the longest (it goes back to the late 1940s) and his range of positions the most extensive. Ironically, the one person he did not talent-spot was his successor, Hu Jintao. Many others he has been linked with and helped. His investments in these people came to fruition in 2012. But putting the success of someone in the leadership line-up of 2012 down to Jiang's support only takes us so far. Those that were promoted were actors in a dynamic and often fast-moving situation. Many failed, and the vast majority didn't even stand a chance. In this context, their biggest patrons in the whole process have been themselves.

We have to depart from a purely patronage- and faction-led framework, therefore, and move more into the realms of politics, working out what sorts of campaigns, policies, public messaging, bureaucratic achievements and ideas leaders are supportive of, instigate or are involved in in modern Chinese politics. Our assessment of all of this is hampered because we are looking at a situation where these sorts of qualities cannot be too overtly demonstrated, because this is a context in which, as yet, there are no open campaigns. Contenders cannot place their achievements out in the clear day. They have to do much under the restraint of covert codes and symbolic negotiations. The arbiters of this are a little-understood inner sanctum of supreme 'deciders', but even they in their turn have to appeal to some notion of wider Party and public support if they have any chance of claiming legitimacy. We understand little about precisely how they do this, and from whom they claim support. The function of understanding and assessing political achievements in this context where opaqueness is regarded as a key tool of power control is more difficult than in multi-party democracies where finding evidence of behaviour is easier. Despite all these caveats, it is clear from all the figures looked at in detail in this chapter and the two preceding ones that they had to meet the expectations of some of their patrons and support networks with real achievements and some kind of evidence that they had ability. That is simply politics, everywhere, every day.

A final dimension in trying to understand the leadership result at the Eighteenth Party Congress is the vexed issue of ideology, of what these people believe. In some ways, they do just believe in themselves, in power and in the importance of maintaining that power, and they act with real ruthlessness to achieve it. There is nothing surprising about this. Political leaders in all systems have to act in similarly focused ways to succeed. Where leaders in China

manage to accrue political capital, how they recruit certain supportive networks to themselves, and manage to distance themselves from others, is important. Some of the leaders above link
into business networks like Zhang Gaoli, but some, like Zhang
Dejiang, stand almost antagonistic to them. Some accrue powerful
local support for their central careers, as Xi Jinping did in his long
career in Fujian, but others have been remarkably fluid in their
commitments to regions. Some carry heavy family networks with
them, as Xi Jinping does. But others have more difficult family
histories, with figures like Yu Zhengsheng almost tragically marred
by his family's experience of the suicide of some of its members,
victimisation, and steep rises and falls in fortune.

If we want to get behind the masks these men wear, then we
have to try not just to work out what they think, but also to understand the environment better in which they are thinking these
things. In their careers, they have been in contexts and situations
in which they have had to deal with tough questions, often in a
very constricted political space. Can we try to go a bit deeper and
enter into this space that they see things from, with the challenges
and the intellectual resources and frameworks that they have available? Perhaps here we can catch a glance of this concealed inner
universe where we might be better able to understand them, and
in that way appreciate more clearly what they might want to do.
In the final chapter, I will move from the material facts of their
lives and the experiences that have shaped them into their mental
world – the ideology that they stand by and that they have chosen
to articulate.

6

THE CONTRADICTIONS OF MODERN CHINA: IDEOLOGY AND ITS ROLE

The Eighteenth Party Congress was the final outcome of a process in which political, not factional or patronage, issues were decisive. The line-up was as it was because of the prevailing of one political philosophy and approach over another. There were family and patron ingredients, and they did factor – but not decisively. We have to view the Eighteenth Party Congress final leadership line-up as a statement of political purpose, and the result of a long and sometimes ferocious argument about where to steer the country in a critical moment in its development. The Eighteenth Party Congress Politburo Standing Committee is a statement of political purpose. That, rather than any other framework, will help us understand it.

One of the great ideological declarations in the Maoist period was the 1957 speech to the Eleventh Plenum of the Supreme State Conference, 'On the correct handling of contradictions among the people'. Mao stated in that speech:

> Never before has our country been as united as it is today. The victories of the bourgeois-democratic revolution and of the socialist revolution and our achievements in social-ist construction have rapidly changed the face of the old China. A still brighter future lies ahead for our motherland. The days of national disunity and chaos which the people

detested are gone, never to return. Led by the working class and the Communist Party, our 600 million people, united as one, are engaged in the great task of building socialism. The unification of our country, the unity of our people and the unity of our various nationalities – these are the basic guarantees for the sure triumph of our cause.

But such optimism was tempered by a caveat:

However, this does not mean that contradictions no longer exist in our society. To imagine that none exist is a naive idea which is at variance with objective reality. We are confronted with two types of social contradictions – those between ourselves and the enemy and those among the people. The two are totally different in nature.[1]

The handling of these contradictions dominated the final two decades of Maoist rule, and led to the vast tumult of the CR in particular, in which classes, tribes and groups were set against each other in ways that produced violent, divisive outcomes, leaving a memory that is powerful to this day amongst the leaders written about in this book.

Apprehension in China about the ability to control the fissures and contradictions in society and the struggle between different classes and groups may be spoken about in more subtle ways than it was under Mao, but the issue has never gone away and haunts the political vocabularies of all post-Mao leaders. The parameters of this internal debate about how to control contradictions are neatly mapped out in statements by two figures from the elite leadership of the Party between 2002 and 2012, Wu Bangguo and Wen Jiabao. Between them they occupy the relative extremes of Party belief, behaviour and thinking over the era of explosive growth and rising political challenge and confusion in the first decades of the twenty-first century. Wu Bangguo, second-ranking member of the Sixteenth and Seventeenth Party Congress Politburo Standing Committees, was an apparatchik from Shanghai, who, as chair of the NPC, became the high priest of hardline conservatism. On 10 March 2011, Wu made a simple declaration at the NPC annual meeting, setting out the Five Noes: No multi-party system; No liberalisation of thinking; No tripartite division of responsibilities between the Party, the state and the courts; No federalism for China; and No privatisation.[2]

For Wen Jiabao, who had become the spokesperson for the liberal wing of the leadership, there were a similar number of options, which stood in stark contrast to Wu's. These were stated in the World Economic Forum in Dalian in September of the same year, and were presented as five areas where deeper reform and opening up were necessary: firstly, building rule of law, changing absolute power and the concentration of power, and reforming the Party and State leadership system; secondly, promoting social fairness and justice; thirdly, maintaining judicial impartiality and independence; fourthly, safeguarding the people's democratic rights, including the right to vote, to information, supervision and participation; and fifthly, combatting corruption.[3]

The statements of Wen Jiabao and Wu Bangguo map out the extremes of the political terrain in contemporary China. For Wu and the many like him, there is a commitment to the primacy of centralised direction and the role of the State as the key source of economic strategic wisdom, and, through its direction by the Party, the delivery of modernity. With Wen, one has engagement with issues of structural reform in which the market is deepened, the boundaries of the State contested, and the energies of private entrepreneurs, non-State actors and others coopted to the project of building a 'strong, rich nation'.

The Politburo as it exists in 2013 is an alliance of leaders of different networks, an assembly of figures that bring different constituencies in the vast modern polity of China into a coalition that has to deliver growth, unity and stability. But it is also an expression of a political vision – the outcome of debates and negotiations through the Party, finalised by elite leadership diktat, which have been prompted as much by ideological commitments as by personal allegiances, and have focused on addressing the fundamental contradictions outlined above. There are two narratives we need to track in this leadership. The first, which has been looked at before in this book, is the narrative of networks and links between figures and groups, tribes, families. Describing this has necessitated looking at the life paths, the commitments, the debts accrued and favours given to and by specific elite figures as they came into greater power. The evidence is the names, the groupings, the stories that each of these leader's lives shows a connection to. But the second narrative is harder to trace, and belongs more to the realm of political purpose, of creating common commitments, aspirations and aims across a successful elite, one that now has guidance of the Party as it pursues what Hu Jintao described as its 'historic mission'.

In order to understand this political purpose, we have to look hard at the way these leaders say they see the world – what is their view of the world around them, and how do they define their key challenges, their main objectives and the outcomes they are driving towards? What sort of language do they use to mobilise people in the broader society for the political purpose they are aiming for? The issue of how they define their problems and challenges perhaps gives the most insight into all the other questions, because the ways in which problems are framed and addressed gives a clue to how they are regarded as being soluble and the sort of outcomes that are being aimed for through this process.

There is at least one thing they do share: a common context within which they speak. This is the acceptance of dialectic that has been embedded in elite Chinese political discourse since the era of Mao. Like Mao, they see a world that is split between alternatives, one where things are 'either–or'; where there are enemies and friends, good and bad; and where the choices they make are between stability or chaos, wealth or poverty, development or backwardness. In this sense, the fifth-generation leadership is still wrestling with a world of contradictoriness in the way that Mao enunciated, despite the almost wholesale changes in society since 1978. Within these polarities modern Chinese leaders try to create a workable policy framework. At the same time, they also attempt to construct an intellectual foundation underpinning these policy positions, something that can be presented as consistent with the previous ones the Party has taken but also flexible enough to confront emerging and new challenges. This has been a project on which many in the Party have expended enormous amounts of energy.

Some members of the Eighteenth Party Congress Standing Committee have written extensively over the past decade contributing to this effort, and in the case of Li Keqiang and Xi Jinping, they have produced doctoral theses, sustained works of intellectual enquiry that at least help us to see from what position they started to look at their key challenges and the kinds of conceptual frameworks that helped in understanding these. But also, in the Party theoretical magazine *Qiushi* (*Seeking Truth*) there have been essays over the last decade by every member of the current Standing Committee. Some are reprints of their speeches at important occasions, some work reports at high-level conferences, but all of them have outlined at least something of the way they see and how they speak about the world. Even in this controlled and harmonised language, there is the chance to see different approaches by each leader, and trace some elements of consensus and some of discord. In this chapter, therefore, I will use some of the essays written by leaders over the last decade in *Qiushi* ('Seeking Truth', the main CPC theoretical magazine), along with Li and Xi's Ph.Ds, to give some idea of the ideological formations that are visible in this new leadership. In particular, I will concentrate on the things that Xi Jinping has written about moral leadership and the Party, the need to conquer 'new spaces for growth' that Li Keqiang has set out, and the ideas that Liu Yunshan has addressed about ideological discipline in a world being turned upside down by social media.

XI JINPING ON THE MORAL AND INTELLECTUAL LEADERSHIP OF THE COMMUNIST PARTY

Contemporary China is a world in which, as the Chinese writer Yu Hua described it, anything can be said about anyone and it will go unchallenged – unless you step into the final area of taboo, that of the elite Party leadership. But as the *New York Times* showed in late 2012 in its treatment of Wen Jiabao and his family wealth, even this area is now under attack.

In a society undergoing such rapid and extensive change, it is no surprise that the traditional vision the Party presents of itself as the entity that delivers unity and modernity is under threat as never before. The Party's moral mandate to rule is under unprecedented challenge from all fronts. Social media subject Party leaders and representatives to what is termed 'public lynching', where they are exposed and humiliated in online postings, with tension between officials and the people growing more critical. Not just its current administrative competence is under the microscope, however, but also its conduct in the past, with debate starting around issues about the ways in which it rose to power; how it exercised power from 1949 onwards; and new evidence presented about the great famines, the CR and the 1989 Tiananmen Square massacre that undermines the orthodox Party explanations for these events. All of these discussions and questions can, and often are, interpreted by Party leaders as threats to its legitimacy. But the Party's control of information and its ability to exercise control have eroded, and too often in recent years it has simply closed down discussion and argument by savage violence. This more than anything undercuts its desire to preserve a morally lofty role in society and an imperious tone towards Chinese people.

Xi Jinping, when he became Party secretary in November 2012, explicitly referred to the issue of corruption because this problem in particular is seen as the most dangerous threat to the Party's moral standing and right to rule unopposed. But corruption was not a new theme for Xi, or something he has only recently started mentioning. It is an issue that he has spoken about many times in his career. In some ways, it has almost become a dominant and identifying theme of his discourse. In 2005, he issued a piece in *Qiushi* called 'Leading cadres at provincial level shall take the lead in keeping Party members' progressiveness'. In this piece he sets out a number of moral demands on cadres, in order to set a better example:

(1) Provincial leaders are high-level leaders of the Party, and they have to preserve their being in the vanguard of society by setting an example.

(2) High cadres need to conduct themselves well. They cannot just be motivated by money, power or 'airs and graces' (more accurately, acquiring mistresses and a luxurious life style). They have to be self-critical, and have a sense of the importance of their social role. In this way they can build trust within society, and reinforce the fabric of society and 'decent' social bonds.

(3) Leaders need to improve their administrative ability. The Party is 'an administrative Party', guiding China into the era in which it is due to become 'a middle-income society'. People's expectations towards governance increase daily. The Party needs to be service-orientated. It needs to be 'scientifically, democratically and legally' administrative.

(4) Leaders need to take the lead in promoting and investing in educational activities.[4]

Xi explicitly refers in this speech to the cancer of corruption. In a later speech on 1 March 2010 to the Party School where he was president, Xi referred to the fact that 'more and more means of drawing cadres into corruption have appeared in society'. 'Power,' he stated, 'is a responsibility'. The greater the power, the greater the responsibility. Power is 'a double-edged sword'.[5] In the era of greater enrichment and of greater temptation, how, therefore, do cadres remain faithful to the founding ideals of the Party? How do they remain good cadres, even as the market overwhelms the world around them, and social media lap at their feet exposing and challenging, and complicating? Speaking at the Party School two years earlier on 1 March 2008, Xi had stated that the Party needed theory, and that without theory it would not succeed. The key theory was 'a scientific viewpoint'. Lauding Marx and Engels, he stated that 'Their theories were not doctrines, but a compass for action and administration.' But more critically, the Communist Party of China had made this blueprint for action imported from the West something applicable to the national conditions in China. The CPC 'will always act according to national conditions'.[6] The key objective of Party leaders, therefore, is to work for the national mission of building a rich, strong country – one that will see productivity increased, the structure of society improved, a Socialist market economy built and Socialist democracy delivered. Clean, not corrupt, officials are the only ones qualified to take the lead in delivering this vision.

For the modern Party in this context, the key questions that Xi outlines are simple ones: 'What is Socialism?', 'How do you build Socialism?', 'What kind of Party should be built?', and 'What kind of development?' along with 'How do you develop?' The question of what sort of Party is wanted is the key one. The Party has to regulate itself, it has to have a sense of moral mission, and of suitability within the hearts of its agents and servants, the cadres that have the most responsibility in running and guiding it. It has to regulate itself and discipline its actions. The vision of development it has must be people-centred, sustainable and just. It has to reacquire the right to use the key terms of moral purpose and worthiness, a right eroded as China has grown rich by the poor behaviour of some officials who fail to look beyond themselves. The narrative of Party history articulated in the canonical Party texts culminating in the 1981 resolution show a path of political development, from idealism to implementation, leading to the grand project, of which Mao is presented as the chief architect, of a unified, dignified country with its autonomy restored to it – master of its own house. Now that the primary stage of Socialism has been created, the key challenge is to improve legality, regulation, governance, modernise the instruments of power and the means by which people participate in this power. The Party has the responsibility to 'construct intellectual theory', and to undertake a reform process that will lead to the building of democracy, fairness, competition and choice. 'Only with a creative country will we become a splendid, rich and strong one.' For this, the Party has an exemplary role: it has to create public trust, and build up social equity.

Xi promoted the concept of the moral responsibility of cadres in a highly personal way quite distinct from Hu Jintao, who avoided personal register in his speeches and talks throughout his time in power. In 2009, Xi visited a place in Lankao celebrating the life of a model worker, Jiao Yulu, who died in 1964. Lauding Jiao's selflessness, Xi appealed to Jiao's spirit of 'not wanting to be a cadre, but to serve'.[7] In Jiao's view of the world, in his view of life, in his values, he represented the best of what a cadre should be – not thinking of private profit but only of public gain. Jiao might not be Lei Feng, the most famous model worker, but he belongs to these starkly worthy figures. The problem, however, is that despite Xi's personal investment in this story and the ways in which he draws it to wider public attention, there are real challenges about what sort of traction this kind of fable might have in a society so radically developing, changing and full of contestation. Do these strategies of attempted moral reinforcement through embodiment in such pure figures drawn from another age and time and seemingly so remote have any real credibility now? The fundamental question that Xi asks, in many of his speeches at the Party School and in pieces from *Qiushi* over the previous decade, is a nostalgic one: how the Party can act not just to assist in society's getting richer, but to maintain the good order of its own key leadership and its original moral function in society, something that he evidently believes was present at its origins. Does the body of theoretical writings of the 'saints and martyrs' of this struggle, people like Mao and Liu Shaoqi, have any real intellectual relevance and power in the twenty-first century?

There are far more vexed questions. The Party has always been linked to power, to the preservation of its powers – even using violence, as it did in 1989, to protect this. Without power, what is the Party? And yet the confines, and meanings, of power in a world atomised after the dawn of social media are fluid, liquid, constantly changing. The Party has an old-fashioned view of power, as something hierarchical, asserted, imposed – not as something that is legitimised, negotiated, transformed and changed as it operates. Xi's formulations against corruption, for instance, strike at this issue of intention and purpose. Why does the Party leadership want to see corruption shrink and disappear? Because they have a fundamental view of human morality, of what is right and wrong? Do they base this on spiritual or religious values, on some kind of ethical principle? Corruption figures in Xi's talks not as a violation of any transcendent moral imperatives but as a factor producing inefficiency, an impediment to further material growth and development. So it is, for this very functional reason, bad. The need to reduce corruption is almost a transactional one. It is done to get trust from society so the whole machine of creating more wealth and GDP can function well again. Officials are corrupt not through any fault of the Party, but because they have not adequately internalised its rules and its values. The Party itself remains faultless; it is the weakness of some of its members that causes problems. No fundamental tenets of Party function and ideology are named as in need of reform in what Xi says. Instead, mistakes are outsourced to those who fail to live up to their responsibilities as good Party leaders and members.

The contradiction here is that the Party has embraced a process of economic diversification and marketisation that has brought with it a concomitant transformation of almost every aspect of social and intellectual life in China while still attempting to preserve the Party's own uncontested position and dominance. Theoretically, the means of doing this are through the exemplary moral behaviour of its cadres, and its own intellectual leadership. But these are under profound threat from the very forces of entrepreneurial energy and opening up of economic opportunities that its policies after 1978 have unleashed. A Party that rose to power as a force for moral leadership against corruption and inequality is now being overwhelmed by those very problems it strove to defeat, its elites drowning in temptation because they are holding in their hands the influence and power that are the most effective means of freeing up access to this vast world of wealth. Xi can deploy exhortations insisting on self-denial and restraint, but in what ways are these persuasive and do they carry any sort of prescriptive weight? The ambition to motivate and mobilise the broad mass of people through appealing to modes of good and right behaviour that are their own reward is almost impossibly difficult when one thinks of how recent the memory of poverty and deprivation in society in China is. The attempt, therefore, to create a compelling narrative that justifies restraint and sells the message of being a good, incorrupt official of the Party delivering its mission of modernity is an ongoing one. It may even be impossible. For this reason it lies at the very heart of the Party's challenge to maintain stability and power in the twenty-first century, and this is utterly central to Xi's world view and ideological interests.

LI KEQIANG: THE URBAN CHALLENGE

Li Keqiang's doctoral thesis, produced at Beijing University in the 1990s, concerned the transformation of the rural economy in China to a semi-urban one, largely focusing on Town and Village

Enterprises and the extraordinary impact they had in the 1980s, allowing surplus labour freed up by increased efficiency and productivity in the agriculture sector to be poured into diverse areas of economic activity. Town and Village Enterprises – TVEs, as they came to be called – were no more than a framework within which a host of interesting new semi-industrial activity happened. In his thesis Li linked industrialisation to urbanisation, and found in the operations of the TVEs the construction of the first phase for rural economies in becoming more geared to urban-type industrialisation and production: 'The reality of modernisation in fact is to see traditional agricultural society change to industrial society.'[8] Industrialisation happens at the sacrifice of agriculture. In an outline of his thesis, Li quotes statistics showing that in 1952, agricultural output made up 56.9 per cent of GDP, and industrial output 43.1 per cent. By 1978, this had changed to 24.8 per cent for agriculture and 75.2 per cent for industry. It is often forgotten, therefore, that the challenge in 1978 was not to create an industrialised nation. China had already started to do that. The real issue was to improve the quality of this industrial productivity.[9] In terms of population, too, there were radical changes over this era. In 1949, on the eve of the Communists coming to power, 89.4 per cent of people lived in the rural areas and 10.6 in towns and cities. By 1978, this had changed slightly to 17.9 per cent in towns and cities, and 82.1 per cent in villages. Li wrote in his thesis of the multiple challenges of managing a phased transition from a rural to a semi-industrial and then a fully industrial economy, and the problems this posed in terms of improving productivity, changing wage structures, the pressure on capital and how it is deployed more efficiently, and the ways in which surplus labour can be used as a major economic asset. 'The main challenge for China's transition,' Li wrote, 'is the modernisation of 80 per cent of its population that still lives in the rural areas'.[10]

Almost two decades later, and no longer as a promising middle-ranking official from the CYL in training at the Central

Party School, Li was directly engaging with a China that, according to the census of 2010, had as many people now in the cities and towns as in the rural areas. This was indeed a massive historic transition. The challenges of how to manage the migration to an industrial, urban economy had already been faced. Now China was on its way to middle-income status, a benchmark set early on in Hu Jintao's period in power. For Li, the main challenge from his time as premier after 2007 was therefore how to achieve 'fast, sustainable growth'. In a report made to the CPPCC on 1 August 2009, Li reflected on the ways of trying to achieve this 'fast, sustainable' growth rate, and the reasons behind why it was such an important priority. One issue had been external, and one internal. The external was simply the impact of the collapse of markets and growth in the developed world after the 2007–8 economic crisis. The internal issue was a series of imbalances and structural problems. Whereas we can therefore see Xi Jinping talking about more broadly abstract, almost philosophical issues, for Li the main priorities were about structures, outputs and specific economic policies. 'The ways in which our economy is picking up are still not stable, nor firm, nor equal,' Li stated, setting out the ways in which the country now needed to face down the negative effects of the global crisis. This included a menu of incentives, from lowering taxes, to allowing better and more efficient market redistribution of investment, support for education, and improving people's livelihood by doing something about corruption. China had a good source for future growth and development, Li stated in this speech, and that was simply within itself, in its huge population, and in the rising living standards they were enjoying now giving momentum for further reform. For 30 years from 1978, he said, the material basis of life had risen, and proved that with stability China could become an urbanised, industrialised country. The issue of the last two decades was a reliance on US and EU consumption in particular, where there had been a vast export market for China's goods. But the 2008 crisis had shown this was a feeble and unreliable basis to build on for long term growth. New sources of growth would now need to be as much from within China, from what Li terms the 'empty spaces' ('fazhan kongjian') that can be developed. With government leadership, the country could now move more into developing these empty spaces.[11] Such spaces included the service sector, new industries, creative industries that China was only just starting to work on, environmental industries, and greater integration between the welfare sector and the economy. Dealing with unemployment and underemployment, and healthcare, were amongst the most important priorities here.

The contradictions in the economy were spelt out in another speech, delivered on 1 June 2010 to provincial and national leaders.[12] Recognising that China needed to speed its growth rate after the impact of collapse of exports in 2009 due to the ongoing problems in developed markets, Li set out a series of issues. China's economic development, he admitted, had come at a high price. It had been unsustainable, taking a terrible toll on the environment, and producing much inequality. There had been overreliance on external markets for growth. In China, the service sector was 42 per cent of GDP. But in developed countries this was 72.5 per cent, and in middle-income countries 53 per cent. Even in other developing countries service sector took up 46 per cent of GDP. China had a structural anomaly here. The main impediments to the delivery of better-quality growth that Li outlined in this speech were related to this sort of structural imbalance. China was overreliant for growth upon external markets; had overlarge income differences, which were partly geographical and partly social; a low service sector; high capital investment levels; and low consumption. All of these had to be addressed if the country was to achieve the main objective – 'relatively fast, sustainable growth'.

Domestic consumption could only be restructured by doing something about demand, and making a fast-urbanising population into a better source of demand: 'Creating internal demand is one of the main routes to sustainable fast growth.' Li states: 'in big countries, internal demand is a key part of GDP growth. In the US and India, it accounts for 92 and 88 per cent of GDP growth. In China it is 72.8 per cent, the lowest of all major countries.'[13] Government alone could not be the source of demand and economic stimulation. Chinese people needed to be key players in this, but in order to do so the government needed to give greater regularity, more predictability, and do more to create a sense of security and wellbeing in people to let them spend more. Housing was critical here, with security of tenure. It was no longer a case, as it had once been, of the government under the Party's guidance ensuring people were well fed and clothed. Things had moved beyond that. Now people wished to be house owners, and even to have houses that were important investment vehicles for them. In the battle to find more spaces that would then be economically productive and generate more GDP, lifting internal demand and consumption through providing a more stable economic environment was one means. The second was to move to a series of other likely growth providers – development of the service sector, development of life-style industries, of environmental sectors, and of better quality goods and brands – things that were largely available only through import from outside China but that it now needed to make bolder moves in order to have indigenous capacity itself.

Li set out a series of challenges China faced from the pattern of its development over the last four decades that would need to be factored in as it moved to conquer these new spaces for growth. The demographics would be an immense burden, with a country that would age quickly as a result of the one-child policies implemented from the 1970s. Labour supply would peak and then decline. China would start to suffer labour shortages in some areas. It would also have an immense pension deficit to start wrestling with. Industrialisation in developed countries took 200 years, and meant that after the initial phase there was time to deal with the negative outcomes, from environmental degradation and resource depletion to social issues. China had undergone this process in only a few decades. The imperative for quick, sustainable growth, however, could not and would not go away.

On housing, Li spoke at more length when addressing a meeting on 16 April 2011. Here, housing figured as a key practical means of constructing the 'harmonious society' of higher-consuming, more secure stakeholders that Hu Jintao had spent much of the previous decade speaking of. Housing, after all, Li acknowledged, has a commodity value, an economic function, a wellbeing value and a social function. It is something that delivers both as a source of growth through the buying, selling and wealth creation of property, but also as a source of security, ownership and belonging. And beyond and around houses, there was the whole living environment that needed to be harmonised and made desirable too – the urban landscape in which people were buying, investing in and owning property.[14]

Another sector that straddled both economic and social wellbeing, and that figured in the armoury of means to create more secure, more highly active consumers, was the healthcare sector. Healthcare, Li stated on 14 November 2011, was a tool of social development, but also a way of increasing domestic demand. It was a critically important, hi-tech sector that needed to be developed. In 1949, life expectancy in China was 35 years. By 2011, this had risen to 73.5 years. For China now, the major issue was the health of the poor, which still lagged behind that of the better-off. Healthcare delivered double benefits in its development. It raised the service-sector proportion of the economy at the same time as it built the infrastructure of a more enfranchised population. Compared to 16 per cent of domestic GDP in the US, Li said, quoting a World Bank statistic, China manages only 5 per cent. In developing healthcare, therefore, China not only does something about this service-sector imbalance, but also delivers on the justice agenda in society.[15]

In Li Keqiang's public statements over the last five years, and in his earlier academic work, one can discern a viable framework for guiding China into an era of deeper industrialisation and greater modernisation, and also a roadmap that addresses its internal structural imbalances by trying to find fresh sources in the economy that lead to sustainable growth rather than being overreliant on the outward environment. In this context, the main objective is to supply a pragmatic framework for a country that will have a stronger services sector, consumption patterns more like those in similar economies, healthcare and other welfare sectors that are parts of the economy, and an integrated strategy through these to deliver on a programme that is about more than just producing raw GDP. This had been articulated from early in the Hu and Wen period, with sociopolitical objectives being sketched out that went beyond simply achieving high levels of growth. However, there seemed little political consensus or will to try to move forward with these. Town elections were frozen, legal reforms were stopped, and the sorts of stagnation occurred that are mentioned in the assessment of the Hu and Wen period given above. Perhaps in Li's comments we can start to envision a strategy to address these issues. Even so, in terms of detailed implementation there is little that Li gives away. At most it is a framework, a clear statement of the problems, and on the whole an analysis of the key problems that most in China would accept. But going from here into the sorts of tactical and strategic choices one needs to make to have any progress on remedying these imbalances remains unclear.

LIU YUNSHAN AND THE SPIRITUAL CIVILISATION MISSION

Of all the members of the current Standing Committee, Liu Yunshan has written the most. This is perhaps unsurprising. He is, after all, a journalist, and for much of the last decade he has had responsibility for the key ideology and propaganda portfolio. If anyone can be called contemporary China's chief ideologue, therefore, Liu can. Throughout his work from 2002, Liu has stressed the need for unified thought. He has done this while talking of a Chinese renaissance, and supporting the ideas of a new era in Chinese development. On 13 August 2009, Liu lauded the great achievements of the Hu era – development, stability, unity, progress and general improvement in living standards. He, more than any other of his colleagues on the Eighteenth Congress Politburo Standing Committee, unpacked the thinking behind the concept of 'scientific development'. He has talked of the achievements of the Party in creating a material basis for developing this 'harmonious society', but also of the function of morality and self regulation and law, and the development of 'Chinese Socialist people'. 'For whether or not a country is able to have long-term stability and peace, that depends in the main part on members of that society and the moral quality of their thinking.'[16]

In meetings of propaganda officials over the last decade, Liu has mapped out the ways in which the Party elite see unified thinking being achieved, and the key elements that they believe such thinking needs to contain. For Liu, propaganda 'creates unity of purpose'. 'Thought work is important,' he also stated in 2005. He even believes that 'propaganda is a kind of science'. But there is also a strong awareness in his speeches of the immense challenges that have been brought by the diversification in Chinese society over the last two decades because of the impact of growth, modernisation and social media. The problem is put clearly enough in 2005: 'Many cadres, and particularly young ones, are not willing to watch our news reports, nor to read out theoretical articles, nor listen to our speeches.'[17] Exposure to the dry, theoretical content and tone of, in particular, a speaker like Hu Jintao helps to explain this. And while Liu knows there is a need to have propaganda with a more personal, approachable tone, and to undertake better political messaging in China, just as in the case of Li Keqiang's prognosis of structural economic issues being clear in their statement of the problems but light on solutions, the same can be said of Liu on Party language and thought work.

Liu does allude in the same 2005 speech to the possibilities offered by technology, and the ways in which this can create the sort of 'empty spaces for growth' in the thought sphere that Li had spoken of in the economic. In November 2006, Liu had stated the need for a new culture, and continued this a year later by referring to the 'splendid culture' China was now engaged in building during the era in which it was growing rich. But his discourse in these sorts of discussions confusingly merges the economic and cultural. The phrase in a speech on the theme of constructing 'spiritual civilisation' he used on 7 September 2007 was 'cultural productivity'. This comes close to sounding as though it is equating culture to something akin to industrial output. Liu does cede that there are important issues about creating new standards, and a need for more cultural diversity, but the sense that culture is merely a side product, an accompaniment to aiding material development, never disappears.[18]

It wasn't just internal developments within the population, and their experience of communication, the media and culture that represented a challenge. In 2008, with the Tibet uprising, the Wenchuan earthquake and the Olympics, the government propaganda organs faced a whole series of news management issues. In a piece issued in June 2008 reflecting on the earthquake news management effort, Liu speaks of the superiority of Chinese Socialism, and the ways in which it is able to respond to disasters and learn lessons from them. While the openness with which China allowed journalists to operate in Sichuan was widely praised after the devastating earthquake happened, less glorious was the way in which it dealt with a scandal over poorly built schools and houses collapsing with the shock while government buildings were unaffected. Liu remains silent on this controversy.

Soft power is something that was on Liu's mind throughout this period. He conveyed the idea that with economic growth, almost as though according to some scientific formula, the country had to have, and indeed merited, international influence. 'Economic and social development have given China an obvious international influence and status and improvement, and this has won for us international and wide understanding and support.'[19] It is this sort of thing that is eroded by the behaviour of corrupt officials, who undermine this new, confident face that China can present to the world. The stability and unity that the Party gives the country offers for Liu the best possible guarantee that the Chinese can deal with crisis. Cadres figure as at the vanguard of this crisis management, improving Western attitudes towards the country, which in turn gives officials enhanced status and dignity both outside and inside China. This slightly unsettling idea that crisis well managed is good publicity is married to another notion – that of a nationalistic mission, in which China preserves its face by being able to cope with crisis and show the opponents outside who believe in a China threat that the country is in fact a good and responsible one, guided by worthy intentions. Why should the Party, finally, not be able to deal with crisis, Liu asks. It was born in an environment full of crises and hardship. It is precisely this that it should be good at.

Liu follows the mantra Li had used of 'sustainable, fast growth'. For Liu, in the ideological and propaganda sphere, the mission is to create a 'rich, strong, cultured, harmonious and modern society'.[20] In this process, creating a master narrative that copes with transformation, reform and transition while maintaining commitment to the statement of a coherent, overarching mission is important, particularly in thought work. The great binary themes of the narrative of Chinese history after 1949 are from class struggle as the key task of the Party under Mao to making economy the key after 1978, from the planned economy from 1949 to embracing the market economy after 1978, from feudalism prior to 1949 to openness after 1978, and from meeting the basic needs of people in terms of clothing and food in the first decades of Chinese Socialism to delivering medium-level development – the sort of goods that Li Keqiang refers to.[21] With so much transformation and experience of change, much of it fast and disruptive, there will be an intense need to have thought work, propaganda work, ideological management, management of public messages, and explanations for the causes of the changes and the rationale behind them. Hu Jintao talked from 2007 onwards of an 'historic mission' for the Party and the PLA of making China a 'rich, strong country'. The changes this had brought almost meant an accompanying mental change, a revolution in the way people viewed their own experiences as Chinese, and how they saw their part in this great transformation. Propaganda work therefore had a critical function in this context of delivering a harmonising and positive narrative, an explanatory framework, for the new condition that people were moving into. Among the public, there was need for 'thought, for morality, for culture and discipline'. Economic developments had led to bewildering social developments, to complexity, and social tensions and contention. There were signs about this across society. People's expectations were becoming higher and higher. Just as there had been a 'great liberation of productivity' in the economy since 1978, so now there was an accompanying 'great liberation of cultural production'.[22] Thought work needs to operate in this area. For the urban and rural divide, too, there was work to do in the propaganda sphere, because the mantra from 2007 was to have a 'spiritual-civilised countryside' – a place where the large inequalities that had appeared could be addressed through better social welfare, better education and the lifting of agricultural taxes.

The financial and social costs of delivering this harmonious, unified thinking and vision, internally and externally, of a spiritual civilisation with Chinese Socialist characteristics were becoming steep. The internet was increasingly a vast battleground between different opinion groups, with censors mandated by various parts of the security State having to play endless technical and vocabulary games to sweep aside specific taboo terms. Signs of cynical disengagement from the very terms of mobilisation that Liu was using, such as 'harmonious society' and 'scientific development', were not hard to find. And the highly circumscribed ways in which he talked of the Party elite's understanding of culture and diversity were indicative of a view that saw the cultural field as linked to practical measures to deliver harmony; to continue contributing to growth; and to do this at the expense sometimes of hearing disruptive, contrasting voices that were either repressed, or drowned out.

CONFRONTING THE GREAT CHALLENGES

From their different standpoints, the leadership have to confront the fundamental structural challenges of a China that has grown fast, but whose growth from now on will be harder won, and will need to become far more sustainable. This is in the face of a fractious, complex, often very unequal society – one in which there are often dramatically extensive spectrums of opinion, in which notions of authority are being contested in multiple ways, some of them virtual, some very much physical. In a society undergoing such a dramatic transition, the categorical statement of what the Party does not want to do and what it does not believe as set out at the start of this chapter by Wu Bangguo may not be fit for purpose. The Party may well do whatever is necessary, and make whatever compromises it has to, jettisoning whatever values and ideas it once held dear, if this means it has a better chance of remaining in power.

The World Bank and Development Research Centre of the State Council jointly issued a report in 2012, *China 2030: Building a Modern, Harmonious and Creative Society*, setting out six key reform areas – areas that were bitterly attacked by the leftist economists mentioned in Chapter 1. This report had the backing of both Wen Jiabao and Li Keqiang. In that sense it can be seen as a statement of macro-economic and political intent. The key areas were:

(1) implementing structural reforms to strengthen the foundation for a market economy;

(2) accelerating the pace of innovation and creating an open innovation system;

(3) seizing the opportunity to go green;

(4)   expanding opportunities and promoting social security for all;

(5)   strengthening the fiscal system;

(6)   seeking mutually beneficial relations with the world.[23]

If these are the broadest policy objectives, then there are questions of how they are phased, the detail of their implementation, the vision for their outcome and finally the critical issue of how the public is mobilised by the Party to work towards them. This is why the issue of the Party and its moral authority in society that Xi alludes to does matter – it needs to have legitimacy and the status in society to be able to push people in the direction outlined above. The option of a charismatic leadership along the lines of Mao Zedong, instilling people with fervour, mobilising them through public mass campaigns, is an unsettling one. Most of the leadership from 2013 have at least some memory of the CR, the apogee of this sort of politics. They are, almost certainly, highly ambiguous about this era, otherwise they would speak more often about it. The cost of social mobilisation in the Maoist style is too high, and has been discredited. How, then, does the Party get people to do what it says if it does not do this, nor take the option of using coercion? There has to be some kind of consent, and the Party has to appeal not just to people's material expectations, but their ideals, aspirations, hopes. That is a far harder task, and one that the discourse of the Hu period never fully attempted.

The indecisive sound of much of what the leaders have said on formal occasions over the last few years, before their final elevation to power, is striking. Much awareness of problems, much understanding of the challenges, but no bold announcement of what direction society really needs to go in. Announcement of safe objectives, like crackdowns on corruption or the need for better-quality growth and unified thinking, but no radical announcement of anything being changed in the political realm – no sense of what or how reform will be achieved here, nor how the participation in decision making and feedback on administration promised by Hu in 2007 will be delivered. Rhetoric about hoping for more legal reform and a greater role for civil society, but not much sense of how or when these changes might happen, or how they might work. There is a sense in their language of a leadership who feel they have space to start to do something, and have fewer constraints than their predecessors, but who also feel that they are at a crossroads where they cannot decide which direction to go in.

The great challenges that the Party faces in its governance as it stands at this crossroads are clear and well known. Growth is important, and will continue to be so. But double-digit growth can no longer continue. The Chinese materially have never been better off. But the signs of a wider discontent and a rising sense of expectations frustrated by the complexity of modern life are appearing. Suicide, depression and mental illness are now becoming part of the landscape of urban and, increasingly, rural life in China. Divorce and instances of people living alone, while low, are rising. The Party can etch out a vision of a rich life, but cannot show through its vision of culture and pride how this will make people happy, nor how its continuing monopoly on power relates to this happiness. It is feared, and admired, but not loved. That means its purchase on people's emotional support is shallow, which in turn creates a sense of insecurity in the Party itself.

The Chinese are now freer than they ever have been. Despite the constraints in daily life, on the whole the vast majority of Chinese live lives where they evade day-to-day State involvement as successfully as their Western counterparts. Like them, many Chinese have a profound dislike of official meddling in their lives, and want the space to live and develop on their own terms. But they live in a polity haunted by the memory of instability and insecurity – a memory that is powerful even though over time it will weaken – of a China bullied, brought to its knees by foreign exploitation and lacking a profound sense of its own identity before 1949, and, more uncomfortably, a country that all too often fell apart in unpleasant campaigns where members of society were pitched against each other during the Maoist era. This leadership remember much of that era from the late 1960s, and for them, while the obsession with stability under Hu and Wen may well lessen, because of this memory it will not go away. The negotiation between stability and freedom will be a long, hard one, and nothing that any of the fifth-generation leaders have said shows that they wish to challenge the parameters of this desire for stability first with freedom afterwards, and only when it does not affect stability.

Throughout this book, we have looked at the relationship between the State and the Party. This is one of the biggest polarities in contemporary China. The Party maintains its privileged status in society, operating almost as a State within a State, a culture within a culture, with its own entry rules, traditions, geography and internal language. It allows nice rhetoric through figures like Wen Jiabao concerning the need to build the rule of law, and to increase regulations and stable rules in society – and yet, at crucial moments, the Party has wished, and looks set to continue wishing, to maintain its freedom to act by fiat and without being accountable or constrained. At what point will this be regarded as an impediment that has to be reined in? At what point will the need for rule of law and regulation mean the Party has to transform and define itself more precisely, and spell out constitutionally where the realms of the Party and the State lie?

For all the historic commitment to equality, China's current inequality is stark, and measurable. But there are dramatic variations even amongst elites, sub-elites, different social and class groups, tribes and families, ethnic and interest groups. This is a society of amazing diversity, despite the outward rhetoric of unity and a cohesive cultural identity. Fundamentally, however, it is a country that is under the direction of a small, and often besieged, super elite – the nearly 3,000 at minister level and above mentioned earlier. These people have huge power formation, and are at the heart of a world of networks and inducements, some of which have been described in this book. For them, the tensions with 'the people' or the masses increase, with the internet and social media in China offering a kind of map of this conflict: flesh searches unleashed on officials; different figures exposed; and then clampdowns, censorship and a range of measures used to try to protect the super elite and rein this in. The cynicism with which the very super elite try to deploy the sorts of moral vocabularies used by Xi Jinping is often exposed too, and the ways in which they frequently seem to be almost fleeing public exposure and contact within their own country is striking. Contradictions between the elite and the masses in Chinese society today are a major source of tension. In this context, can this elite achieve the final balancing act of preserving its privileged position in society, while at the same time allowing the networks around it to be enriched; will it have the legitimacy and moral standing in the future to convince society to make sacrifices when a 'crossroads' moment comes and important strategic decisions about the country's development need to be made? Will it be able to communicate in a coherent way with a society that is more fractious, more expectant, more demanding and more diffuse? These are essentially the immense challenges these leaders face as they take China into the second decade of the twenty-first century, on a country's journey towards middle-income status, and the pursuit of a 'dream' that will only be fulfilled if they can find answers to these problems.

CONCLUSION

This book has looked at the networks that we find around the new leadership in China who came into power at the Eighteenth Party Congress in 2012. It has been an attempt to map and understand a little more the dynamism of these networks, and both the political as well as the personal meaning that they carry.

Within the marketplace of power in contemporary China, where power is akin to a force or kind of energy acting on the world at the very same time as it is being shaped and directed by that same world, it is possible to draw out with the new leaders a list of influences on this power that help to give it traction and make it effective. Part of the usefulness of this exercise is to understand the transactional influence of certain factors – the ways in which they supplement, assist and promote power interests and networks associated with them. But in all of this, as I have attempted to argue throughout this book, one should never lose sight of the political parameters. China is not a monolithic polity now – the Communist Party is more like a coalition of interests, broad and extensive, rather than a narrowly defined band of elites who are able to act with complete freedom. In this environment there is competition for influence, and the promotion of some interests over others, accompanied by a whole set of different strategies by which to gain competitive advantage in this endeavour. Just as the economic terrain in China has been deeply marketised since 1978, so too has the geography of influence and politics.

Despite this highly practical side of power promotion, I have stressed through this book that one must also never lose sight of the more abstract political objectives. Figures in China today want power for material rewards and status, but also to defend certain historic and current principles and belief systems. In this sense, abstract politics, politics about ideological issues like the role of the State or the free market matter in contemporary China – matter despite the strenuous efforts of some of the elite to impose a highly standardised language of consensus and harmony. Under the surface of this bland language there are still stark disagreements among different groups in society about the choices that China needs to make in the short-to-long-term future, the key challenges it faces and how these are best articulated, and above all the optimal framework within which to see both the interpretation of these challenges, and how to face them.

I have used the seven members of the Eighteenth Party Congress Standing Committee as a cross-section of China's political super elite, a foundation upon which one can try to build up a deeper awareness of the operations of networks within Chinese society more broadly. Of course, Chinese society is immensely diverse – socially, economically, ethnically. Part of the problem of the current leadership is that in terms of age, gender and ethnicity it is superficially very narrow. But even within this group, as I have attempted to show, there are differences: different paths that people have taken to reach where they are, different world views, different ideological underpinnings – and most important of all, different views of power and of the kinds of debts and obligations that these super-elite figures are under. They are the visible tip of the gargantuan iceberg of modern Chinese society, and so, while they offer a highly circumscribed 'control group' by which to understand where the country stands and where it might be going, and what the specific configurations of power are, they offer a natural starting point. We can see distilled amongst them the sorts of dynamics, power negotiations, tensions and competition that can generically be found throughout the rest of society. This makes them worth understanding more deeply for their importance, not

just to the rest of the world as China becomes an increasingly significant global actor, but to the composition of influence and the
energies of power within China itself.

In terms of the sorts of fields of influence one sees in this super
elite, the most efficient approach is simply to break these down
into discrete areas. Using these, one can come up with a mode of
evaluation. Whoever is able to recruit the energies of these areas of
influence the most is best placed to be a winner in the whole process of becoming a leader.

Family matters, of course. In a society structured along the lines
Fei Xiaotong outlined in 1947, the most inelastic of the elastic
links binding people together are family ones. They are visible,
hard to walk away from, and carry important traditional obligations and levels of duty. The founding fathers of the Communist
Party over nine decades before came from a tight-knit community.
Many were from specific geographic locations in China. Of the
earliest membership – fewer than 60 in 1921 – more than half were
from Hunan province.[1] We cannot overinterpret the depth of these
links, and of course the CPC underwent many changes in the decades before it came to power. Even so, the trust and sense of common purpose and identity forged in the early struggles of the Party
among a relatively small revolutionary elite were something that
their children and heirs, once they came to power, stood to inherit.
Talk of a tightly definable princeling faction over the last few years
has become too neat. The princelings are not a cohesive grouping,
as the different fates of Bo Xilai and Xi Jinping make clear. Precise
definitions of what makes a princeling are also frustratingly elusive.
But tribal alliances based on family links are an important factor.
In the run-up to November 2012, there was much evidence of
family meetings, and of the immense input that family groupings
had, leveraging their links to former elite leaders. Even so, some
were dismayed at the path the Party was taking, and some more
conciliatory. One saw within these family groupings much contestation, and something like a fight for the idea of the soul of the

Party, linked to its historic mission and traditions. Family links can
be useful in the promotion of a political career. But alone, they are
more neutral and perhaps more liquid as a source of influence than
might have been thought. Family links give a natural network that
can be used well – but alone have little true influence, and at times
might be an impediment, as inherited elite links in any society are.
It is a question of the person using them.

Provincial links are critically important. It is true that on the whole
the path to Beijing lies through the provinces. Of the seven figures I
have looked at in detail in this book, all had provincial careers, though
of varying depth. Wang Qishan's was the most brief, Xi Jinping and
Zhang Dejiang's extensive and broad. There are questions of the best
provinces to give one leverage, and the experiences one had there to
give greater career progression. For some, like Zhang Gaoli, their
provincial achievements were in terms of GDP growth. Others, like
Zhang Dejiang and Li Keqiang, proved themselves as crisis managers.
Elite politics in China is now very competitive. There are sophisticated
and complex means of assessment. In this leadership, Liu Yunshan
proves a politician can be elevated with no provincial senior leadership
experience at all. Management of provinces gives signs of ability, and
can supply political networks through the Central Committee and
other groups that are useful. But being a successful provincial leader
alone is not enough. Bo Xilai was popular, innovative and successful in
Liaoning and Chongqing. But that didn't help in the end.

Business and money are key, and becoming more important.
There has never been a money-making machine like the CPC. It
has assisted in creation of the world's second largest economy, and
the accrual of over USD 3.5 trillion of foreign reserves. The CPC
has uniquely married a Marxist ideology with ruthless capitalist
productivity. It has pragmatically acknowledged the role of entrepreneurs and enfranchised them within the Party. Building benign
business links is critically important, and is often done through
provincial careers. Zhang Gaoli leveraged business links acquired
in Fujian and Shenzhen to get major investments into Shandong

and Tianjin. Zheng Dejiang did not let a North Korean training in economics stand in the way of allowing private-sector business to continue to thrive in Zhejiang. Lobbying for business, helping business and finding support in business form a major political and economic function of modern Chinese leaders. And while the business networks have no direct say in the elite leadership outcomes, even in their nominal role in the CPPCC and the Central Committee, whether for State or non-State companies, they are key allies to get on side, because for one of the most powerful measures for success – GDP growth – they are so critical. Business links are also the source of reward for patronage, with elite politicians operating in complex ways to get allies and friends into State and non-State positions. This appears in the immensely sensitive area of family links around elite leaders to business, as Wen Jiabao in particular illustrates.

But even despite all this money, patronage is also important. However the other issues above figure, one of the lessons of the Eighteenth Party Congress was that having support from the tiny collection of former elite leaders, from Jiang Zemin to Zhu Rongji, or Hu Jintao, was important. There is a sliding scale here. From a combination of planned and unplanned causes, Jiang Zemin's influence was greater than had been expected in brokering the outcome of the Congress in 2012. In the future, this may change, with Hu Jintao choosing a different way of exercising influence. What is clear is that having the proactive and positive support of such elite retired leaders was worth immense and patient effort, by figures like Zhang Gaoli with his recruitment of Jiang Zemin to his cause, and Li Keqiang with his expert cultivation first of Hu Jintao and then of Wen Jiabao.

Military and institutional ties are also valuable. Less important than perhaps it once was, having at least some links to important entities like the military is also something we have to consider. Xi Jinping had this unique link. Bo Xilai's having some links into the military through his father's influence was perhaps one of the more unsettling issues about him for the other members of the elite. Military contacts and links to security or other powerful and partly cohesive entities in the Party-political apparatus are useful, although precisely how they operate is poorly understood. In the great consultative process that China has undertaken in the last few years to settle the new leadership, the voice of the military probably acts as powerful if it actively opposes, but not so powerful in actively promoting. A potential leader with poor relations with the military is not likely to get far. A leader firmly promoted by the military would raise hackles. Military links therefore are best if benign rather than forceful.

We can assess how the leadership performs against these different 'zones of influence' to see what sort of networks they have. This gives us at least some idea of the concept of network accrual. Of the seven, therefore, we can list them with the clear links that they have to the above networks:

> Xi Jingping: Family, military, business, provincial, elite
>   support
> Li Keqiang: Family, provincial, business, some elite
>   support
> Wang Qishan: Family (inherited), provincial (brief), busi-
>   ness (central and intellectual), elite support
> Zhang Gaoli: Provincial, elite support, business
> Zhang Dejiang: Provincial, elite support, business
> Yu Zhengsheng: Family, provincial, business, elite
> Liu Yunshan: Business (intellectual, central), some elite
>   support

The conclusion is pretty clear. The greatest networks to go for in contemporary China are elite support and business. The political rationale for Xi is that he alone combined the full range of networks. Family and provincial links are helpful. Least influential are intellectual and military network support. The CPC is like a partly family-run business on this model.

One network that goes without saying in the listing above is the Party itself – the networks within the Party that support and enable someone to lead it and succeed in it. In this sense, the Party is in a permanent process of lobbying itself, and undergoing inward reconfiguration of different sectors of interest and circles of negotiation. While we can look at the mechanics of network formation that have been attended to throughout this book, therefore, we also have to shift our sight to the second dimension – political intentions and objectives. The sorts of issues set out in the final chapter gave the parameters of concern for the future development of China that statements by these seven leaders show is on their minds. But we can say that one of the most pressing, and least publicly discussed, is the issue of the Party and its governance of itself.

The Party has undertaken consultation on its internal regulation over the last decade, and in some senses has shifted the priority to this area of intra-Party democracy. The strategy seems to be that it preserves its privileged role in society by being exemplary in modernising its governance modes before they spread to the rest of society. It is likely that this intention will continue – even while there is more urgent talk of the need for legal regularity in society more broadly. There is nothing about the backgrounds and previous statements of the current seven that shows they would wish to challenge the role of the Party or fundamentally redefine it despite this. For all of them, the key task is to ensure that it maintains its stable, unique role in society. In that case, the key questions for them revolve around how best the Party governs. In an era of deepening contestation between different groups, with inequality already established (although its broad levels might be slowing down), how is the Party able to attend to the different, and sometimes wholly divergent, needs of groups across society now, and broker compromise without itself coming across as the biggest source of vested interest? How does the Party try to maintain some kind of moral mandate in an environment in which it is so deeply implicated and frequently seen as a part of the problem, rather than as some source of adjudication? What sort of concord with transparency does it need, and what concessions does it make to other groups and institutions in order to maintain control over its key strategic areas – and how does it define those areas?

Related to this is the set of questions around how the Party embraces deeper rule of law, allowing government and institutions to have more space in society, and rolling out the frontiers of civil society in ways that do not lead its own position to be undermined. Does it construct a 'bird in the cage' legal scenario, where legality can regulate everything but not invade and challenge the Party itself? Or does the Party start preparing for the scenario of more complete legal reform, finding frameworks in which this process is not viewed as an existential threat but as something that will and should happen in the natural evolution of the Party as a modern force?

This whole leadership transition has also raised a starkly clear set of issues about how the Party mobilises the public and relates to it, shifting away from the sterile and unsatisfying language of communication that was used in the Hu period, and trying to claim more emotional connection with the broader public in the country through the identification of fresher vocabularies and narratives, and a more dynamic and modern model of authority. Can the Party embark on a period of more charismatic leadership, despite the historic memory stains of the Maoist period, with its profound experience of the expense of charismatic rule but lack of any kind of accountability framework? Will it be able to carry important segments of the population when decisions have to be made, and some interests sacrificed for the good of others? How can it recruit and mobilise people and create a sense of cohesive emotional belonging in them at a time when the Party stands the risk of being seen as simply promoting its own interests?

The new leadership stand at the centre of the attempt to sort out these challenges. The simple objective they are guardians of is to create a strong, rich country by 2020, one that will double its GDP and be a middle-income country. This alone will be a staggering achievement. They want a China that will once more stand at the centre of international affairs, reacquiring what they believe was its historic status in the dawn of modernity two centuries ago, before its tragic and destructive first encounters with Western colonialism. They want a society in which they can claim that Chinese people are the masters of their own affairs, and have a living standard that is comparable to that of much of the developed world. They want a China that is innovative and able to produce its own intellectual property, its own version of Apple or Samsung, and one where Chinese companies will be recognisable on the global stage, and a Chinese president will be as visible and respected as a US one. They want a China that is appreciated for its contribution to global development and to the solution of global environmental and sustainability challenges; a society urbanised, modernised and technologised; a China that receives increasing numbers of Nobel prizes – perhaps even a China whose films and cultural products will be appreciated, influential and admired throughout the rest of the world.

This, in essence, lies at the heart of the dream that Xi Jinping has talked of throughout 2013. He sits at the head of a leadership that want to buck the trend in a country that, in the last 150 years, has all too often collapsed in disarray and failure when it has tried to take on the West. This generation know that they can be different from this – that they can guide the country in such a way that it does not need to fragment or disintegrate into disunity or be overwhelmed by internal instability. But this leadership also know that in order to become materially more successful, more wealthy and more powerful they will have to deal with the immense challenges outlined above. Nothing will make China any easier to rule for the Party as its current leaders take this path towards what they believe is their country's historic mission. Whatever path they seek to take, one thing is almost certain: the fragmented, sometimes fractious worlds within China of different networks and power groups will need to be mobilised and made to work together as never before in order to deliver this dream of a great, rich country. That is why, for this generation of leaders with their worlds of connections around them, the stakes are so high, as they take the journey into the twenty-first century.

NOTES

INTRODUCTION: THE NETWORKED LEADERSHIP

1 Report issued by Xinhua, 'Details of intentional homicide trial of Bogu Kailai, Zhang Xiaojun' (11 August 2012). Available at http://news.xinhuanet.com/english/bilingual/2012-08/11/c_131777892.htm (accessed 7 December 2013).

2 Ibid.

3 Specifics of the Heywood case are set out in Jamil Anderlini, *The Bo Xilai Scandal: Power, Death and Politics in China* (London: Penguin, 2012); and John Garnaut, *The Rise and Fall of the House of Bo* (London: Penguin, 2012).

4 This was detailed in Wang's trial in September 2012, at which he was given a guilty verdict and sentenced to 15 years in jail. See Edward Wong, 'Police Chief in Chinese murder scandal convicted and sentenced to 15 years', *New York Times*, 23 September 2012.

5 Personal communication.

6 See Elizabeth Perry, *Anyuan: Mining China's Revolutionary Tradition* (Berkeley: University of California Press, 2012).

7 Yang Jisheng, *Tombstone: The Untold Story of Mao's Great Famine* (Harmondsworth: Penguin, 2012) is a translation of the two originals available in Hong Kong.

8 Known as 'Liandong' in Chinese. Duan Ruoshi, personal communication.

9 Wang Hui, *The End of the Revolution: China and the Limits of Modernity* (London: Verso, 2009), p. 9.

1. POWER AND THE POLITBURO

1 This account is taken from the *Tai Kung Pao* website, which was available at http://news.163.com/13/0418/08/8SNSUGH10001124J_all.html#p1 on 18 April 2013, but then promptly erased. *Tai Kung Pao* issued an apology the next day.

2 Rowan Callick, *Party Time: Who Runs China and How* (Collingwood, VIC: Black, 2013), p. 167.

3 Cheng Li's work on factions can be found best in *China's Leaders: The New Generation* (Lanham, MD: Rowman Littlefield, 2001); and on the *China Leadership Monitor* issued by the Hoover Institute in Stanford. Available at www.hoover.org/publications/china-leadership-monitor (accessed 7 December 2013).

4 Yan Jiaqi and Gao Gao wrote about this extensively in Yan Jiaqi (嚴家其) and Gao Gao (高皋), *Wenhua dageming' shinianshi 1966–1976* (文化大革命十年史 [*The History of the Ten Years of Turbulence*]) (Tianjin: Renmin Chubanshi, 1986).

5 For its cultural aspects, see Paul Clark, *The Chinese Cultural Revolution: A History* (Cambridge University Press, 2008).

6 Gao Tian (高天), *Xi Li Shibada Gonglue* (习李十八大攻略 [*A Walkthrough of the 18th CPC National Congress led by Xi and Li*]) (Hong Kong: Xianggang Wenhua Yishu Chubanshe, 2011)],' p. 373.

7 Xia Fei (夏飞) and Cheng Gongyi (程恭义), *Zhengzhiju Qi-Changwei* (政治局七常委 [*The Seven Members of the Central Politburo Standing Committee*]) (Hong Kong: Mingjing Chubanshe, 2012), p. 413.

8 Bo Zhiyue presents some of these models in the first chapter of 中共十八大政治繼承持續、變遷與挑戰 (*Chinese Communists' 18th Party Congress and Political Succession: Continuities, Changes and Challenges*), ed. Xu Siqin (徐斯勤) and Chen Desheng (陳德昇) (Taipei: Yinke Wenxue Shenghuo Zazhi Chuban Youxian Gongsi, 2012), pp. 9–27.

9 A presentation of the 'elitist'-versus-'grassroots' bifurcation is in Cheng Li, 'The end of the CPC's resilient authoritarianism? A tripartite assessment of shifting power in China', *The China Quarterly* 211 (2012): 595–624, particularly pp. 612–13.

10 Xia and Cheng, *Zhengzhiju Qi-Changwei*, p. 158.

11 Ibid., p. 164.

12 Kjeld Eric Brødsgaard, 'Cadres and personnel management in the CPC', *China: An International Journal* 10.2 (2012): 69–83 (p. 72).

13 An example of a highly granular analysis of the shifts in patronage from elite figures like Jiang, to Hu, and then to Xi, and the generational divisions and interdivisions can be found in Alice Miller, 'The new Party Politburo leadership', *China Leadership Monitor* 40 (2013), pp. 7–8. Available at http://media.hoover.org/sites/default/files/documents/CLM40AM.pdf (accessed 12 May 2013).

14 An example of this is Bo Zhiyue, *China's Elite Politics: Governance and Democratization* (Singapore: World Scientific, 2010).

15 On speculation over the Jiang-to-Hu leadership transition, see the *China Leadership Monitor*, and, in particular, H. Lyman Miller, 'The road to the Sixteenth Party Congress', *China Leadership Monitor* 1 (2002). Available at http://media.hoover.org/sites/default/files/documents/clm1_LM.pdf (accessed 9 December 2013).

16 For the context of this, see Liang Zhang, Andrew J. Nathan, Perry Link and Orville Schell (eds), *The Tiananmen Papers* (New York: PublicAffairs, 2002).

17 Gao, *Xi Li Shibada Gonglue*, p. 94. Assessments of Jiang can be found in Willy Lo-Lap Lam, *The Era of Jiang Zemin* (Upper Saddle River, NJ: Prentice Hall, 1999); Bruce Gilley, *Tiger on the Brink: Jiang Zemin and China's New Elite* (Berkeley: University of California Press, 1998); and, more controversially because of its hagiographic tone, Robert Lawrence Kuhn, *The Man who Changed China: The Life and Legacy of Jiang Zemin* (New York: Crown, 2005).

18 Wang Hui, *The End of the Revolution: China and the Limits of Modernity* (London: Verso, 2009), p. 6.

19 These are sketched out to some extent in Mark Leonard, *What Does China Think?* (New York: PublicAffairs, 2008); and also in more detail in Joseph Fewsmith, *China since Tiananmen: From Deng Xiaoping to Hu Jintao* (Cambridge University Press, 2008).

20 See Mao Yushi, and the attacks on him: Raymond Li, 'Liberal economist Mao Yushi warns of a "leftist revival" in China', *South China Morning Post* (27 May 2013). Available at www.scmp.com/news/china/article/1246186/liberal-economist-mao-yushi-warns-leftist-revival-china?page=all (accessed 9 December 2013).

21 See A. Greer Meisels, 'Lessons learned in China from the collapse of the Soviet Union', University of Sidney China Studies Centre Policy Paper 3 (2013). Available at http://sydney.edu.au/china_studies_centre/images/content/ccpublications/policy_paper_series/2013/Lessons-learned-in-China-from-the-collapse-of-the-Soviet-Union.shtml.pdf (accessed 9 December 2013).

22 Shi Guangjian (石光劍) and Wu Jingying (吴晶莹), *Zhonggong Shibada* (中共十八大 [*The 18th CPC National Congress*]) (Hong Kong: Mingjing Chubanshe, 2012), pp. 96–106.

23 See Kerry Brown, 'The Communist of China and ideology', *China: An International Journal* 10.2 (2012): 52–68 for an overview of this.

24 Michel Foucault, *Power*, Vol. 3 of *The Essential Works*, 3 vols, ed. James D. Faubion, trans. Robert Hurley et al. (Harmondsworth: Penguin, 2000) p. 340.

25 See Kerry Brown, *Hu Jintao: China's Silent Ruler* (Singapore: World Scientific, 2012).

26 Zygmunt Bauman, *Liquid Modernity* (Cambridge: Polity, 2000), p. 1.

27 Ibid., p. 6.

28 Fei Xiaotong, *From the Soil: The Foundations of Chinese Society* (Berkeley: University of California Press, 1992 [1947]), p. 37.

29 Ibid., p. 41.

30 Ibid., p. 43.

31 Ibid., pp. 62–3.

32 Ibid., p. 65.

33 Ibid.

34 Chen Yifan (陈亦凡), *Zhonggong Ba-Da-Jiazu* (中共八大家族 [*Eight Big Families of the Communist Party of China*]) (Hong Kong: Mingjing Chubanshe, 2013), pp. 25–6.

35 Ibid., p. 27.

36 Ibid., p. 29.

37 Bloomberg News, 'Heirs of Mao's comrades rise as new capitalist nobility' (27 December 2012). Available at www.bloomberg.com/news/2012-12-26/immortals-beget-china-capitalism-from-citic-to-godfather-of-golf.html (accessed 9 December 2013).

38 Tom Phillips, 'Heirs of Communist China's Eight Immortals "have amassed huge wealth"', *Daily Telegraph* (27 December 2012). Available at www.telegraph.co.uk/news/worldnews/asia/china/9767514/Heirs-of-Communist-Chinas-Eight-Immortals-have-amassed-huge-wealth.html (accessed 9 December 2013).

39 Mark Edward Lewis, *The Early Chinese Empires: Qin and Han* (Cambridge, MA: Belknap Press, 2007), p. 164.

40 Ibid., pp. 164–5.

41 Richard McGregor, *The Party: The Secret World of China's Communist Rulers* (London: Allen Lane, 2010), esp. Chapter 1, pp. 1–34.

42 Luo Changping (罗昌平) and Rao Zhi (饶智), 'Gonggong qundai' ('公共裙带' ['The public mistress']), *Caijing zazhi*, 2011 (4).

43 Xia and Cheng, *Zhengzhiju Qi-Changwei*, p. 325.

44 See in particular 'Who governs: China's political elites', Part 1 of Bo, *China's Elite Politics*, for a granular analysis of the personnel on the Central Committee of the Seventeenth Party Congress and the specific offices they hold to merit membership of this.

45 See Bruce Dickson and Jie Chen, *Allies of the State: China's Private Entrepreneurs and Democratic Change* (Cambridge, MA: Harvard University Press, 2010); Yasheng Huang, *Selling China: Foreign Direct Investment during the Reform*

Era (Cambridge University Press, 2003); and Sonja Opper and Victor Nee, *Capitalism from Below: Markets and Institutional Change in China* (Cambridge, MA: Harvard University Press, 2012).

46 This is powerfully and trenchantly discussed in Evgeny Morozov, *The Net Delusion: The Dark Side of Internet Freedom* (New York: PublicAffairs, 2012).

47 The US-based website, *China Digital Times*, documents many examples of this. Please see http://chinadigitaltimes.net/ (accessed 31 December 2013).

48 Yang Guobin, *The Power of the Internet in China: Citizen Activism Online* (New York: Columbia University Press, 2011).

2. THE LONG AND WINDING ROAD TO THE EIGHTEENTH PARTY CONGRESS

1 See Warren Sun and Frederick Teiwes, 'China's new economic policy under Hua Guofeng: Party consensus and Party myths', *The China Journal* 66 (July 2011), 1–23 for a re-evaluation of Hua; and Robert Weatherley, *Mao's Forgotten Successor: The Political Career of Hua Guofeng* (Basingstoke: Palgrave Macmillan, 2010) for a study of his career.

2 The full text of the Constitution of the CPC is available at http://news.xin-huanet.com/english/special/18cpcnc/2012-11/18/c_131982575.htm (accessed 24 December 2013).

3 Xia and Cheng, *Zhengzhiju Qi-Changwei*, p. 151.

4 Gao, *Xi Li Shibada Gonglue*, p. 379.

5 Willy Wo-Lap Lam, 'Zeng Qinghong: A man to watch', *China Brief* 2.21 (31 December 2002).

6 Lindsay Beck, 'Hatchet man to henchman: China's Zeng bows out' (21 October 2007). Available at http://uk.reuters.com/article/2007/10/21/uk-china-party-zeng-qinghong-idUSPEK824520071021 (accessed 12 December 2013).

7 Li Yuan and Wang Xiaobing, 'Giant power groups privatisation under fire', *Caijing*. Available at http://english.caijing.com.cn/2007-01-08/100015623.html (accessed 24 December 2013).

8 John Garnaut, 'A family affair', *Foreign Policy* (31 May 2012). Available at www.foreignpolicy.com/articles/2012/05/30/a_family_affair#sthash.AshY3vIt.dpbs (accessed 12 December 2013).

9 Gao, *Xi Li Shibada Gonglue*, p. 26.

10 Wu Ming (吴鸣), *Xi jinping Zhuan* (习近平传 [*A Biography of Xi Jinping*]) (Hong Kong: Xianggang Wenhua Yishu Chubanshe, 2008), p. 299.

11 Ibid., p. 300.

12 For examples, see Kerry Brown, 'Hu Jintao's legacy', *Foreign Policy* (7 November 2012). Available at www.foreignpolicy.com/articles/2012/11/07/hu_jintao_s_gamble (accessed 12 December 2013); and 'What did Hu Jintao and Wen Jiabao do for China?' (14 March 2013). Availabe at www.bbc.co.uk/news/world-asia-china-21669780 (accessed 12 December 2013).

13 Gao, *Xi Li Shibada Gonglue*, p. 148.

14 Quoted in ibid., p. 68.

15 Ibid., pp. 152–6.

16 Jao Ho Chung (ed.), *China's Crisis Management* (London: Routledge, 2011).

17 Xia Handong (夏寒冬), Cheng Gongyi (程恭义) and Xia Fei (夏飞), *Zhonggong Shibada Changwei* (中共十八大常委 [*The Eighteenth Central Politburo Standing Committee*]) (Hong Kong: Mingjing Chubanshe, 2012), p. 43.

18 Liao Jiang, 'Hu Jintao de Fen'e you duo da: Cong wu xhong quanhui kan shi ba da', *Da Shi Qing*, 2011 (2).

19 Shi and Wu, *Zhonggong Shibada*, p. 240.

20 Ibid., p. 217.

21 Gao, *Xi Li Shibada Gonglue*, pp. 168–9.

22 Quotes at transcript of talk, available at www.transcripts.cnn.com/ TRANSCRIPTS/1010/03/fzgps.01.html (accessed 4 May 2013).

23 Shi and Wu, *Zhonggong Shibada*, p. 78

24 Gao, *Xi Li Shibada Gonglue*, p. 162.

25 Shi and Wu, *Zhonggong Shibada*, pp. 111–13.

26 Ibid., p. 116.

27 BBC News, 'Book critical of Chinese PM Wen Jiabao goes on sale' (16 August 2010). Available at www.bbc.co.uk/news/world-asia-pacific-10983310 (accessed 12 December 2013).

28 Yu Jie, *Wen Jiabao: China's Best Actor* (Hong Kong: New Century Press, 2010).

29 William Yan, 'Chinese dissident details alleged torture', *Washington Post*, 19 January 2012.

30 Shi and Wu, *Zhonggong Shibada*, p. 125.

31 Hannah Beech, 'Is China's ex-leader Jiang Zemin dead? Local censors don't want any speculation', *Time*, 6 July 2011.

32 Xia, Cheng and Xia, *Zhonggong Shibada Changwei*, p. 15.

33 Shi and Wu, *Zhonggong Shibada*, p. 85.

34 On this, see the reports of Bo's life in Cheng, 'The end of the CPC's resilient author-itarianism?'; John Garnaut, 'A family affair'; and Duan Ruoshi, 'Remembrances'.

35 Xia and Cheng, *Zhengzhiju Qi-Changwei*, p. 28.

36 Ibid., p. 69.

37 Gao, *Xi Li Shibada Gonglue*, p. 255.

38 Ibid., p. 263.

39 Ibid., pp. 272, 273.

40 Ibid., p. 274.

41 Ibid., p. 275.

42 Xia and Cheng, *Zhengzhiju, Qi-Changwei*, p. 345.

43 Ibid., p. 346.

44 Gao, *Xi Li Shibada Gonglue*, pp. 263–6; Xia and Cheng, *Zhengzhiju Qi-Changwei*, p. 70.

45 Li Junru, *What Do You Know about the Communist Party of China* (Beijing: Foreign Languages Press, 2011), p. 66.

46 See Kate Westgarth, 'China in 2020: The leadership and the Party', in *China 2020: The Next Decade for the People's Republic of China*, ed. Kerry Brown (Oxford: Chandos, 2011), pp. 1–21.

47 Shi and Wu, *Zhonggong Shibada*, pp. 32–4.

48 Ibid., p. 260.

49 Peter Hartcher, 'Church and China face critical test', *Sydney Morning Herald*, 12 March 2013.

50 Shi Jingtao, 'Beidaihe meeting on leadership succession ends, say analysts', *South China Morning Post* (16 August 2012). Available at www.scmp.com/ news/china/article/1015715/beidaihe-meeting-leadership-succession-ends-say-analysts (accessed 18 December 2013).

51 Shi and Wu, *Zhonggong Shibada*, p. 228.

52 Ryan Manuel, 'Xi Jinping's recent absence: Back spasm or knee jerk?' (30 September 2012). Available at www.eastasiaforum.org/2012/09/30/xi-jinpings-recent-absence-back-spasm-or-knee-jerk/ (accessed 12 December 2013).

53 Kerry Brown, 'Analysis: Hu Jintao's speech' (8 November 2012). Available at www.bbc.co.uk/news/world-asia-china-20248100 (accessed 12 December 2013).
54 Chan Koonchung, *The Fat Years* (London: Doubleday, 2011).

3. THE NEW EMPEROR: XI JINPING

1 Taken from BBC News, 'Full text: China's new Party chief Xi Jinping's speech' (15 November 2012). Available at www.bbc.co.uk/news/world-asia-china-20338586 (accessed 11 May 2013).
2 Robert A. Caro, *The Years of Lyndon Johnson*, 4 vols to date, Vol. 4: *The Passage of Power* (London: The Bodley Head, 2012), p. xiv.
3 Yongnian Zheng, *The Chinese Communist Party as Organizational Emperor: Culture, Reproduction and Transformation* (London: Routledge, 2009).
4 Jason Miks, 'Who is Xi Jinping?', *The Diplomat*, 20 October 2010.
5 Tania Branigan, 'Profile: Xi Jinping', *Guardian*, 13 February 2012.
6 Wu, *Xi Jinping Zhuan*, pp. 33–4.
7 Shi and Wu, *Zhonggong Shibada*, p. 155.
8 Wu, *Xi Jinping Zhuan*, p. 38.
9 Shi and Wu, *Zhonggong Shibada*, p. 211.
10 Ibid., p. 153.
11 Richard Curt Krause, *The Cultural Revolution: A Very Short Introduction* (Oxford University Press, 2012), pp. 1–2.
12 Xi himself had made one reference, in 2000, to his experiences at this time:

I had been expelled from the high school for children of high ranking party members and then caught by Kang Sheng's wife Cao Yi'ou's red guard group, who accused me of all manner of bad things. I was called a gang leader because I was stubborn, and because I said that I had done nothing wrong. I did not want to be kicked around and did not give in to the red guards. I was only 14. The red guards asked:

'How serious do you yourself think your crimes are?'
'You can estimate it yourselves. Is it enough to execute me?'
'We can execute you a hundred times.'

To my mind there was no difference between being executed a hundred times or once, so why be afraid of a hundred times? The red guards wanted to scare me saying that now I was to feel the democratic dictatorship of the people, and that I only had five minutes left. Afterwards they said that I was to read quotations from Chairman Mao every single day until late at night. Then they decided to send me to a youth prison [...] At the same time – it was in December 1968 – Chairman Mao issued a new instruction: *Young students should be sent into the countryside to learn from the peasants.* I immediately went to the school to be sent into the countryside so that I could follow Chairman Mao's instruction. They considered that at the school eventually deciding that I was to go to Yan'an. It was like being sent into exile [...]

When I was sent to the countryside, I was very young. It was something I was forced to. At the time I did not think very far and did not at all think of the importance of cooperating. While others in the village every day went up the mountain slopes and worked, I did as I chose, and people got a very bad impression of me. Some months later I was sent back to Beijing and placed in a 'study group'. When six months later I was let out, I thought a lot

about whether I should return to the village. At last I called upon my uncle, who before 1949 had worked in a base area in the Taihang Mountains. At the time he, my aunt and my mother were active in revolutionary work. All of them are people who have meant a lot to me. My uncle told me about his work then, and about how decisive it is to cooperate with the people among whom you are. That settled it. I went back to the village, got down to work and cooperated. In a matter of a year I did the same work as people in the village, lived in the same way as they and worked hard. People saw that I had changed. They accepted me. (http://nias.ku.dk/news/interview-2000-china%E2%80%99s-vice-president-xi-jinping-translated-western-language-first-time (accessed 18 December 2013))
I am very grateful to Carsten Boyer Thorgerson for alerting me to this account.

13 Xinhua, 'Wen says that China needs political reform, warns of another Cultural Revolution if without'. Available at http://news.xinhuanet.com/english/china/2012–03/14/c_131466552.htm (accessed 11 May 2013).

14 Tania Branigan, 'Red songs ring out in Chinese city's new Cultural Revolution', *Guardian* (22 April 2011). Available at www.guardian.co.uk/world/2011/apr/22/red-songs-chinese-cultural-revolution (accessed 11 May 2013).

15 'Resolution on certain questions in the history of our Party since the founding of the People's Republic of China' (27 June 1981). Available at www.marxists.org/subject/china/documents/cpc/history/01.htm (accessed 11 May 2013).

16 Wu, *Xi Jinping Zhuan*, p. 136.

17 Ibid., p. 137.

18 Ibid., p. 128.

19 Ibid., p. 95.

20 Ibid., p. 156.

21 Ibid., p. 157.

22 Ibid., p. 159.

23 Ibid., p. 160.

24 The whole case is dealt with in Oliver August, *Inside the Red Mansion: On the Trail of China's Most Wanted Man* (New York: Houghton Mifflin, 2007).

25 Wu, *Xi Jinping Zhuan*, p. 204.

26 Ibid., p. 205.

27 Shi and Wu, *Zhonggong Shibada*, quoted from Bloomberg source, p. 167.

28 Ibid., p. 191; Cheng and Xia, *Zhengzhiju Qi-Changwei*, p. 111.

29 Shi and Wu, *Zhonggong Shibada*, p. 190; Cheng and Xia, *Zhengzhiju Qi-Changwei*, p. 111.

30 Bloomberg News, 'Xi Jinping millionaire relations reveal fortunes of the elite' (29 June 2012). Available at www.bloomberg.com/news/2012-06-29/xi-jinping-millionaire-relations-reveal-fortunes-of-elite.html (accessed 11 May 2013).

31 Shi and Wu, *Zhonggong Shibada*, p. 168.

32 Ibid., p. 211.

33 Willy Lam, 'Xi Jinping's Chongqing tour: Gang of princelings gains clout', *China Brief* 10.25 (17 December 2010).

34 Xia and Cheng, *Zhengzhiju Qi-Changwei*, p. 34.

35 Ibid., p. 37.

36 Shi and Wu, *Zhonggong Shibada*, p. 54.

37 On Xi's military links, see also Xia and Cheng, *Zhengzhiju Qi-Changwei*, p. 122.

38 The two have apparently been 'close friends since the late 1970s' according to John Garnaut, 'Xi's war drums', *Foreign Policy* (May/June 2013). Available at

www.foreignpolicy.com/articles/2013/04/29/xis_war_drums (accessed 11 May 2013).
39 Xia and Cheng, *Zhengzhiju Qi-Changwei*, p. 125.
40 Wu, *Xi Jinping Zhuan*, pp. 362–3.
41 Ibid., 367.

4. THE LAWYER: PREMIER LI KEQIANG

1 Cheng, *China's Leaders*, p. 10.
2 Gao, *Xi Li Shibada Gonglue*, p. 70.
3 Ibid., p. 61.
4 Ibid. While some observers said that this showed a new sort of outreach by Chinese leaders to the world, and a new line on internationalisation (Hu and Wen never sullying their mouths with foreign languages and sticking rigidly to Mandarin Chinese wherever they went), others were less charitable, with some mocking Li's pronunciation, saying that he said 'world' like the word 'war', and 'attract' as though he were saying 'attack'. In fact, Jiang Zemin and Zhu Rongji had been keener on using their language skills, with Jiang particularly loquacious on his visits abroad.
5 Ibid., p. 62.
6 Hosting Li has one advantage, however. The fact that his wife is a US-trained academic able to speak English, and has evidently taught him well, means he is able to speak directly without being swamped by translators. And his breaking out into an alien tongue in Hong Kong suggests (though cannot prove) a more receptive view of non-Chinese cultures. That, at least, is the theory.
7 Xia and Cheng, *Zhengzhiju Qi-Changwei*, p. 149.
8 Ibid., p. 158.
9 Gao, *Xi Li Shibada Gonglue*, p. 76. Wang was to end up as one of the key ringleaders blamed by the government in 1989 and put in prison. He was exiled to the US in the 1990s.
10 Li Keqiang (李克强), 'Guanyu fazhi-xitong kongzhi-guochengde tantao' ('关于法制系统控制过程的探讨' ['On the control process of the legal system']), *Qian kexue zazhi*, 1981 (4): 56–9; Gong Xiangrui (龚祥瑞) and Li Keqiang (李克强), 'Falu gongzuo de jisuanji-hua' ('法律工作的计算机化' ['The Computerization of Legal Affairs']), *Faxue zazhi*, 1983 (3): 16–20.
11 Xia and Cheng, *Zhengzhiju Qi-Changwei*, p. 159.
12 Ma Rong, *Population and Society in Contemporary Tibet* (Hong Kong University Press, 2011), pp. 175–6.
13 Jonathan Watts, *When a Billion Chinese Jump: How China Will Save Mankind* (London: Faber and Faber, 2010).
14 Yu Jianrong, 'Maintaining a baseline of social stability: Speech before the Beijing Lawyers Association' (December 2009). Available at http://chinadigitaltimes.net/2010/03/yu-jianrong-maintaining-a-baseline-of-social-stability-part-i/ (accessed 12 May 2013).
15 Christian Godel and Lynette Ong, 'Social unrest in China', Europe China Research and Advice Network (September 2012), p. 41. Available at www.euecran.eu/Long%20Papers/ECRAN%20Social%20Unrest%20in%20China_%20Christian%20Gobel%20and%20Lynette%20H.%20Ong.pdf (accessed 14 May 2013).
16 Xia and Cheng, *Zhengzhiju Qi-Changwei*, p. 51.

17 Gao, *Xi Li Shibada Gonglue*, p. 78.

18 John Gittings, 'The AIDS scandal China could not hush up', *Guardian*, 11 June 2001.

19 'Blood Debts', *The Economist* (18 January 2007). Available at http://www.economist.com/node/8554778 (accessed 29 December 2013).

20 Cheng Li, 'China's two Li's: Frontrunners in the race to succeed Hu Jintao', *China Leadership Monitor* 22 (2007), 10.

21 Quoting the State Administration for Coal Mine Safety in 2010, Xinhua said that deaths from coal mine accidents came to 3,215 in 2008; 'China's coal mine accidents fall 13.2% in Jan.–Sept.', *China Daily* (12 October 2010). Available at http://www.chinadaily.com.cn/china/2010–10/12/content_11398186.htm (accessed 22 December 2013).

22 Xia and Cheng, *Zhengzhiju Qi-Changwei*, pp. 164–5.

23 Ibid., p. 164.

24 Ibid., p. 113.

25 Ibid.

26 Ibid., p. 138.

27 Paul Maidment, 'China's Li delivers a polished future', *Forbes* (28 June 2010). Available at www.forbes.com/sites/davos/2010/01/28/chinas-li-delivers-a-polished-future/ (accessed 22 December 2013).

28 Kathrin Hillie, 'Li Keqiang: Quiet man facing economic test', *Financial Times*, 22 March 2013.

29 Other reports impute the initial enthusiasm for this book to Wang Qishan.

30 Jamil Anderlini, 'China's ever greater expectations', *Financial Times*, 8 November 2012. See also Xia and Cheng, *Zhengzhiju Qi-Changwei*, p. 144.

5. THE STARS AROUND THE TWO SUNS: THE OTHER FIVE

1 From Rick Carew, 'Will China buy the world? The Beijing debate', China Real Time Report, *The Wall Street Journal* (10 March 2009). Available at http://blogs.wsj.com/chinarealtime/tag/xiang-wenbo/ (accessed 18 May 2013).

2 Some of these challenges are covered in Kerry Brown, 'No reverse gear', CLSA (September 2008). Available at www.kerry-brown.co.uk/files/clsa_paper_final.pdf (accessed 18 May 2013).

3 Xia and Cheng, *Zhengzhiju Qi-Changwei*, p. 200.

4 Gao, *Xi Li Shibada Gonglue*, p. 310.

5 Ibid., p. 311.

6 Xia and Cheng, *Zhengzhiju Qi-Changwei*, p. 223.

7 Jason Dean, 'Wikileaks: Singapore's Lee rates China's Leaders', China Real Time Report, *The Wall Street Journal* (30 November 2010). Available at http://blogs.wsj.com/chinarealtime/2010/11/30/wikileaks-singapores-lee-rates-chinas-leaders/ (accessed 18 May 2013).

8 Xia and Cheng, *Zhengzhiju Qi-Changwei*, p. 212.

9 Gao, *Xi Li Shibada Gonglue*, p. 308.

10 Xia and Cheng, *Zhengzhiju Qi-Changwei*, p. 225.

11 Bloomberg News, 'China risks talent mismatch as Wang gets discipline job' (14 November 2012). Available at www.bloomberg.com/news/2012-11-14/xi-li-named-to-communist-party-panel-clearing-way-to-top-posts.html (accessed 30 December 2013).

12 Andrew Wedeman, *Double Paradox: Rapid Growth and Rising Corruption in China* (Ithaca, NY and London: Cornell University Press, 2012), pp. 1–2.

13 Ibid., p. 108.

14 Gao, *Xi Li Shibada Gonglue*, p. 349.

15 Ibid.

16 Ibid., p. 350.

17 Xia and Cheng, *Zhengzhiju Qi-Changwei*, pp. 329–31.

18 Gao, *Xi Li Shibada Gonglue*, p. 352.

19 Ibid., 366.

20 Benjamin Kang-Lim, 'China princeling emerges from defection scandal', Reuters (19 June 2007). Available at www.reuters.com/article/2007/06/19/us-china-party-yu-idUSPEK15174020070619 (accessed 30 December 2013).

21 Ibid.

22 Gao, *Xi Li Shibada Gonglue*, p. 368.

23 Ibid., pp. 368–9.

24 Thomas Campanella, *The Concrete Dragon: China's Urban Revolution and What It Means for the World* (New York: Princeton Architectural Press, 2008), p. 42.

25 Gao, *Xi Li Shibada Gonglue*, p. 389.

26 Ibid., p. 392.

27 Xia and Cheng, *Zhengzhiju Qi-Changwei*, p. 76.

28 Gao, *Xi Li Shibada Gonglue*, pp. 387, 391.

29 Xia and Cheng, *Zhengzhiju Qi-Changwei*, p. 262.

30 Ibid., p. 257.

31 Ibid.

32 AsiaNews.it, 'Corruption charges against judges and police in Tianjin, one suicide' (6 June 2007). Available at www.asianews.it/news-en/Corruption-charges-against-judges-and-police-in-Tianjin,-one-suicide-9545.html (accessed 30 December 2013).

33 Frank Pieke, *The Good Communist: Elite Training and State Building in Today's China* (Cambridge University Press, 2009), p. 1.

34 Gao, *Xi Li Shibada Gonglue*, p. 327.

35 Shi and Wu, *Zhonggong Shibada*, p. 287.

36 'Sun Zhigang's brutal killers sentenced', *China Daily* (10 June 2003). Available at www.chinadaily.com.cn/en/doc/2003-06/10/content_168514.htm (accessed 30 December 2013).

37 Gao, *Xi Li Shibada Gonglue*, p. 329.

38 Ibid., p. 331.

39 Ibid., p. 332.

40 Willy Wo-Lap Lam, *Chinese Politics in the Hu Jintao Era: New Leaders, New Challenges* (New York and London: M. E. Sharpe, 2006), pp. 130–1.

41 AsiaNews.it, 'Government defends Dongzhou massacre' (19 December 2005). Available at www.asianews.it/news-en/Government-defends-Dongzhou-massacre-4907.html (accessed 30 December 2013). Quoted in Gao, *Xi Li Shibada Gonglue*, p. 336.

42 Gao, *Xi Li Shibada Gonglue*, p. 343.

43 Xia and Cheng, *Zhengzhiju Qi-Changwei*, pp. 195–6.

44 Shi and Wu, *Zhonggong Shibada*, p. 296.

45 Ibid., p. 298.

46 Associated Press, 'Ding Guangen, former China propaganda chief, dies at 83', *New York Times* (22 July 2012). Available at http://www.nytimes.com/2012/07/23/world/asia/ding-guangen-former-china-propaganda-chief-dies-at-83.html?_r=0 (accessed 30 December 2013).

47 Xia and Cheng, *Zhengzhiju Qi-Changwei*, p. 244.

48 Ibid., 241.

49 'Xi Jinping: The new era. The power emerges from the 18th Congress', briefing produced by China Trade Winds (December 2012), p. 24.

50 Kenneth Tan, 'Busted: CCTV's RMB77 low-income tenant, 2011's first internet star', *Shanghaiist* (2 January 2011). Available at http://shanghaiist. com/2011/01/02/cctvs_rmb77_low-income_tenant_buste.php (accessed 30 December 2013).

51 'Xi Jinping: The new era', p. 24.

6. THE CONTRADICTIONS OF MODERN CHINA: IDEOLOGY AND ITS ROLE

1 Mao Zedong, 'On the correct handling of contradictions among the people', in *Selected Works of Mao Tse-tung*. Available at www.marxists.org/reference/archive/ mao/selected-works/volume-5/mswv5_58.htm (accessed 19 May 2013).

2 Gao, *Xi Li Shibada Gonglue*, p. 173.

3 Ibid., 175.

4 Xi Jinping (习近平), 'Shengji lingdao ganbu bixu daitou baochi gongchandangy-uan de xianjinxing' ('省级领导干部必须带头保持共产党员的先进性' ['Leading cadres at provincial level shall take the lead in keeping Party members' progressiveness']), *Qiushi zazhi*, 2005 (5). Available at www.qstheory.cn/ (accessed 5 April 2013).

5 Xi Jinping (习近平), 'Shenru xuexi Zhongguo tese-shehui-zhuyi Lilun tixi, nuli zhangwo Makesi zhuyi lichang guandian fangfa' ('深入学习中国特色社会主义理论体系 努力掌握马克思主义立场观点方法' ['Thoroughly study the system of theories of Socialism with Chinese characteristics, make great efforts in mastering the viewpoints and methods of Marxism']), *Qiushi zazhi*, 2010 (7). Available at www.qstheory.cn/ (accessed 5 April 2013).

6 From Xi Jinping (习近平), 'Guanyu Zhongguo tese-shehui-zhuyi lilun tixi de jidian xuexi tihui he renshi' ('关于中国特色社会主义理论体系的几点学习体会和认识' ['Some learning attainment and understanding of the system of theories of Socialism with Chinese characteristics']), *Qiushi zazhi*, 2008 (7). Available at www.qstheory.cn/ (accessed 5 April 2013).

7 Xi Jinping (习近平), 'Jiehe xin de shiji dali hongyang Jiao Yulu Jingshen' ('结合新的实际大力弘扬焦裕禄精神' ['Combine with the new reality of China, strongly carry forward the Jiao Yulu Spirit'), *Qiushi zazhi*, 2009 (10). Available at www. qstheory.cn/ (accessed 5 April 2013).

8 Li Keqiang (李克强), 'Lun wo guo jingji de sanyuan jiegou' ('论我国经济的三元结构 (博士学位论文)' ['The tri-structure of China's economy: Doctoral thesis']), *Zhongguo shehui-kexue*, 1991 (3): 65–82 (p. 65).

9 Ibid., p. 67.

10 Ibid., p. 79.

11 Xi Jinping (习近平). 'Shizhong jianchi he chongfen fahui dang de dete youshi' ('始终坚持和充分发挥党的独特优势' ['Firmly insist on and fully exert the unique advantages of the CPC']), *Qiushi zazhi*, 2012 (15). Available at www.qstheory. cn/ (accessed 5 April 2013).

12 Xi Jinping (习近平), 'Shizhong jianchi he chongfen fahui dang de dete youshi' ('始终坚持和充分发挥党的独特优势' ['Firmly insist on and fully exert the unique advantages of the CPC']), *Qiushi zazhi*, 2012 (15). Available at www.qstheory. cn/ (accessed 5 April 2013).

13 Li Keqiang (李克强), 'Guanyu tiaozheng jingji jiegou cujin chixu fazhande jige wenti' ('李克强: 关于调整经济结构促进持续发展的几个问题' ['Some problems of adjusting economic structure and promoting continuous development']), *Qiushi zazhi*, 2010 (11). Available at www.qstheory.cn/ (accessed 5 April 2013).

14 Li Keqiang (李克强), 'Da guimo shishi baozhang-xing anju-gongcheng, zhubu wanshan zhufang zhengce he gongying tixi' ('大规模实施保障性安居工程，逐步完善住房政策和供应体系' ['Widely implement the affordable housing projects, progressively improve the housing policies and housing supply systems']), *Qiushi zazhi*, 2011 (8). Available at www.qstheory.cn/ (accessed 5 April 2013).

15 Li Keqiang (李克强), 'Buduan shenhua yigai, tuidong jianli fuhe guoqing huiji quanmin de yiyao-weisheng tizhi' ('不断深化医改，推动建立符合国情惠及全民的医药卫生体制' ['Continue to deepen the reform of healthcare systems and promote the establishment of a health system that tallies with the national conditions and benefits all people']), *Qiushi zazhi*, 2011 (22). Available at www.qstheory.cn/ (accessed 5 April 2013).

16 Liu Yunshan (刘云山), 'Anzhao goujian shehui-zhuyi hexie shehui yaoqiu shenhua tuozhan chuangxin xuanchuan sixiang gongzuo' ('按照构建社会主义和谐社会要求深化拓展创新宣传思想工作' ['Based on the requirements of constructing Socialist harmonious society, deepen, expand in scope and innovate propaganda of ideological work']), *Qiushi zazhi*, 2005 (19). Available at www.qstheory.cn/ (accessed 5 April 2013).

17 Ibid.

18 Liu Yunshan (刘云山), 'Qishi yu sikao' ('启示与思考' ['Enlightenment and thought']), *Qiushi zazhi*, 2008 (19). Available at www.qstheory.cn/ (accessed 5 April 2013).

19 Ibid.

20 Liu Yunshan (刘云山), 'Huigu yu zhanwang' ('回顾与展望' ['Review and Prospect']), *Qiushi zazhi*, 2009 (1). Available at www.qstheory.cn/ (accessed 5 April 2013).

21 Ibid.

22 Ibid.

23 World Bank and Development Research Centre for State Council, PRC, *China 2030: Building a Modern, Harmonious and Creative Society* (Washington, DC: World Bank, 2013), pp. xxi–xxiii. Available at http://documents.worldbank.org/curated/en/2013/03/17494829/china-2030-building-modern-harmonious-creative-society (accessed 31 December 2013).

CONCLUSION

1 Hans van de Ven, *From Friend to Comrade: The Founding of the Chinese Communist Party, 1920–1927* (Berkeley: University of California Press, 1991), p. 68.

SELECT BIBLIOGRAPHY OF CHINESE SOURCES

BOOKS

陈亦凡. 中共八大家族. 香港: 明镜出版社, 2013. Chen Yifan, *Zhonggong Ba-Da-Jiazu*, Xianggang: Mingjing Chubanshe, 2013. Chen Yifan, *Eight Big Families of the Communist Party of China*, Hong Kong: Mingjing Chubanshe, 2013

高天. 习李十八大攻略. 香港: 香港文化艺术出版社, 2011. Gao Tian, *Xi Li Shibada Gonglue*, Xianggang: Xianggang Wenhua Yishu Chubanshe, 2011. Gao Tian, *A Walkthrough of the 18th CPC National Congress led by Xi and Li*, Hong Kong: Xianggang Wenhua Yishu Chubanshe, 2011.

石光剑, 吴晶莹. 中共十八大. 香港: 明镜出版社, 2012. Shi Guangjian and Wu Jingying, *Zhonggong Shibada*, Xianggang: Mingjing Chubanshe, 2012. Shi Guangjian and Wu Jingying, *The 18th CPC National Congress*, Hong Kong: Mingjing Chubanshe, 2012.

吴鸣. 习近平传. 香港: 香港文化艺术出版社, 2008. Wu Ming, *Xi Jinping Zhuan*, Xianggang: Xianggang Wenhua Yishu Chubanshe, 2008. Wu Ming, *A Biography of Xi Jinping*, Hong Kong: Xianggang Wenhua Yishu Chubanshe, 2008.

夏飞, 程恭义. 政治局七常委. 香港: 明镜出版社, 2012. Xia Fei and Cheng Gongyi, *Zhengzhiju Qi-Changwei*, Xianggang: Mingjing Chubanshe, 2012; Xia Fei and Cheng Gongyi, *The Seven Members of the Central Politburo Standing Committee*, Hong Kong: Mingjing Chubanshe, 2012.

夏寒冬, 程恭义, 夏飞. 中共十八大常委. 香港: 明镜出版社, 2012. Xia Handong, Cheng Gongyi and Xia Fei, *Zhonggong Shibada Changwei*, Xianggang: Mingjing Chubanshe, 2012. Xia Handong, Cheng Gongyi and Xia Fei, *The 18th Central Politburo Standing Committee*, Hong Kong: Mingjing Chubanshe, 2012.

徐斯勤, 陈德昇. 中共十八大政治继承-持续、变迁与挑战. 台北: 印刻文学生活杂志出版有限公司, 2012. Xu Siqin and Chen Desheng, *Zhonggong Shibada Zhengzhi Jicheng – Chixu, Bianqian yu Tiaozhan*, Taibei: Yinke Wenxue Shenghuo Zazhi Chuban Youxian Gongsi, 2012. Xu Siqin and Chen Desheng, *The 18th CPC National Congress and Political Succession: Continuities, Changes and Challenges*, Taipei: Yinke Wenxue Shenghuo Zazhi Chuban Youxian Gongsi, 2012.

ARTICLES AND DISSERTATIONS

习近平. '中国农村市场化研究-申请清华大学法学博士学位论文'.博士论文, 清华大学, 2001. Xi Jinping, 'Zhongguo Nongcun Shichanghua Yanjiu: Shenqing

Qinghua daxue faxue boshi xuewei lunwen'. Xi Jinping, 'A tentative study on China's rural marketisation' (doctoral dissertation, Tsinghua University, 2001).

习近平. '解放思想、实事求是要 一 以贯之–重读邓小平同志 "解放思想，实事求是，团结一致向前看"'.求是杂志, 1999 (1). Xi Jinping, 'Jiefang-sixiang, shishi-qiushi yao yiyiguanzhi – Chong du Deng Xiaoping tongzhi "Jiefang-sixiang, shishi-qiushi, tuanjie-yizhi xiangqian kan"', Qiushi zazhi, 1999 (1). Xi Jinping, 'Freeing up the mind, seeking truth from facts should be consistent with the fundamental principle: Reread Deng Xiaoping's "Emancipate the mind, seek truth from facts and unite as one in looking to the future"', Qiushi, 1999 (1). Available at www.qstheory.cn/ (accessed 5 April 2013).

习近平. '省级领导干部必顽带头保持共产党员的先进性'. 求是杂志, 2005 (5). Xi Jinping, 'Shengji lingdao ganbu bixu daitou baochi gongchandangyuan de xianjinxing', Qiushi zazhi, 2005 (5). Xi Jinping, 'Leading cadres at provincial level shall take the lead in keeping Party members' progressiveness', Qiushi, 2005 (5). Available at www.qstheory.cn/ (accessed 5 April 2013).

习近平. '以建设社会主义新农村为主题，深入开展农村先进性教育活动'.求是杂志, 2006 (8). Xi Jinping. 'Yi jianshe shehui-zhuyi xin-nongcun wei zhuti, shenru kaizhan nongcun xianjinxing jiaoyu huodong', Qiushi zazhi, 2006 (8). Xi Jinping, 'Make building new Socialist countryside as the theme, deeply promote rural progressiveness education campaign', Qiushi, 2006 (8). Available at www.qstheory.cn/ (accessed 5 April 2013).

习近平. '加强基层基础工作，夯实社会和谐之基'. 求是杂志, 21 (2006). Xi Jinping, 'Jiaqiang jiceng jichu gongzuo, hangshi shehui hexie zhi ji', Qiushi zazhi, 2006 (21). Xi Jinping, 'Strengthen community-level basic work, stamp the foundation of social harmony', Qiushi, 2006 (21). Available at www.qstheory.cn/ (accessed 5 April 2013).

习近平. '善学善思，善做善成'. 求是杂志, 2007 (9). Xi Jinping. 'Shanxue shansi, shanzuo shancheng', Qiushi zazhi, 2007 (9). Xi Jinping, 'Be good at learning, thinking, implementation and succeeding', Qiushi, 2007 (9).

习近平. '关于中国特色社会主义理论体系的几点学习体会和认识'. 求是杂志, 2008 (7). Xi Jinping, 'Guanyu Zhongguo tese-shehui-zhuyi lilun tixi de jidian xuexi tihui he renshi', Qiushi zazhi, 2008 (7). Xi Jinping, 'Some learning attainment and understanding of the system of theories of Socialism with Chinese characteristics', Qiushi, 2008 (7). Available at www.qstheory.cn/ (accessed 5 April 2013).

习近平. '结合新的实际大力弘扬焦裕禄精神'. 求是杂志, 2009 (10). Xi Jinping, 'Jiehe xin de shiji dali hongyang Jiao Yulu Jingshen', Qiushi zazhi, 2009 (10). Xi Jinping, 'Combine with the new reality of China, strongly carry forward the Jiao Yulu Spirit', Qiushi, 2009 (10). Available at www.qstheory.cn/ (accessed 5 April 2013).

习近平. '深入学习中国特色社会主义理论体系，努力掌握马克思主义立场观点方法'. 求是杂志, 2010 (7). Xi Jinping, 'Shenru xuexi Zhongguo tese-shehui-zhuyi Lilun tixi, nuli zhangwo Makesi zhuyi lichang guandian fangfa', Qiushi zazhi, 2010 (7). Xi Jinping, 'Thoroughly study the system of theories of Socialism with Chinese characteristics, make great efforts in mastering the viewpoints and methods of Marxism', Qiushi, 2010 (7). Available at www.qstheory.cn/ (accessed 5 April 2013).

习近平. '努力克服不良文风，积极倡导优良文风'. 求是杂志, 2010 (10). Xi Jinping, 'Nuli kefu buliang-wenfeng, jiji changdao youliang-wenfeng', Qiushi zazhi, 2010 (10). Xi Jinping, 'Make great efforts to inhibit the unhealthy writing style and strongly promote the fine style of writing', Qiushi, 2010 (10). Available at www.qstheory.cn/ (accessed 5 April 2013).

习近平. '关键在于落实'. 求是杂志, 2011 (6). Xi Jinping, 'Guanjian zaiyu luoshi', Qiushi zazhi, 2011 (6). Xi Jinping, 'Implementation is the key', Qiushi, 2011 (6). Available at www.qstheory.cn/ (accessed 5 April 2013).

习近平. '扎实做好保持党的纯洁性各<工作'. 求是杂志, 2012 (6). Xi Jinping, 'Zhashi zuo hao baochi dang de chunjie-xing gexiang gongzuo', *Qiushi zazhi*, 2012 (6). Xi Jinping, 'Solid steps shall be taken in maintaining the Party's purity', *Qiushi*, 2012 (6). Available at www.qstheory.cn/ (accessed 5 April 2013).

习近平. '始终坚持和充分发挥党的独特优势'. 求是杂志, 2012 (15). Xi Jinping. 'Shizhong jianchi he chongfen fahui dang de dete youshi', *Qiushi zazhi*, 2012 (15). Xi Jinping, 'Firmly insist on and fully exert the unique advantages of the CPC', *Qiushi*, 2012 (15). Available at www.qstheory.cn/ (accessed 5 April 2013).

习近平. '认真学习党章, 严格遵守党章 (2012年11月16日)'. 求是杂志, 2012 (23). Xi Jinping, 'Renzhen xuexi dangzhang, yange zhunshou dangzhang (2012-11-16)', *Qiushi zazhi*, 2012 (23). Xi Jinping, 'Seriously study and strictly adhere to the Party Constitution'. *Qiushi*, 2012 (23). Available at www.qstheory.cn/ (accessed 5 April 2013).

习近平. '紧紧围绕坚持和发展中国特色社会主义, 学习宣传贯彻党的十八大精神 (2012年11月17日)'. 求是杂志, 2012 (23). Xi Jinping, 'Jinjin weirao jianchi he fazhan Zhongguo-tese-shehui-zhuyi, xuexi xuanchuan guanche dang de Shibadajingshen (2012-11-17)', *Qiushi zazhi*, 2012 (23). Xi Jinping, 'Based on upholding and building Socialism with Chinese characteristics to learn, propagate and implement the spirit of the 18th CPC National Congress (2012–11-17)', *Qiushi*, 2012 (23). Available at www.qstheory.cn/ (accessed 5 April 2013).

习近平. '全面贯彻落实党的十八大精神要突出抓好六个方面工作 (2012年11月15日)'. 求是杂志, 2013 (1). Xi Jinping, 'Quanmian guanche luoshi dang de Shibada jingshen yao tuchu zhuahao liu-ge fangmian gongzuo (2012-11-15)', *Qiushi zazhi*, 2013 (1). Xi Jinping, 'Comprehensive implementation of the spirit of the 18th CPC National Congress shall focus on six aspects, *Qiushi*, 2013 (1). Available at www.qstheory.cn/ (accessed 5 April 2013).

李克强. '关于法制系统控制过程的探讨'. 潜科学杂志, 1981 (4): 56–9. Li Keqiang. 'Guanyu fazhi-xitong kongzhi-guocheng de tantao', *Qian kexue zazhi*, 1981 (4): 56–9. Li Keqiang, On the control process of the legal system, *Potential Science Magazine*, 1981 (4): 56–9.

龚祥瑞, 李克强. '法律工作的计算机化'. 法学杂志, 1983 (3): 16–20. Gong Xiangrui and Li Keqiang, 'Falu gongzuo de jisuanji-hua', *Faxue zazhi*, 1983 (3): 16–20. Gong Xiangrui and Li Keqiang, 'The Computerization of Legal Affairs', *Law Science Magazine*, 1983 (3): 16–20.

李克强. '论我国经济的三元结构 (博士学位论文)'. 中国社会科学, 1991 (3): 65–82. Li Keqiang, 'Lun wo guo jingji de sanyuan jiegou', *Zhongguo shehui-kexue*, 1991 (3): 65–82. Li Keqiang, 'The tri-structure of China's economy: Doctoral thesis', *China Social Science*, 1991 (3): 65–82.

李克强. '保持经济平稳较快发展'. 求是杂志, 2009 (15). Li Keqiang. 'Baochi jingji pingwen jiaokuai fazhan', *Qiushi zazhi*, 2009 (15). Li Keqiang, 'Maintain steady and robust growth of the economy', *Qiushi*, 2009 (15). Available at www.qstheory.cn/ (accessed 5 April 2013).

李克强. '李克强: 关于调整经济结构促进持续发展的几个问题'. 求是杂志, 2010 (11). Li Keqiang, 'Guanyu tiaozheng jingji jiegou cujin chixu fazhande jige wenti', *Qiushi zazhi*, 2010 (11). Li Keqiang, 'Some problems of adjusting economic structure and promoting continuous development', *Qiushi*, 2010 (11). Available at www.qstheory.cn/ (accessed 5 April 2013).

李克强. '大规模实施保障性安居工程, 逐步完善住房政策和供应体系'. 求是杂志, 2011 (8). Li Keqiang, 'Da guimo shishi baozhang-xing anju-gongcheng, zhubu wanshan zhufang zhengce he gongying tixi', *Qiushi zazhi*, 2011 (8). Li Keqiang, 'Widely implement the affordable housing projects, progressively improve the housing policies and housing supply systems', *Qiushi*, 2011 (8). Available at www.qstheory.cn/ (accessed 5 April 2013).

李克强. '不断深化医改，推动建立符合国情惠及全民的医药卫生体制'. 求是杂志, 2011 (22). Li Keqiang, 'Buduan shenhua yigai, tuidong jianli fuhe guoqing huiji quan-min de yiyao-weisheng tizhi', *Qiushi zazhi*, 2011 (22). Li Keqiang, 'Continue to deepen the reform of healthcare systems and promote the establishment of a health system that tallies with the national conditions and benefits all people', *Qiushi*, 2011 (22). Available at www.qstheory.cn/ (accessed 5 April 2013).

李克强. '在改革开放进程中深入实施扩大内需战略'. 求是杂志, 2012 (4). Li Keqiang, 'Zai gaige-kaifang jincheng zhong shenru-shishi kuoda neixu zhanlue', *Qiushi zazhi*, 2012 (4). Li Keqiang, 'Deeply implement the strategy of boosting domes-tic demand in the process of reform and opening-up, *Qiushi*, 2012 (4). Available at www.qstheory.cn/ (accessed 5 April 2013).

刘云山. '以 "三个代表" 重要思想为指导，大力繁荣发展哲学社会科学'. 求是杂志, 2002 (16). Liu Yunshan, 'Yi "Sange-daibiao" zhongyao sixiang wei zhidao, dali fanrong fazhan zhexue shehui-kexue'. *Qiushi zazhi*, 2002 (16). Liu Yunshan, 'Following the guidance of Three Represents, vigorously develop philosophical social science, *Qiushi*, 2002 (16). Available at www.qstheory.cn/ (accessed 5 April 2013).

刘云山. '充分认识哲学社会科学面临的形势任务，充分发挥国家社科基金的重要作用'. 求是杂志, 2005 (10). Liu Yunshan. 'Chongfen renshi zhexue shehui-kexue mian-lin de xingshi-renwu, chongfen fahui guojia sheke-jijin de zhongyao zuoyong', *Qiushi zazhi*, 2005 (10). Liu Yunshan, 'Thoroughly understand the new envi-ronment and tasks in philosophical social science and fully exert the important function of National Social Science Foundation', *Qiushi*, 2005 (10). Available at www.qstheory.cn/ (accessed 5 April 2013).

刘云山. '按照构建社会主义和谐社会要求深化拓展创新宣传思想工作'. 求是杂志, 2005 (19). Liu Yunshan, 'Anzhao goujian shehui-zhuyi hexie shehui yaoqiu shenhua tuozhan chuangxin xuanchuan sixiang gongzuo', *Qiushi zazhi*, 2005 (19). Liu Yunshan, 'Based on the requirements of constructing Socialist harmonious society, deepen, expand in scope and innovate propaganda of ideological work', *Qiushi*, 2005 (19). Available at www.qstheory.cn/ (accessed 5 April 2013).

刘云山. '大力实施 "四个一批" 人才工程，切实加强宣传文化工作队伍建设'. 求是杂志, 2006 (11). Liu Yunshan, 'Dali shishi "Sige-yipi" rencai gongcheng, qieshi jiaqiang xuanchuan wenhua gongzuo duiwu jianshe', *Qiushi zazhi*, 2006 (11). Liu Yunshan, Vigorously exert four batches of talent project, realistically strengthen propaganda staff training', *Qiushi*, 2006 (11). Available at www. qstheory.cn/ (accessed 5 April 2013).

刘云山. '精心组织文艺精品创作生产，更加自觉更加主动地推动文艺大发展大繁荣–在第十届精神文明建设 "五个一工程" 表彰座谈会上的喇话 (2007年9月7日)"'. 求是杂志, 2007 (19). Liu Yunshan, 'Jingxin zuzhi wenyi jingpin chuangzuo shengchan, gengjia zijue zhudong de tuidong wenyi fazhan da fanrong – zai di-shi jie jin-gshen-wenming jianshe "Wuge-yi gongcheng" biaozhang zuotanhui shang de jianghua (2007-09-07)', *Qiushi zazhi*, 2007 (19). Liu Yunshan, 'Elaborately organize creation and production of high-quality literature and arts, further actively promoting the prosperous development of literature and arts – talk given in the 9th session of construction of spiritual civilization Five–One Project Awards commendation meeting', *Qiushi*, 2007 (19). Available at www.qstheory. cn/ (accessed 5 April 2013).

刘云山. '毫不动摇地高举中国特色社会主义伟大旗帜–学习党的十七大报告的体会'. 求是杂志, 2008 (2). Liu Yunshan, 'Haobu-dongyao de gaoju Zhongguo tese she-hui-zhuyi weida-qizhi – xuexi dang de Shiqida baogao de tihui', *Qiushi zazhi*, 2008 (2). Liu Yunshan, 'Firmly hold high the great banner of Socialism with Chinese characteristics: Some learning attainment of the report of the 17th CPC National Congress', *Qiushi*, 2008 (2). Available at www.qstheory.cn/ (accessed 5 April 2013).

刘云山. '启示与思考'. 求是杂志, 2008 (19). Liu Yunshan, 'Qishi yu sikao', *Qiushi zazhi*, 2008 (19). Liu Yunshan, 'Enlightenment and thought', *Qiushi*, 2008 (19). Available at www.qstheory.cn/ (accessed 5 April 2013).

刘云山. '回顾与展望'. 求是杂志, 2009 (1). Liu Yunshan, 'Huigu yu zhanwang', *Qiushi zazhi*, 2009 (1). Liu Yunshan, 'Review and prospect', *Qiushi*, 2009 (1). Available at www.qstheory.cn/ (accessed 5 April 2013).

刘云山. '把握正确方向，发扬优良传统，坚持改革创新，在新的历史起点上继续推动哲学社会科学繁荣发展'. 求是杂志, 2009 (13). Liu Yunshan, 'Bawo zhengque fangxiang, fayang youliang chuantong, jianchi gaige chuangxin, zai xinde lishi qidian shang jixu tuidong zhexue shehui-kexue fanrong fazhan', *Qiushi zazhi*, 2009 (13). Liu Yunshan, 'Understand right directions, carry forward fine traditions, adhere to reform and innovation, continuously promote flourishing development of philosophical social science from a new historical starting point', *Qiushi*, 2009 (13). Available at www.qstheory.cn/ (accessed 5 April 2013).

刘云山. '推动农村精神文明建设再上新台阶'. 求是杂志, 2009 (20). Liu Yunshan, 'Tuidong nongcun jingshen-wenming jianshe zai shang xin taijie', *Qiushi zazhi*, 2009 (20). Liu Yunshan, Promote construction of rural spiritual civilization to a new level, *Qiushi*, 2009 (20). Available at www.qstheory.cn/ (accessed 5 April 2013).

刘云山. '中国应对国际金融危机的实践和启示–在第五次中越两党理论研讨会上的主旨报告'. 求是杂志, 2010 (1). Liu Yunshan, 'Zhongguo yingdui guoji jinrong weiji de shijian he qishi – zai di-wu ci Zhong Yue liang-dang lilun yantaohui shang de zhuzhi baogao', *Qiushi zazhi*, 2010 (1). Liu Yunshan, 'Enlightenment of China's experience in coping with the international financial crisis: The report given on the Fifth Sino-Vietnam Communist Party Symposium', *Qiushi*, 2010 (1). Available at www.qstheory.cn/ (accessed 5 April 2013).

刘云山. '扎实推进学习型党组织建设'. 求是杂志, 2010 (9). Liu Yunshan, 'Zhashi tuijin xuexi-xingdang-zuzhi jianshe', *Qiushi zazhi*, 2010 (9). Liu Yunshan, 'Solid steps shall be taken in promoting building of learning Party organization', *Qiushi*, 2010 (9). Available at www.qstheory.cn/ (accessed 5 April 2013).

刘云山. '中国特色社会主义文化建设的实践探索和理论思考–在第六次中越两党理论研讨会上的主旨报告 (2010年9月8日)'. 求是杂志, 2010 (20). Liu Yunshan. 'Zhongguo tese shehui-zhuyi wenhua jianshe de shijian tansuo he lilun sikao – zai di-liu ci Zhong Yue liang-dang lilun yantaohui shang de zhuzhi baogao (2010-09-08)', *Qiushi zazhi*, 2010 (20). Liu Yunshan, 'Practical exploration and theoretical thinking of the Socialist cultural construction with Chinese characteristics: Report given on the Sixth Sino-Vietnam Communist Party Symposium (2010-09-08)', *Qiushi*, 2010 (20). Available at www.qstheory.cn/ (accessed 5 April 2013).

刘云山. '立足中国国情，坚持改革创新，探索具有自身特色的社会主义现代化道路–在第一次中老两党理论研讨会上的主旨报告 (2010年10月22日)'. 求是杂志, 2010 (22). Liu Yunshan, 'Lizu Zhongguo guoqing, jianchi gaige chuangxin, tansuo juyou zishen tese de shehui-zhuyi xiandaihua daolu – zai di-yi ci Zhong Lao liang-dang lilun yantaohui shang de zhuzhi baogao (2010-10-22)', *Qiushi zazhi*, 2010 (22). Liu Yunshan, 'Based on China's realities, adhere to reform and innovation and explore the path of Socialist modernization with own characteristics: The report given at the First Sino-Laos Communist Party Symposium (2010-10-22)', *Qiushi*, 2010 (22). Available at www.qstheory.cn/ (accessed 5 April 2013).

刘云山. '为了谁，依靠谁，我是谁–关于贯彻党的群众路线的几点思考'. 求是杂志, 2011 (16). Liu Yunshan, 'Weile shui, yikao shui, wo shi shui – guanyu guanche dang de qunzhong luxian de jidian sikao', *Qiushi zazhi* 2011 (16). Liu Yunshan, 'Who do we represent, who do we rely on, and who are we? Thoughts on implementing the Party's mass line', *Qiushi*, 2011 (16). Available at www.qstheory.cn/ (accessed 5 April 2013).

刘云山. '切实做好新形势下的群众工作–在第七次中越两党理论研讨会上的主旨报告'. 求是杂志, 2011 (24). Liu Yunshan, 'Qieshi zuohao xin xingshi xia de qunzhong gongzuo – zai di-qi ci Zhong Yue liang-dang lilun yantaohui shang de zhuzhi baogao', *Qiushi zazhi*, 2011 (24). Liu Yunshan, 'Realistically implement mass work under new circumstances: Report given on the Seventh Sino-Vietnam Communist Party Symposium, *Qiushi*, 2011 (24). Available at www.qstheory.cn/ (accessed 5 April 2013).

刘云山. '深入学习党的文化建设理论，推动十七届六中全会精神贯彻落实'. 求是杂志, 2012 (5). Liu Yunshan, 'Shenru xuexi dang de wenhua jianshe lilun, tuidong Shiqijie-Liuzhongquanhui jingshen guanche luoshi', *Qiushi zazhi*, 2012 (5). Liu Yunshan, 'Thoroughly study the theories of the Party's cultural progress and vigorously promote the guiding thought of the Sixth Plenary Session of the 17th CPC Central Committee', *Qiushi*, 2012 (5). Available at www.qstheory.cn/ (accessed 5 April 2013).

刘云山. '不断深化思想认识，努力把握工作规律，推动学习型党组织建设向广度深度拓展'. 求是杂志, 2012 (9). Liu Yunshan, 'Buduan shenhua sixiang renshi, nuli bawo gongzuo guilu, tuidong xuexi-xing dang-zuzhi jianshe xiang guangdu shendu tuozhan', *Qiushi zazhi*, 2012 (9). Liu Yunshan, 'Continue to deepen thinking and understanding, strenuously grasp the rules of work and promote the building of a learning Party organization in depth and breadth', *Qiushi*, 2012 (9). Available at www.qstheory.cn/ (accessed 5 April 2013).

刘云山. '以崇高文化理想和艺术追求推动我国文艺繁荣发展'. 求是杂志, 2012 (20). Liu Yunshan, 'Yi chonggao wenhua lixiang he yishu zhuiqiu tuidong wo guo wenyi fanrong fazhan', *Qiushi zazhi*, 2012 (20). Liu Yunshan, 'Using lofty cultural ideas and artistic pursuit to promote prosperous development of China's literature and arts', *Qiushi*, 2012 (20).

张德江. '大力推进煤矿瓦斯抽采利用'. 求是杂志, 2009 (24). Zhang Dejiang, 'Dali tuijin meikuang wasi choucai liyong', *Qiushi zazhi*, 2009 (24). Zhang Dejiang, 'Vigorously promote extraction and utilisation of coal mine gas', *Qiushi*, 2009 (24). Available at www.qstheory.cn/ (accessed 5 April 2013).

张德江. '落实政策措施，提高企业素质，努力把中小企业发展提高到新水平'. 求是杂志, 2011 (24). Zhang Dejiang, 'Luoshi zhengce cuoshi, tigao qiye suzhi, nuli ba zhong-xiao qiye fazhan tigao dao xin shuiping', *Qiushi zazhi*, 2011 (24). Zhang Dejiang, 'Implement policies and measures, improve enterprises' qualities and strenuously develop small and medium size enterprises to a new level', *Qiushi*, 2011 (24). Available at www.qstheory.cn/ (accessed 5 April 2013).

俞正声. '以科学发展观为指导，促进中部地区崛起'. 求是杂志, 2005 (7). Yu Zhengsheng, 'Yi Kexuefazhanguan wei zhidao, cujin zhongbu diqu jueqi', *Qiushi zazhi*, 2005 (7). Yu Zhengsheng, 'Following the guidance of the scientific outlook on development, promote the rise of the central region', *Qiushi*, 2005 (7). Available at www.qstheory.cn/ (accessed 5 April 2013).

俞正声. '创新转型谋发展，服务群众促和谐，围绕实现"十二五"良好开局创先争优'. 求是杂志, 2011 (7). Yu Zhengsheng, 'Chuangxin zhuanxing mou fazhan, fuwu qunzhong cu hexie, weirao shixian "Shi-er-wu" lianghao kaiju chuangxian zhengyou', *Qiushi zazhi*, 2011 (7). Yu Zhengsheng, 'Explore development opportunities through innovation and transformation, serve the people to promote harmonious society and excel at work for a good beginning of the implementation of the twelfth five-year plan', *Qiushi*, 2011 (7). Available at www.qstheory.cn/ (accessed 5 April 2013).

俞正声. '深入贯彻落实科学发展观，大力推进上海创新驱动转型发展'. 求是杂志, 2012 (17). Yu Zhengsheng, 'Shenru guanche luoshi Kexuefazhanguan, dali tuijin Shanghai chuangxin qudong zhuanxing fazhan', *Qiushi zazhi*, 2012 (17). Yu Zhengsheng, 'Deeply implement the scientific outlook on development, vigorously promote Shanghai's innovation-driven transformation and development', *Qiushi*, 2012 (17). Available at www.qstheory.cn/ (accessed 5 April 2013).

王岐山. '深入学习贯彻党的十八大精神，努力开创党风廉政建设和反腐败斗争新局面–在中国共产党第十八届中央纪律检查委员会第二次全体会晦上的工作报告 (2013年1月21日)'. *人民日报*, 2013-02-26. Wang Qishan, 'Shenru xuexi guanche dang de Shibada jingshen, nuli kaichuang dangfeng lianzheng jianshe he fanfu douzheng xin jumian – zai Zhongguo Gongchandang di-shibajie Zhongyang Jilu Jiancha Weiyuanhui di-er ci quanti huiyi shang de gongzuo baogao (2013-01-21)', *Renmin ribao*, 2013-02-26. Wang Qishan, 'Thoroughly study and implement the spirit of the 18th CPC National Congress, for making new progress in improving Party conduct, promoting integrity and combating corruption: Working report of the second plenary session of the 18th CPC Central Commission for Discipline Inspection (2013-01-21)', *People's Daily*, 26 February 2013.

张高丽. '努力打造自主品牌'. 求是杂志, 2006 (4). Zhang Gaoli, 'Nuli dazao zizhu pinpai', *Qiushi zazhi*, 2006 (4). Zhang Gaoli, 'Make great effort in building Chinese indigenous brands', *Qiushi*, 2006 (4). Available at www.qstheory.cn/ (accessed 5 April 2013).

张高丽. '重在武装思想，解决问题，取得实效；推动科学发展，和谐发展，率先发展'. *求是杂志*, 2009 (17). Zhang Gaoli, 'Zhong zai wuzhuang sixiang, jiejue wenti, qude shixiao, tuidong kexue fazhan, hexie fazhan, shuaixian fazhan', *Qiushi zazhi*, 2009 (17). Zhang Gaoli, 'Focus on arming oneself with thoughts, solving problems and achieving actual effects, promoting scientific development, harmonious development and proactive development', *Qiushi*, 2009 (17). Available at www.qstheory.cn/ (accessed 5 April 2013).

张高丽. '深入推进三‹重点工作，努力营造良好发展环境'. *求是杂志*, 2010 (16). Zhang Gaoli, 'Shenru tuijin sanxiang zhongdian gongzuo, nuli yingzao lianghao fazhan huanjing', *Qiushi zazhi*, 2010 (16). Zhang Gaoli, 'Work harder on three important issues of work, make great efforts in creating a favourable environment for development', *Qiushi*, 2010 (16). Available at www.qstheory.cn/ (accessed 5 April 2013).

张高丽. '加快滨海新区开发开放，当好科学发展的排头兵'. *求是杂志*, 2012 (14). Zhang Gaoli, 'Jiakuai Binhai Xinqu kaifa kaifang, dang hao kexue fazhan de paitoubing', *Qiushi zazhi*, 2012 (14). Zhang Gaoli, 'Speed up the development and opening-up of Binhai new area, to be a model vanguard of scientific development', *Qiushi*, 2012 (14). Available at www.qstheory.cn/ (accessed 5 April 2013).

由冀. '十八大习近平掌军执政的前景. 台北: 习李体制、人事调整与政策取向: 持续与变迁研讨会, 2013-03-29. You Ji. 'Shibada Xi Jinping zhangjun zhizheng de qianjing'. Taibei: Xi Li tizhi, renshi tiaozheng yu zhengce quxiang: chixu yu bianqian yantaohui, 2013-03-29. You Ji, 'Prospects of Xi's governance and ruling of the PLA and the Party after the Eighteenth CPC National Congress. Xi's and Li's systems, personnel changes and policy preferences: Continuities, changes and challenges. Unpublished conference paper, Eighteenth CPC National Congress, Taipei, 29 March 2013.

罗昌平，饶智. '公共裙带'. 财经杂志, 2011 (4). Luo Changping and Rao Zhi, 'Gonggong qundai', *Caijing zazhi*, 2011 (4). Luo Changping and Rao Zhi, 'The public mistress', *Caijing*, 2011 (4).

INDEX